MONTCALM & WOLFE

MONTCALM & WOLFE

TWO MEN WHO FOREVER CHANGED

THE COURSE OF CANADIAN HISTORY

ROCH CARRIER

TRANSLATED BY DONALD WINKLER

HarperCollins*PublishersLtd*

Montcalm & Wolfe
Copyright © 2014 by Roch Carrier.
English language translation © 2014 by Donald Winkler.
All rights reserved.

Published by HarperCollins Publishers Ltd
Simultaneously published in the French language by Les Éditions Libre Expression
under the title 'Montcalm et Wolfe."

HarperCollins books may be purchased for educational, business,
or sales promotional use through our Special Markets Department.

HarperCollins Publishers Ltd
2 Bloor Street East, 20th Floor
Toronto, Ontario, Canada
M4W 1A8

www.harpercollins.ca

Library and Archives Canada Cataloguing in Publication
information is available upon request

ISBN 978-1-44343-688-5

Printed and bound in the United States of America
RRD 9 8 7 6 5 4 3 2 1

Contents

Prelude

Two generals serving enemy nations would die in Quebec City in a battle that took place far, very far, from their native lands. Louis-Joseph de Montcalm was French; James Wolfe was English. Wolfe was the person I most despised during my French Canadian adolescence. He had usurped the land of my ancestors, the land that was mine. It had not yet occurred to me that my French forebears had themselves appropriated a territory already inhabited by numerous peoples.

As a young poet, in France, I rode my motor scooter hundreds of kilometres on a pilgrimage to Candiac where, before his manor house, I might pay homage to Lieutenant-General Montcalm, our history's great hero, who had been unable to save my country. And I promised myself then that one day I would try to understand why.

Blessed as we are to be living in an age when intolerance and racial prejudice have been expunged from the human spirit, it is perhaps difficult for us now to acknowledge that such sentiments existed in the past. My ancestors, three or four centuries ago, their leaders, their allies, their enemies, were not proponents of politically correct thinking. In this book I have tried my best to be true to the ethos forming the backdrop to their conflicts and their stories.

A castle, a river, and so many wars

Wolfe and Montcalm were both descended from families in service to their kings.

The Montcalm family, "an ancient house of Rouergue" (Aveyron), had been "known from the end of the thirteenth century, the time of Simon de Montcalm, seigneur of Viala & Cornus." In the fifteenth century, a member of the Montcalm family was chief judge for the court in Nîmes, a Montcalm was highly placed at the Holy See in Rome, and another was the *maître d'hôtel* for Charles VIII and then for Louis XII. In the sixteenth century, François de Montcalm was a ship's captain.

Several members of the Montcalm family had shed blood for their king. Captain Louis de Montcalm, born in 1563, died in 1587 of a wound he had received at the siege of Marguerittes, a town being defended by Protestants. In 1629, after surrendering in a besieged La Rochelle, Cardinal Armand du Plessis de Richelieu sought help from another Louis de Montcalm, born in 1583, to negotiate peace terms with the Protestants. In Lombardy, while trying to stop German troops from coming to the aid of Spaniards on whom Richelieu had declared war, Maréchal François de Montcalm died in 1632 in the region of Valtellina, in northern Italy. Eleven years later, the infantry captain Jacques de Montcalm was killed in the same place. Maurice de Montcalm, twenty-five years old, a captain in the regiment of the Grand Condé during the war with Holland, was injured by a cannonball during the siege of Naarden. When the Spanish occupied the fort of Bellegarde in 1674, in the Pyrenees on the border between France and Spain, Louis de Montcalm (the fourth of that name) was wounded during an attempt to dislodge them. He died the following year. In 1677, at the Battle of Cassel in Holland, where the troops of William of Orange faced off against those of Philippe d'Orléans, brother of Louis XIV, Gaspard de Montcalm, a cavalry captain, was seriously hurt. The same day, his brother Daniel was killed at the age of thirty-two.

The Montcalms, like many Languedoc nobles, were fervent partisans of the Protestant faction in the Cévennes, but Jean-Louis de Montcalm, at the age of seventeen, renounced his Protestantism in the chapel of the Bishop of Grenoble. Appalled, his parents disinherited this wayward son. Louis-Daniel de Montcalm, born in 1676, also wanted to become a Catholic. He had met a fetching Catholic woman. As she was also a very rich heiress, their son's conversion was forgivable in his parents' eyes. Louis-Daniel de Montcalm married his fiancée in 1708.

A first child was born to them in 1710: a daughter, Louise-Françoise-Thérèse. The future lieutenant-general who would be defeated at Quebec, Louis-Joseph de Montcalm, came into the world in Candiac, near Nîmes, on February 28, 1712. Like his ancestor Jean de Montcalm, born in 1407, he would hold, among other titles, that of seigneur of the hamlet of Saint-Véran. His mother saw to it that her son was baptized as soon as possible in the Catholic Church. The next year, the Treaty of Utrecht brought relative peace to France, which had agreed to cede the land of Acadia, in New France, to the English.

Little Louis-Joseph, who now had a second sister, Louise-Charlotte, born in 1714, was delicate. His godmother, who was his maternal great-grandmother, watched over him with doting tenderness during his first years, at the castle of Roquemaure. Louis-Joseph would never forget this home with its crenellated walls built atop a black rock, nor the Rhone River, beside whose banks he took his first steps. It was near another great river, in Quebec, far from his "little village," that he would take his last.

Snails and ground-up earthworms,
whisked into milk with cloves

The Woulfes, ancestors of James Wolfe, lived in southern Wales. In the sixteenth century, they immigrated to western Ireland, where they acquired lands and possessions. Having converted to Catholicism, the Woulfes were prominent citizens in Limerick. James Woulfe became one of the city's overseers. Sir Edward Seymour, an uncle of King Edward VI of England, married the daughter of Morgan Woulfe.

James I of England, opting for the Anglicans as his power base, banished the Catholics in 1604. On November 5, 1605, a band of Catholics tried to explode thirty or so barrels of gunpowder in the House of Lords, where the king was presiding over the opening of Parliament. The persecution of Catholics intensified. In Ireland, George Woulfe, then sheriff of Limerick, refused to swear allegiance to James I. He did not recognize the authority of this king newly arrived from Scotland, and as a Catholic, he could not accept that the Pope would no longer be his religious leader. James I relieved him of his responsibilities in 1613.

Politics and religion created discord among George Woulfe's three sons. In 1649, Oliver Cromwell and three thousand "Ironsides," fanatic cavalry troopers, descended on Ireland, putting "the women and children of Drogheda to the sword with the Bible text *God is love* pasted around the mouth of his cannon," in the words of James Joyce. Lieutenant-Colonel Edward Woulfe was at Cromwell's side. His two brothers, George and Francis Woulfe, were in the opposite camp. George, the great-grandfather of the future Major-General James Wolfe, was one of the key defenders of Limerick when the city was besieged in 1651. Francis was a Franciscan monk. Each in his own way offered resistance to the English army, but Limerick fell into the hands of its enemies. Francis was hanged. George was able to escape. The Catholic families were dispossessed. A good thirty members of the Woulfe families sought refuge on the continent, some in Paris and elsewhere in France.

Captain George Woulfe, for his part, chose Yorkshire in the north of England, a region that offered commercial opportunities. The weaving industry was growing rapidly in this agricultural county. The fugitive changed the spelling of his name, becoming a Wolfe, and he embraced Protestantism. His wife bore him two sons. Edward became an officer in the army, but when King James II of England converted to Catholicism, the king took away his commission. Shortly thereafter, William of Orange ousted James II, and Edward Wolfe became a captain in 1690. For thirteen years, he served the king throughout the Mediterranean and in the Low Countries, where he was wounded. His commission was renewed once more in 1702, by Queen Anne. Then, having retired to York, he urged his two sons to follow in his footsteps.

The elder, Edward, who would be Major-General James Wolfe's father, received an ensign's commission in a regiment of navy fusiliers in 1702, while his brother, Walter, became an ensign in an Irish infantry regiment. Edward fought in Flanders under John Churchill, Duke of Marlborough. In 1706, he took part in the defeat of Franco-Spanish troops at Ramillies (Belgium), then served in Scotland in

1715. Despite his youth, his qualities and experience earned him a promotion to the rank of lieutenant-colonel in 1717.

In 1720, after the scandal-ridden collapse of the South Sea Company, which had held the monopoly for trade with the Spanish colonies in America, England enjoyed twenty years of peace. Edward Wolfe was employed building roads in the countryside. In 1724, he married Henrietta Thompson. The daughter of a good Yorkshire family, she had an imposing dignity and a great beauty. After living with Henrietta's parents for two years in York, Edward and his wife bought a three-gabled house on a modest property in Westerham, amid wooded, rolling hills. Forty kilometres from London, the lieutenant-colonel would be closer to where decisions were being made.

Their son, James Wolfe, was born on January 2, 1727, in the Westerham presbytery because the family home was undergoing repairs. Henrietta, his mother, was alone at the moment of birth. His father was away with his regiment. The news of the day, in the gazettes, was that a woman in the countryside had given birth to six rabbits! Two years later, James had a little brother: Edward.

As their father was almost always absent on account of his military obligations, the two children were raised by a demanding mother. Ambitious, she made no secret of the fact that she had more respect for a family that made its own fortune than for one that inherited its social rank.

The two sons of this strong woman had fragile constitutions. Both were often sick despite the precautions their mother took, keeping them indoors to protect them from airborne perils. She devised medicines to cleanse their humours: snails and ground-up earthworms, whisked into milk and mixed with bear's foot, angelica, and cloves.

When their father came home, his conversation naturally revolved around military matters. The children listened to stories describing a world unknown to them.

3

"Obedience, docility, and a wholehearted compliance"

At the age of six, in 1718, Louis-Joseph de Montcalm was placed with a tutor in Grenoble; Louis Dumas, born out of wedlock, was the half-brother of his pupil's father. He was a learned man who was always studying. He had lived in England and maintained close ties with Dutch correspondents. The child was introduced to French, Greek, Latin, philosophy, the exact sciences, and music. The little one tired easily, and his mind often wandered. As soon as Louis-Joseph had learned to write, Dumas insisted that he compose weekly reports for his parents concerning his activities, his progress, and the recent happenings in the city and at court.

In 1719, a little brother made his appearance in the Montcalm family: Jean-Louis-Pierre. At the age of two and a half, the child knew the alphabet, and at three, he was reading Greek and Latin. At five, he was translating from Hebrew.

Once Louis-Joseph de Montcalm had reached the age of twelve, in 1724, he was enlisted, with the rank of ensign, in the Hainaut Infantry Regiment where his father was lieutenant-colonel. The tutor, who found that his pupil had an "aversion to writing," was concerned for his future: "I have been thinking about Monsieur de Montcalm's limited aptitudes and talent," he wrote to the father. "What will become of him? Where will he excel?"

Reacting a little later to this verdict, Louis-Joseph wrote to his father: "In a few words, I pride myself on the following: 1) being an honest man, of good habits, a virtuous and good Christian; 2) being a middling reader, knowing the Greek and Latin languages as well as most people in this world, mastering the four rules of arithmetic, having some knowledge of history, geography, and French and Latin literature, valuing sound judgment, even if I have it not, and cherishing in particular the sciences and arts of which I am ignorant; 3) what I set above all else: obedience, docility, and a wholehearted compliance to your orders and those of my dear mother, along with a deference for the counsels of Monsieur Dumas; 4) where the body is concerned, to take up arms and mount horseback as much as my meagre talents will permit me."

At the age of twenty, Captain Louis-Joseph de Montcalm did not neglect his studies. He was determined to further his education. Louis Dumas had him read Aristophanes's *The Birds*. In this play, two Athenians weary of the conflicts dividing the city's citizens escape to the realm of the birds to found a new city between heaven and earth. It was essential to know the classic Greek texts, Dumas believed, in a time when an aristocracy of the sword was being embraced by a well-educated bourgeoisie. Montcalm also took lessons in riding, fencing, sword, and foil, before being posted to the garrison of Fort-Louis, in Alsace. He was then transferred to Strasbourg. In this fortress built by the engineer Vauban, Montcalm was one of the 6,000 soldiers protecting the 26,000 inhabitants of that city, most of them Protestants. Shortly afterward, he was sent to Mézières, on the Meuse River, then to the garrison of Charlemont at Givet in the Ardennes, where he became an officer.

Stanisław I Leszczyński of Poland, who lost his crown after being defeated by Peter the Great of Russia in 1709, had been replaced by Augustus II. Upon the latter's death in 1733, Stanisław

I was called upon by the Polish diet to remount the throne. Supported by Austria and Russia, Augustus III, the son of Augustus II, laid claim to the crown of Stanisław I, whose daughter, Marie Leszczyńska, was now the wife of the King of France. Louis XV came to the aid of his father-in-law. The French army marched through Lorraine, Germany, and Italy. The Hainaut Regiment, to which Montcalm belonged, formed part of this army of the Rhine. In October 1733, it surrounded the town of Kehl, opposite Strasbourg, which surrendered.

Back with his family, Montcalm attended the marriage of his sister Louise-Charlotte to Gilbert de Massilian, chief judge in Montpellier. Montcalm had two other sisters: Louise-Françoise, his elder, who in 1728 married Baron Antoine Jean Viel, seigneur of Lunas, advisor to the king at Languedoc's finance and revenue court, and his youngest sister, Macrine, born in 1723.

In the spring of 1734, the Hainaut Regiment took part in the siege of Philippsburg in Germany, a campaign the young Captain Montcalm judged to be "premature." He complained to his brother-in-law Antoine Viel, a man of substance and influence, that he had no tent, no bed, no equipment. "Fortunately," he said, "I have two horses, twelve shirts, and a pair of tin trunks." On June 3, the French began to dig their trenches in front of the city. A month and a half later, on July 18, the enemy army's commander, Prince Eugène de Savoie-Carignan, a Frenchman fighting for Austria, was forced to surrender. Montcalm relished the victory. The town was "rubble," he told his father, "not a house worth living in; … nothing but stench and infection."

The Rhine army fought no other battle. Montcalm, capitalizing on the inactivity, read Greek writers and began to learn German. But not all was study: there was this young Calvinist girl he was thinking of marrying "in hope of making a conversion," he said ironically to his father, who had himself converted in order to marry his mother.

After his father's death in September of 1735, Louis-Joseph saw that a new chapter in his life was beginning. He would soon be twenty-four years old. Was that not a time to start a family? Given his class, Montcalm was expected to forge an advantageous union, but he also wanted to experience love. A friend of the family, the Marquis Philippe-Charles de La Fare, offered him useful advice and became his intermediary.

On the night of October 2, 1736, in a ceremony lit by hundreds of candles, Captain Louis-Joseph de Montcalm married Angélique Louise Talon du Boulay, daughter of the Marquis Antoine Omer Talon du Boulay, colonel in the Orléans Regiment. Cardinal André Hercule de Fleury, former tutor of Louis XV and now prime minister, appended his signature to the bottom of the marriage contract. Young Captain Montcalm would for some years lead a peaceful life on his rural property in Candiac, in the company of his young wife and his dear mother.

4

"I am very sorry, dear Mamma, that you doubt my love"

James Wolfe was eleven years old when his family moved to Greenwich in 1738. A pastor named Samuel Swindon had opened a school there for the sons of army and navy officers. If James, very tall for his age, played games with his comrades, he took little pleasure in it. He preferred to be alone and to lose himself in tales of ancient wars. Pastor Swindon, who had his eye on James, saw in the young man the qualities of a future officer.

At that time, the English people were outraged at the brutality with which the Spanish were attacking their ships. King George II strengthened his navy's presence in the West Indies and Latin America. The Spanish shored up their fortresses. In 1739, Admiral Edward Vernon seized control of their naval base at Portobelo, on the north of the Isthmus of Panama. Suddenly, thanks to this victory, the English saw the Spanish as vulnerable. The English Admiralty immediately decided to send a fleet, first to Jamaica, where it would join that of Admiral Vernon and bolster it: the goal was to deal a final blow to the Spanish in the West Indies.

James's father, Edward Wolfe, now an adjutant-general, took part in the expedition with his First Infantry Regiment for the navy.

One of the privileges of senior officers was to be accompanied by volunteers. James begged his father to take him along. In that, the father saw the answer to his prayers! His son would follow in his footsteps and those of his forebears. But Henrietta Wolfe feared for the health of her frail adolescent. Using emotional blackmail, she tried in vain to turn her son away from his obsession with distant seas.

For the red-uniformed soldiers, called "lobsters" by the populace, the pay was poor, the discipline harsh, the lodgings wretched; they often shared stables with animals. If you enlisted in the army, it was because you were desperate . . . or the son of a military man. Those privileged by class or good fortune bought officers' commissions, which were for sale. James's father, however, felt that a soldier, without title, penniless, but courageous, had a chance to set his foot on the promotional ladder.

In July 1740, with his rough and ready companions, the gangly adolescent found himself in camp, in a tent. To preclude the anticipated desertions, the members of the expedition had to be assembled on an island, the Isle of Wight in the English Channel.

The equipment was late arriving, the conscripts were late reporting, the officers had not yet shown up. The arms had not been delivered, and the ships were not yet refitted. After waiting two months, they were at last ready to cast off, but the winds were unfavourable. Meanwhile, the Spanish in the West Indies had received warnings that the expedition was in the offing, and they were making their own preparations to defend against it.

James Wolfe was unhappy. His mother accused him of not loving her, because he had left home. That left him shaken. At the beginning of August, the son replied to his mother: "I am very sorry, dear Mamma, that you doubt my love." Commiserating, he added: "I'm sorry to hear that your head is so bad." Mother and son were never so close as when they spoke of their respective maladies.

The fleet didn't take to sea until October. The soldiers were crammed into transport vessels where they would live and sleep one on top of the other for the long crossing, surviving on meat and salt fish. The ship that would bear him to the Caribbean had not even weighed anchor when James Wolfe became paler than usual. If he risked a mouthful of food, his stomach rejected it. The adolescent was already seasick—so sick that he had to disembark at Portsmouth. What a disaster for the young dreamer! What a humiliation for his father, the adjutant-general Edward Wolfe!

5

"Bloody and memorable affairs"

Peace has a very short season. France, in 1741, joined a coalition with Prussia, Spain, and Bavaria to try to prevent Maria Theresa from succeeding her father, Charles VI, to the Austrian throne. Marquis de La Fare, lieutenant-general of the French army, marched on Bohemia. Captain Louis-Joseph de Montcalm asked the marquis, his protector, who had advised him in the matter of his marriage, if he would grant Montcalm the favour of taking him on as his aide-de-camp. The marquis granted the request.

In 1742, the French army succeeded in entering the city of Prague, which was soon surrounded by eighty thousand soldiers. During a sortie against these many enemies, Captain Montcalm was injured by an exploding bomb. The French army, plagued by bad weather, shortages, and illness, beat a retreat. This time, aide-de-camp Montcalm got a taste of defeat.

In the autumn, having learned of the death of his brother-in-law Antoine Viel, he showed himself to be a responsible head of the family. "Your children, if God grants me life, will be as dear to me as my own," he wrote to the widow, his sister Louise-Françoise.

Having been promoted, in March of 1743, to the rank of colonel in the Auxerrois Regiment, Montcalm was honoured, the next year, with the title of Chevalier of the Order of Saint-Louis, founded by

Louis XIV. This distinction was conferred only after ten years of distinguished service, and the recipient had to be Catholic.

When hostilities were renewed, the Austrian and Sardinian forces in Italy went to ground. After months of frustrating inaction, the French and Spanish worked together to force the Sardinian king to retreat. During their advance, more than five hundred men were killed or wounded. There were many desertions. As the enemy closed in, the Sardinians emptied out their houses; furniture, food, fodder, tools were all spirited away on the backs of mules. At the end of this inglorious campaign, Montcalm settled in Montpellier for the winter.

In March 1744, Colonel Montcalm returned to his regiment. Twenty kilometres from the French border, six thousand Sardinians were blocking Spanish and French access to the Château-Dauphin valley, the only route to the valleys of Piedmont that lay farther on. The Sardinians had built low stone walls and cut down fifty thousand trees whose trunks, scattered pell-mell, broke up the enemy ranks. They had mined the rocks to make them more jagged and had spread the debris over the fields to make marching more difficult. In April, the thirty thousand Frenchmen of Louis François de Bourbon, Prince of Conti, drove the Piedmontese from the fort at Mont Alban, and made off with their animals and the enormous quantity of food they needed for themselves. In July, the Franco-Spanish troops occupied Château-Dauphin, even though it was defended by the Austrians, the English, 35,000 foot soldiers of the King of Sardinia, twenty-four battalions of mercenaries, and a cavalry of ten thousand horses. In the month of August, the French took the citadel of Saint-Elme at Villefranche after bombarding it for three days. During this campaign, which dragged on until December 20, Colonel Montcalm was charged with "a number of duties," but he did not participate, he reported, in "bloody and memorable affairs."

After these events, Montcalm was assigned with his men to a garrison in Menton. Several times, he had to interrupt the winter truce to go off and punish Barbets, Sardinian militias that rose up and provoked skirmishes in the Genoese countryside. In the spring of 1745, his regiment was responsible for making sure that information, instructions, food, forage, animals, tools, arms, and munitions were delivered to the appropriate units.

The following year, the Barbets were positioned near Acqui, a small Piedmont town known for its sulphur spring. As Montcalm's four battalions approached to drive them off, the Barbets slipped away. Montcalm and his men, on difficult terrain, gave chase, surprised them, and took 150 prisoners. They then rejoined the Franco-Spanish army, which on June 16 suffered a costly defeat at the hands of the Austrians at Piacenza. Among the many soldiers who lost their lives was Montcalm's nephew, the son of his elder sister, who was already a widow. As for Montcalm, he received sabre blows to his forehead, the back of his head, and a shoulder blade, and suffered a severed artery. Covered in blood, he was captured by the Austrians. His regiment, which was "wiped out," he reported to his mother, "did badly," but "less badly than the others." It "was the last to take flight." "Our religion served us well," he explained.

When the foes exchanged prisoners, Montcalm was freed and returned to France. Despite the defeat, Louis XV, at a ceremony in Paris, promoted him to the rank of brigadier.

In 1747, Montcalm joined the staff of Louis Charles Armand Fouquet, Chevalier of Belle-Isle, who was commander of the Franco-Spanish army in Italy. At Assietta, a high plateau in the Alps, the King of Sardinia's troops once again repelled the French, cutting down four thousand men. The Chevalier of Belle-Isle and several officers were killed. Montcalm's forehead was split open by a ball.

During these campaigns in territory that was uneven, mountainous, bristling with woodland, carved out by rivers, Brigadier Montcalm learned to identify locations that provided natural protection for camps, to choose the best routes for convoys, to recognize openings from which the adversary might appear, to take advantage of possibilities offered by a particular terrain, to assess the strengths and weaknesses of enemy positions: all vital knowledge for a general who had to make crucial decisions.

6

The deadly encounter with a one-eyed,
one-armed, one-legged hero

Suffering from seasickness, James Wolfe was thus unable to join his father on his campaign to the West Indies. When Admiral Vernon appeared before Cartagena, Colombia, in March 1741, with 160 ships, his soldiers were weakened by seasickness and long inaction. Many were suffering from scurvy. On April 20, the assault was finally launched against Fort Saint-Lazare. The English found that their ladders were too short to scale the ramparts. And the grenades they launched didn't explode: their shells were too thickly moulded. The defenders' bombardments scattered the troops. In the course of a desperate rout, six hundred redcoats were felled by English muskets. A few days later, from island to island, the indigenous populace spread the news that Blas de Lezo, a warrior who had only one eye, one arm, and one leg, had with his 2,500 men repelled 24,000 Englishmen!

Enfeebled by their wretched physical condition, the English could not fight off yellow fever, dysentery, and malaria. More than ten thousand soldiers and crew members fell victim to tropical diseases. Planned attacks against other Spanish outposts, such as the post in Cuba, were put off. In his letters written from the West Indies, James Wolfe's father told the story of the sad campaign and swore never again to participate in a mission where naval and land troops would have to combine their efforts. Edward Wolfe would return home only two years later.

The expedition to Cartagena represented a humiliating failure for James Wolfe as well. His merciless schoolmates at the Swindon Academy poured scorn on this warrior who wanted to conquer exotic lands but who became seasick at the very sight of his vessel! All his life, James Wolfe would be haunted by his awareness of how fragile he was at sea. "Salt water" and he were "bitter enemies," he confessed. And he would never forget the tales his father told of the Cartagena fiasco; they would dog his memory.

Even if he feared not having the right stuff to be a navy fusilier, he dared not shatter the paternal dream. On November 14, 1741, at the age of fourteen, he joined the regiment of his father, Adjutant-General Edward Wolfe, as a fusilier.

For his mother, Henrietta, it was hard to accept that her son, whose health was so delicate, would have to live on ships rocked by waves, among men ridden with illnesses. His father soon began to suspect that when hostilities ended, this regiment formed for a specific purpose would likely be dissolved. Would not an older, well-established infantry regiment offer his son a more promising future?

In her efforts to have her son's commission changed, Henrietta Wolfe sought support from members of her family and influential friends. Adjutant-General Wolfe, for his part, talked to his military colleagues. While waiting, James Wolfe studied Latin and mathematics. Aware that physical weakness could compromise his career, he embarked on a regime of strenuous exercise. On March 27, 1742, a proud James Wolfe showed off his new commission to his fellow students at the Swindon Academy: with the rank of ensign, he would be standard-bearer for the 12th Infantry Regiment.

In an England greatly demoralized following its defeats in the West Indies, merchants feared that if the French, with their allies, were to take control of the Low Countries, they would revive the Ostend Company that had rivalled the English in India. Charles VI of Austria had dissolved this company as a token of thanks for England's support of his Pragmatic Sanction, which in the absence of a male heir ensured that Maria Theresa would succeed him. And so the British Parliament voted a resolution stipulating that the army would go to the Low Countries to help the Austrians combat the French. Thus began England's participation in the War of the Austrian Succession.

Before the troops left on April 27, 1742, King George II, along with his two sons, the Prince of Wales and the Duke of Cumberland, passed them in review at Blackheath. James Wolfe bore the colours of the 12th Infantry Regiment.

The army arrived at Ostend on May 10 and set off immediately. Crossing through Bruges, James Wolfe and his younger brother, Edward, intrigued by the facades of polished brick, the vaulted doorways, the belfries, and the canals criss-crossing the city, were taken aback by the scorn heaped on them by the people lining the roads. At the age of fifteen, James had no idea that these people, whose country was occupied by the Austrians, wanted only to live in peace without being imposed upon by invaders. At Ghent, the English soldiers were billeted with the inhabitants, who did not hide their resentment. Since the army's arrival, the price of goods had increased. Quarrels were frequent. In the market, an English officer picked up a piece of meat to see if it was fresh. The butcher, assuming he was being robbed, slashed the officer in the face with a knife. One of the officer's comrades drew his sword and ran the butcher through. Other merchants ran forward with their cleavers. The soldiers brandished their weapons. The cavalry was summoned. By the end of the brawl, several bloodied townspeople and soldiers were dead.

James Wolfe and his brother, who did not find their soldier comrades particularly likeable, enjoyed wandering through Ghent's narrow streets and along its canals. They admired the ancient fortifications. The people seemed poorer than those of Westerham. Often dressed in rags, many wore large wooden shoes. The two adolescents eyed the young girls and tried to talk with the populace.

Three months went by very slowly for this idle army. James took flute lessons. He reported to his mother that the food was excellent, that rum and brandy were cheap, and that the ladies were "very civil and speak French."

James was lodged in a dimly lit room. Chilled, his fingers numb from the cold, he worked at his flute. Twice a week, he went to the opera and the theatre. He tried to learn a few words of French, so he could approach the young girls.

Enemies tend not to do battle during the winter. However, in February 1743, to the great surprise of the officers and soldiers, John Dalrymple, Major-General Stair, gave his army marching orders. Destination: the centre of Germany. French troops had been spotted in that direction. The weather was bad: cold rain, wind that cut through wet clothing. Muddy roads. Having arrived at Liège, James confessed to his mother: "My strength is not so great as I imagined." The sickly adolescent had pains in his knees and hips. At Tongres, the family he was to be billeted with refused to let him in. He went to the city hall to complain, and "one of the most courteous men" he had ever met agreed to lodge him.

To continue his route, James Wolfe rented a horse, which he shared with his brother, Edward. Each rode it for one day and the next went on foot, turn and turn about. On April 7, 1743, there was snow up to their knees. In the villages around Bonn, the peasants refused to sell supplies to the English soldiers. Fortunately, in the city, James and his brother feasted on eggs, bacon, and "sour bread."

Sixty thousand French, under the orders of Marshal Adrien Maurice de Noailles, marched to meet Marshal Stair's troops. In June 1743, some thirty-two kilometres from Frankfurt, Noailles's army almost surrounded Stair's troops in the narrow Main River valley, walled with mountains. If Noailles had completely succeeded in this operation, the British would have been cut off from all reinforcements. James Wolfe, who had just been appointed interim adjutant, knew, given his position, that food and forage were going to be in short supply: "I don't know how it will be possible to get provisions. . . . The French are burning all the villages on the other side of the Main and we are ravaging the country on this side." James was proud to inform his father that he was becoming used to expending the effort his duties demanded.

King George II, accompanied by his son William Augustus, Duke of Cumberland, visited his troops and gave them the order to pull back. But the route was blocked near Dettingen by thirty thousand French who awaited them with menacing artillery on flat and open terrain. Red-faced, brandishing his sword, George II galloped on horseback ahead of the front line from one flank to the other. He roared, he swore, he exhorted his troops to resist. The Grey Musketeers cavalry charged. The king's horse bolted and threw His Majesty to the ground. The musketeers mowed down the English front line. The French and British cavalries locked horns.

When the British were readying their muskets to shoot, the French dropped to the ground, and after the shots, they rose and marched in "intolerably good order," maintaining a fire that sowed confusion in the enemy. In the end, the English troops threw themselves on the French with such fury that they carried the day.

This was James Wolfe's first battle. The young officer saw what he called "the stupidity of war." He was enormously impressed by the Duke of Cumberland, who, under balls and shot, fought on despite his bloody leg. The adolescent had the privilege of approaching this man who was the king's son. He wrote proudly to his parents: "I had several times the honour of speaking to him." James's brother, Edward, had to go back to London for medical treatment. The British army returned to its winter quarters. James, at the age of sixteen, was promoted to the rank of lieutenant.

The following year, in the summer of 1744, the French army in the Low Countries took possession of strategic towns such as Ypres, despite the fact that the Anglo-Austrian coalition army counted 65,000 men. Its new commander, Marshal George Wade, could not decide what action to take. Allied contingents deserted.

Having become captain of the 4th Infantry Regiment, James Wolfe spent the winter in Ghent, where he learned of his brother's death from "consumption," or tuberculosis. James had never suspected that Edward's health was so poor. He confessed to his mother that he had "many difficult hours," knowing that he had not shared his brother's last breaths. Desolate, Henrietta hoped to be comforted by the presence of her other son. She begged her husband to overcome "some obstacles" to bring James to England, but the young captain refused to abandon his regiment.

The Duke of Cumberland replaced the ineffective Marshal Wade. The king's son was only twenty-three. Barely arrived in the Low Countries, he decided to liberate Tournai. This former capital of the French dominion in Flanders, fortified by the engineer Vauban, had been besieged since April 26, 1745, by forty thousand French soldiers.

Louis XV and his heir apparent accompanied the French forces. This was the first time since the Battle of Poitiers in 1356 that a king and his heir had honoured the French army with their presence.

After an early advantage, the French were forced to retreat, but their commander, Marshal Maurice de Saxe, rallied his troops, and eight kilometres from Tournai, on treeless terrain, he threw up redoubts and dug trenches. On this field at Fontenoy, on May 11, 1745, the 53,000 men of the Duke of Cumberland—English, Austrian, Dutch, and Hanoverian—were defeated in a bloody confrontation: the English and their allies left some six thousand soldiers on the battlefield.

Posted to Ghent, the 4th Regiment escaped the massacre, but the officers talked among themselves. What had caused the English defeat? How could damaging delays be avoided? How could they achieve a better cohesion of allied detachments? How could they improve discipline among the rank and file? James Wolfe listened attentively to the conversations.

7

"No individual corps had been wanting in their duty"

Following the promulgation of the Act of Settlement in 1701, only a Protestant king could accede to the English throne. King James II had embraced the Catholic faith, had married a Catholic Italian princess, and had fled to France, forced by a coup d'état. Succession to the throne was thus out of the question for his son, James Francis Edward Stuart. James II's grandson, Charles Edward Stuart, who had grown up in Rome where the Pope had provided a residence for his father, now asked the French to support his legitimate claim to the English throne. The French navy, which feared the British navy, used the pretext of bad weather over the Channel to make itself scarce. Disappointed, Charles Edward Stuart recruited a dozen men, and with them, in two modest vessels, he crossed the Channel.

He landed in Scotland on July 25, 1745, and began urging the Highlanders to march with him to take possession of the English throne. Many believed in his divine right to a throne of which his grandfather and father had been unjustly deprived. As for the reigning king, George II, he was a foreigner from the German house of Hanover. And so three hundred men from the MacDonald clan and seven hundred from the Cameron clan agreed to follow "Bonnie Prince Charlie," as Charles Edward Stuart was called. This armed band, growing in numbers every day, succeeded in taking Edinburgh. Bonnie Prince Charlie took up residence in Holyrood Palace, where he held court.

As might be expected, the British forces in Scotland set off in pursuit of Bonnie Prince Charlie, who was quite prepared to come out from Edinburgh and confront them. Many soldiers in the English army were conscripts. When they heard the rallying cries of the Scottish clans, they panicked. To stop them from fleeing, their officers threatened to shoot them down. But the soldiers could not get very far in any case, as their way was blocked by a ditch and a wall. In five minutes, a thousand of them were massacred by the partisans of the Young Pretender to the throne.

King George II, alarmed, recalled seven regiments from Flanders, including the 4th Infantry Regiment belonging to Captain James Wolfe, who had not seen England for three years. The 4th Regiment was quartered in Newcastle upon Tyne. Several weeks passed without any action being taken. Meanwhile, Bonnie Prince Charlie's troops were besieging Carlisle in the northeast of England.

Called upon at last, James Wolfe's regiment covered ninety-five kilometres from hill to hill, in deep snow. The terrain was rough, the cold was harsh. By the time the royal troops arrived at Carlisle, the town had already fallen to the Jacobites. The Young Pretender occupied the castle. In the ranks of the Royal Army, many were happy not to have to fight the fierce Scots. James Wolfe was disappointed to hear even the officers expressing their relief.

London was on the verge of panic. Bonnie Prince Charlie, supported by six thousand men, had now reached Derby, two hundred kilometres away. More reinforcements were urgently summoned from Flanders, but Bonnie Prince Charlie and the clans suddenly decided to return to the Scottish Highlands. In pursuit of the

Jacobites, General Henry Hawley led his men toward Stirling, in Scotland.

Informed on the way that Bonnie Prince Charlie and his men were nearby, the general stopped at Falkirk. He was convinced that the Jacobites would not dare to approach his nine thousand soldiers. But on January 17, 1746, to the astonishment of his Scottish officers, the Young Pretender attacked the English in their camp while they were eating. Confusion reigned. General Hawley was nowhere to be seen.

In fact, he was dining in peace, and in private, with a countess, a few kilometres away. When he arrived, out of breath, fulminating, cursing, the Highlanders were well dug in. Under a driving winter rain, Hawley spurred on his cavalry, then his infantry, to dislodge them. Bonnie Prince Charlie's Highlanders tossed away their muskets: the downpour had soaked their fuses and their powder. Claymores in hand, they charged the British ranks, scattering their left flank. The right flank, where Captain Wolfe was shivering, retreated, leaving its cannons stuck in the mud.

After the lucrative pillage that followed their victory, many of the Highlanders returned to their lands, proud of the booty they carried with them. His numbers depleted, Bonnie Prince Charlie set his sights on Stirling Castle, perched on a rocky height. Protected by three steep cliffs, the fortified castle proved untakeable.

The Duke of Cumberland travelled up and down this territory that had furnished so many fighters for the Young Pretender, punishing the rebels and forcing them to proclaim their loyalty to King George II. At the end of February 1746, he entered Aberdeen. There he met James Wolfe once more and made him aide-de-camp to Lieutenant-General Hawley.

The residence allotted to the general belonged to Lady Gordon, a supporter of Bonnie Prince Charlie, who had had to seek refuge under another roof. All her goods had been confiscated except the clothes she was wearing. General Hawley proposed to speak to the duke, so that Lady Gordon might keep her personal effects. To this end, he sent his new aide-de-camp to pay her a visit. She asked whether she might keep her tea. Wolfe replied that tea was very rare, and that it would be much appreciated by the officers. She would also like to keep her chocolate. "The officers are very fond of chocolate," said the aide-de-camp. Could she keep her porcelain? "The officers are lovers of porcelain," he assured her. Could she keep the portrait of her son? "How old is he?" asked Wolfe. "Fourteen years old." "Where is he? Madame, you should have declared your son," the implacable young officer advised her.

After Hawley intervened, Cumberland returned all Lady Gordon's personal possessions to her. When she sent someone to pick up a pair of pants for her son, along with tea and flour, Wolfe refused her request. Lady Gordon supported Charles Edward Stuart; as an officer of the British Royal Army, Wolfe was persuaded that his duty was to punish the enemy.

In April 1746, the Royal Army set out for the west coast. Some distance away, Bonnie Prince Charlie's Highlanders were roaming the countryside in search of food. On some days, all they had to eat was a single biscuit. Since Falkirk, almost half of the Young Pretender's partisans had slipped away. Those who remained were exhausted and disillusioned. Dissension was rife.

On April 16, in the wind and rain, Bonnie Prince Charlie gathered together on Culloden Moor what was left of his army. The Duke of Cumberland arrived there at midday. He positioned his troops. The rain stopped. He gave his officers the following instructions: when the Highlanders charged, every infantryman was to stand ready to plant his bayonet not in the enemy facing him but in the enemy's neighbour to the right, under the raised arm brandishing the claymore. In that way, the soldier would avoid sticking his weapon into the attacker's wooden shield. Cumberland promised victory if the troops heeded this advice.

Ten English cannons discharged a volley of shots. The Highlanders retreated. Bonnie Prince Charlie rallied them. They charged the English, but on the flat terrain they were mowed down. For a short moment, the Cameron clan surrounded James Wolfe's 4th Regiment. Another regiment came to its aid.

Once the attack on foot was repulsed, Lieutenant-General Hawley's horsemen charged Bonnie Prince Charlie's supporters. "Those ruffians," as Wolfe called them, were dispersed. The cavalry went after them, and 1,500 were left in the blood-soaked earth where they fell. What is more, seven hundred prisoners were punished by Cumberland, whom the Jacobites called "the butcher." The next day, in a letter to his mother, Wolfe declared that in this victorious battle "no individual corps had been wanting in their duty."

After his triumph at Culloden, the Duke of Cumberland continued to sow terror in the Highland Jacobites until July. He then returned to England with much of his army. The rest spread out through Scotland to intimidate the rebels. Captain Wolfe was assigned to a company charged with rebuilding the fort at Inversnaid, on the banks of Loch Lomond. He spent the Christmas holidays in London with his family, where they celebrated the promotion of his father, Edward Wolfe, to the rank of lieutenant-general.

8

So much learned, so much to learn...

The French took advantage of the absence of the British troops summoned to Scotland to themselves deploy in the Low Countries. The 4th Infantry Regiment was reassigned to Flanders. James Wolfe was now twenty years old. Camped not far from Liège, he made the acquaintance of a Miss Lacey, the daughter of a general serving with the Austrian troops. Soon the young officer had to proceed on his way. James wrote often, and profusely, to Miss Lacey. His approach was playful, but he became very serious when he spoke to her about the red frock coat he had ordered: would she closely supervise the work of the tailor?

Flush with his success in Scotland, the Duke of Cumberland was made commander-in-chief of the allied armies, which included Austria, the United Provinces, Piedmont, Sardinia, and Saxony. At the head of a hundred thousand fighters, the duke launched a first offensive in the Low Countries. In his haste to surprise the French, he was ill prepared; his soldiers were short of munitions! He also discovered that the French army was more disciplined than the Highlanders. Wanting to capitalize on the Allies' predicament, Marshal de Saxe, the French commander, marched his troops on Maastricht.

On July 2, 1747, in the village of Lauffeldt, five kilometres from Maastricht, Cumberland's army fended off the French three times. On the French troops' fourth attempt, the French bayonets dislodged the Allies, who lost 5,700 men, killed or wounded. The victory cost the French some ten thousand men. During the confrontation, James Wolfe was hit in the body by a bullet.

After ten days in the hospital, he was able to return to service. In the regiment, his comrades teased him about a young girl he'd arranged to meet at the church. But from the Duke of Cumberland himself, he received formal thanks for the role he'd played in the recent battle.

Late in the autumn, he received permission to return to London. During his stay, he was dazzled by Elizabeth Lawson, one of the Princess of Wales's maids of honour. Her father was a baron, her mother was niece to a count, and her uncle was a general. At first, the two lovebirds kept their mutual feelings secret. When James finally confided in his parents, they were far from happy: Miss Lawson would bring her husband a dowry of only twelve thousand pounds. Henrietta Wolfe knew a charming young lady, Kitty Ann Hoskins, with thirty thousand pounds to her name. . . .

In the spring of 1748, James Wolfe was posted to Holland with a German detachment in the pay of England. His mission was to find munitions, food, and brandy for the soldiers and feed for the animals, as well as wagons for transport. Even though he would have preferred a more martial assignment, he applied himself energetically to the task at hand.

To the Allies' surprise, the French suddenly appeared before Maastricht in April 1748. Fearing to lose the city, the Allies' representatives in Aix-la-Chapelle agreed to make concessions. The monarchs signed a treaty that put an end to the War of the Austrian Succession. All the conquered territories were returned. The French withdrew from the Low Countries and gave back Madras, in India, to the East India Company. Cape Breton Island, occupied in Canada by the English, was returned to France.

James Wolfe would have liked to take advantage of this peace to further his education. He wanted to learn how foreign armies recruited and trained their soldiers. His request for study leave was turned down because the 4th Regiment would soon be recalled to England, it was said, and new responsibilities would await the officers. For six months, James fretted, inactive, to no purpose. He resented wasting all that time. He accused his superiors of being indifferent to his desire to improve himself. His mother, always concerned for the health of her overly thin son, sent him medicines. He was grateful: "Your green oil in particular was of singular service to me, for a hurt I received by the falling of my horse (not *from* my horse), and that's well likewise." Henrietta Wolfe did her son another favour: she went herself to provide a wigmaker with her son's exact measurements. A "trustworthy" sergeant came to pick up the wig in London and to deliver it to Glasgow. In return, James, a good son, informed his mother, who had need of false teeth, that in Paris they knew how to install teeth that were artificial. Did they also know how to do that in London? he asked. He had lost a tooth in combat.

James Wolfe had time to reflect. Over the last years, he had experienced fear, he had faced death. He had known the elation of fighting and not dying. He had learned that an army couldn't win without destroying its enemy. He had served under generals who were "dotards" and "brainless swashbucklers." With Cumberland, he had observed how a leader could instill courage and strength in his soldiers. He had witnessed corruption, favouritism, and laxness in the king's army. Was Captain James Wolfe, at the age of twenty-one, still a young man? At the beginning of winter, 1748, he returned to his parents. Despite their disapproval, he was still courting Elizabeth Lawson.

9

Peace, family, and rural beauty

After the signing of the Treaty of Aix-la-Chapelle on July 18, 1748, Louis-Joseph de Montcalm returned to France with his regiment and to its garrison in Tonnerre, in Burgundy. Surrounded by vineyards on green hills, it was an ancient city. Marguerite de Bourgogne, sister-in-law of Saint Louis, was entombed there in a chapel she had had built in 1293. Sensitive to history, Montcalm was also mindful of his career. If a brigadier thought of becoming a general, he had to be where decisions were made. Montcalm went up to Paris.

The War of the Austrian Succession had taken its toll on the royal treasury. In February 1749, Louis XV reduced the number of his regiments. That of Montcalm was merged with the Flanders Regiment. Brigadier Montcalm lost the allowance that went along with his position, but he was being considered as the commander of a new unit of grenadiers. He showed little interest, however, in commanding men who became grenadiers largely by virtue of their height. Two new cavalry regiments were also being created. In April 1749, Montcalm accepted the title of *mestre de camp*, or regiment commander. This might have been considered a demotion, but Montcalm's goal was to found one of these new regiments. And it would carry his name . . .

And so Montcalm returned to Candiac. He owed his domain to a reward his ancestor Louis II de Montcalm had received from King Louis XIII, around 1630. The castle was built with stones from the ramparts of Nîmes, destroyed in 1623. Surrounded by his mother, his wife, and his children, Montcalm again took up the life of a *seigneur* in the château where he and so many of his ancestors were born and had lived. He oversaw the work being done in the fields and woods. He had oaks planted, as well as olive and almond trees. He spent time in his mill, where oil was extracted from olives. He took care of the castle at Candiac and the lands at Vestric. From the Languedoc sky, the sun beat down. In the fields, the lavender was fragrant. He gathered his thoughts while reading ancient writers. But the spell was broken by a disagreement over property rights, which turned into a prolonged trial.

More than anything, he relished his role as a father. Angélique Louise bore him ten children. Some died at an early age: "We must, my most dear and best loved friend, resign ourselves to the will of Providence," he wrote to console his wife while he was in the midst of a campaign. A few years later, on the death of another child, he said to her: "God did not want this soul to be sullied on earth." Six of their children survived: "One might think that that is much for a modest fortune," said Montcalm, "and especially with four girls; but does God ever leave his children in need?"

Every autumn, his two boys left for a Jesuit college in Paris. He and his wife knew the rector. With his mother and his wife, Montcalm spent the winter in Montpellier, where he had many friends. When the Estates of Languedoc opposed the imposition of a new tax, the *seigneur* of Candiac and Vestric took part in the debate. During other deliberations, Montcalm pleaded the cause of regional prerogatives.

The *mestre de camp* also fulfilled his military duties. Conscientious in putting together his regiment, Montcalm went to consult with cavalry inspectors concerning the best exercises to introduce. He went to oversee his regiment's manoeuvres at Limoges, then known as the "holy city." In its convents, monasteries, and colleges, Ursulines, Benedictines, and Jesuits expounded Catholic doctrine. Many penitents prayed to God, flagellated themselves, lived on public charity, walked barefoot, and dressed in long hooded robes, inveighing against the "corpulent" clergy. Why did the *mestre de camp* Montcalm choose to station his regiment in this city? Perhaps he wanted to be sure that God would be on the side of his cavalry. Montcalm wrote: "Spiritual exercises, proportional to their needs, did not stand in the way of their being trained every day, either on foot or on horseback."

The honour of having a regiment that carried his name cost him dearly. In October 1752, Montcalm asked for a pension. He let it be known to the secretary of state for war, Marc-Pierre de Voyer de Paulmy d'Argenson, that he had served in the king's army for thirty-one years, that he had participated in eleven campaigns, that he had been wounded five times, that he had been made prisoner, and that he had never hesitated to draw on his modest fortune to support his regiment. In the autumn of 1755, he was called up to Paris by the minister.

10

*"It is not in our interest to quarrel
with any but the French"*

At the beginning of January 1749, James Wolfe, now promoted
to the rank of major and assigned to the 20th Infantry
Regiment, was in Stirling, in Scotland. With the regiment colonel
appearing only occasionally to inspect the troops, the lieutenant-colonel was the de facto commander. On reporting to his
regiment, however, Wolfe learned that the lieutenant-colonel
was absent: Edward Cornwallis had in fact been named governor
of Nova Scotia, in Canada. Therefore, Major Wolfe had to take
command of the regiment. At twenty-two, he was younger than
most of his officers.

After the defeat of Bonnie Prince Charlie at Culloden Moor,
George II's soldiers had hunted down Highlanders who had supported
the Young Pretender. They hanged many. They put farms to the
torch and confiscated the lands of Jacobite leaders. England annulled
traditional judicial and political powers; the Highlanders now had to
submit to the same laws as other Scots. They were forbidden to carry
arms and even to wear their distinctive kilt. The Celtic language was
banned. The Scottish Episcopal Church had to swear allegiance to
George II. English garrisons stationed in Scotland would see to the
application of these laws. That was James Wolfe's mission.

Not only was Stirling "filthy and full of drunkards," but its climate was wretched. Wolfe imposed strict standards of cleanliness on his regiment. He required that the officers do the rounds in their quarters every night between nine and eleven. If they found one of their soldiers too thin or too pale, they had to take appropriate measures to restore his health. Any soldier who left his watch without authorization from his officer was harshly punished. Soldiers had to avoid any dispute with the citizens. If there was some commotion, they were not to mix with the crowd.

Barely two weeks later, the regiment was transferred to Glasgow, a city of twenty thousand inhabitants whom Wolfe regarded as hypocritical and disloyal. After a few weeks, the town was less disagreeable. The women seemed not to fear the soldiers. Was he still dreaming of Elizabeth Lawson? He confessed to a friend, "If I'm kept long here, the fire will be extinguished."

The commander of an English regiment was an important personage: he represented the king. In Glasgow, James Wolfe had expenses: his lodging, his food, his servant, his laundry, his horse and its feed, and so on. He asked his parents for help. His father refused to get involved; his son had to assume his own obligations. His mother, of course, made the old soldier relent, and he contributed to his son's serving the king.

Every Sunday, Major Wolfe made a point of attending the service at the Kirk (the Scottish church), even if "Scotch preachers are excessive blockheads." He submitted to this ordeal to show the people how tolerant the king was. In the early summer, a fire threatened a whole city neighbourhood. Wolfe deployed his regiment to help the populace: the soldiers saved their houses. After that, his men helped build roads. When Lord John Sackville, the colonel, came to inspect his regiment later in June, he was so pleased with what Wolfe had accomplished that he promised to help him in his career.

Wolfe hired two tutors from the University of Glasgow: one for Latin and the other for mathematics, which "can help in judgment." In August, under a cloudy sky, he grew restless. He went hunting to perfect his aim and thought back on past campaigns: "A battle gained is, I believe, the highest joy mankind is capable of receiving, to him who commands." He was also concerned: a skin infection on his hand, could that be scurvy? Should he drink water from a spring with medicinal properties? His mother suggested he drink, rather, goat's whey to "put right the bad juices" within him. Was he still very thin? Yes, he replied to his mother, but there was some advantage in that: the surgeons could have "a clear view of them in me, distinct from fat or fleshy impediment."

Wolfe carried on a correspondence with George Keppel, Lord Bury, who had just succeeded Lord Sackville as his regiment colonel. Wolfe had earned the respect of Lord Sackville, a fellow Freemason and an influential member of London's high society. Now he had to gain the confidence of Lord Bury, who was already a family friend.

Who would replace Lord Cornwallis, lieutenant-colonel of the 20th Regiment? Perhaps the Duke of Cumberland would remember Major Wolfe.

In March 1750, surrounded by his officers, Lieutenant-Colonel James Wolfe celebrated, at a regimental dinner, the commission he was about to receive at the age of twenty-three. This promotion, along with vigorous exercise on the moor, did more for him than goat's milk and baths: suddenly, he felt himself "as hard as flint."

His flame for Elizabeth Lawson had not gone out. Edward Wolfe reproached his son, in very blunt words, for persisting in his error. His parents even stopped writing to him. Was his father going to disinherit James in order to force Elizabeth's father to reject this fiancé with nothing to his name? Despite his parents' silence, James continued to send them letters.

Two years earlier, he had hoped to visit the European continent, to improve his French, to observe how foreign armies prepared for war. Now he dreamed of attending the School of Infantry and Engineering in Metz, France. Lord Bury granted him a leave but required that he stay in Great Britain. Did his superiors fear that, like many British officers, he would be recruited by a foreign army? Had he not from time to time expressed an interest in such an experience?

Disappointed, unhappy that the Duke of Cumberland had not allowed him to go abroad, he arrived at his parents' home in London, in November 1750. His father would not tolerate his saying anything negative about the duke. Then the subject of Elizabeth Lawson came up. Why would James not consent to being introduced to Miss Hoskins? Not so innocently, Henrietta Wolfe related some stories about Miss Lawson's past life. The young man flared up, lost his temper, left the family house, and threw himself into the streets of London.

He skirted walls, wandered beneath the arches of the Vauxhall Pleasure Gardens, through the Chinese Garden, around the Obelisk, and stopped to listen to musicians. In revolt against his parents, he got drunk, squandered his money in low dives, visited brothels in Covent Garden, and followed boys into sordid rooms. To a friend, he confessed: "I lived in the idlest, dissolute, abandoned manner that could be conceived, and that not out of vice." He became so sick that he asked to be taken back to his parents. Once he had recovered, he agreed to be introduced to Miss Hoskins. Too late. She had just become engaged. A few months later, she brought her husband a dowry of thirty thousand pounds. It took a long time for General Wolfe and his wife to forgive James for not being that husband.

In April 1751, Wolfe returned to his 20th Regiment at Banff, in Scotland. For six months, there was again only silence between the young man and his parents. James went to Peterhead, where the water from a mineral spring did wonders for his lungs, his stomach, and the pains in his chest. Along with this water, a distinguished doctor recommended an internal ingestion of soap. He immediately praised this treatment to his mother. Their emotional bond was renewed. Henrietta sent her son several pounds of chocolate.

At the end of September, Wolfe's regiment was at Inverness. The rain, and later the November snows, gave him rheumatism. The young officer had served almost three years in Scotland. What future did the lieutenant-colonel have? He saw officers with service records inferior to his receiving promotions. Was Lord Bury slowing his advancement? Despite his unease, Wolfe told himself: "It's my duty to be here and that silences me."

The city's inhabitants, who were still loyal to Bonnie Prince Charlie, did not hide their aversion to George II's soldiers. James Wolfe was determined to win their confidence. He returned to the Kirk and made a profession of faith to the pastor. On his orders, his infantrymen became pious soldiers. The lieutenant-colonel also encouraged them to attend dances, where they encountered "an assembly of rebel females, MacDonald, Frazer, and McIntoch," who were "truly wild." Wolfe danced with the daughter of a clan chief who had been killed at the Battle of Culloden. Little by little, he and his men found themselves accepted by the population.

Wolfe visited the site of the Battle of Culloden where, he believed, the commander of the Royal Army had exposed his men to needless risks. And in his opinion, the pursuit of the enemy had not been zealous enough; the Royal Army ought to have inflicted greater damage.

In the spring of 1752, Lord Bury came to inspect his regiment.

The members of the Inverness Council, although in large part supporters of the Young Pretender, invited Lord Bury, colonel of the English regiment assigned to the city, to celebrate with them the birthday of the Duke of Cumberland, victor at Culloden. This remarkable civility was a product of Wolfe's conciliatory initiatives. Lord Bury, with the gross foolhardiness of an occupier, proposed that the council put off its celebrations to the next day, which was the anniversary of the English victory. Of course, the losing party refused to honour its own defeat. Outraged, Lord Bury warned the council that he would be unable to exert control over his soldiers, who would see this rebuff as an insult to the army. And so the council acceded to the wishes of Lord Bury.

Eager to visit the other garrisons, the colonel asked Wolfe to accompany him. If the ambitious lieutenant-colonel felt humiliated at having to carry the colonel's powder horn and flints, he nevertheless had an opportunity to chat with him. Lord Bury must have heard Wolfe talk about his strong desire to travel, to educate himself, and to be engaged in military action that went beyond having a civilizing influence on the population. Wolfe spoke frankly: he had served so long in this 20th Regiment that at times the very sight of one of his soldiers was abhorrent to him. Lord Bury promised to champion his request for a leave, and James Wolfe continued to follow him from garrison to garrison: Perth, Dublin, Cork, Bristol . . .

In Ireland, he made a pilgrimage to the site of the Battle of the Boyne. Having defeated the Catholic king James II in 1690, the Protestant king William III secured Protestant supremacy in Ireland. James Wolfe noted: "There is not another piece of ground in the world that I could take so much pleasure to observe."

He returned to London in August 1752. His parents had moved into a new property in Blackheath, near Greenwich Park. There was no talk of Miss Lawson or Miss Hoskins. James had received permission to travel abroad for a period of six months. In October, he left for Paris. His parents advanced him the money, and Lord Bury gave him a letter of introduction to his own father, who was English ambassador in France. Wolfe was so excited that he forgot to be seasick on the boat. Five days later, he was in Paris.

The first thing he did was to hire a French tutor. Then he signed up for fencing and riding lessons. He even took up dance. At six feet two inches, James Wolfe was much taller than most men of his time. His hair was red, his skin was pale. His eyes were grey-blue, his nose was long and turned-up. He had a high receding fore-head. Even if he didn't have the strong jaw of a warrior, Lieutenant-Colonel Wolfe did not pass unnoticed. Was not learning to dance the minuet without provoking laughter a rather frivolous goal for a soldier? He remarked: "The fortune of a military man seems to depend almost as much on his exteriors as upon things that are in reality more estimable and praiseworthy." He attended theatre and opera but was always in bed by eleven o'clock. The English ambassador, Lord Albemarle, father of Lord Bury, invited James Wolfe to family dinners. He also invited him to official dinners where he met important French personages and the delegates of foreign countries.

The ambassador even introduced him to Louis XV's court, where, in "splendour and magnificence," Wolfe saw "how a multitude of men and women were assembled to bow and pay their compliments in a most submissive manner to a creature of their own species."

On January 10, 1753, thanks to the good offices of Lord Albemarle, Wolfe, along with other English guests, was presented to King Louis XV and the royal family. Then the guests were received by Madame de Pompadour, the king's mistress, in a room where she was busy curling her hair. One of her companions informed James Wolfe that among the 3,525 volumes in her personal library were translations into French of *Tom Jones*, *Robinson Crusoe*, and *Moll Flanders*.

James Wolfe did not try to insinuate himself into the circle of Paris beauties, because he would have had to spend a fortune he didn't possess. What is more, they received at an hour when he was climbing into bed so as to be fresh for his morning exercises. As for the men of Paris, he accused them of preferring witty words to noble acts. From them, he could learn "how to persuade you that I am what I am not." He was not tempted by such pretensions.

France was at that time in the throes of another religious controversy. Three or four years earlier, the archbishop of Paris, Christophe de Beaumont du Repaire, had instructed priests, before administering the last rites, to demand *billets de confession* attesting to the fact that the dying had endorsed the anti-Jansenist Bull *Unigenitus*. Parliament, for its part, forbade priests to refuse anyone such sacraments. The king intervened, prohibiting Parliament from involving itself in the issue. Parliament reacted on April 9, 1753, protesting to the king, who responded by exiling the Parliament to Pontoise. As the officer of a foreign army, Wolfe refrained from commenting on French politics, but he nonetheless thought that churchmen were the authors of almost all the evils that had plagued Europe since the introduction of Christianity. Wolfe also observed: "The English are not favourites here; they [the French] can't help looking upon us as enemies, and I believe they are right."

For the young lieutenant-colonel, French civilization's greatest achievement was the invention of the umbrella. Its use, he thought, could be exported to Britain. Beyond that, he appreciated the "art" of the dentist who filled two of his teeth with lead.

Louis XV's Royal Army had invited the Prussian and Austrian armies to participate in manoeuvres. Lord Albemarle thought

James could be England's observing officer. Excited by the prospect of seeing "at least half of Europe's armies at work," Wolfe requested the necessary authorization from Lord Bury, who ordered him instead to rejoin his regiment in Glasgow, where his presence was urgently needed. The major who in Wolfe's absence had assumed command was ill.

On April 22, Wolfe, en route for Glasgow, was being shaken and rattled about in one of the new post-chaises. Although he was extremely unhappy to be missing out on an experience that had been his dream, he would do his duty. When he arrived in Glasgow, where he reunited with the 20th Regiment, he found that the major had just died of apoplexy. Too many amorous liaisons had worn him down, Wolfe was told, and he had to console the man's widow and little daughter. Later, during the showing of the colours, an ensign fainted. During the dinner offered by the lieutenant-colonel on the occasion of his return from Paris, another ensign collapsed. Then Wolfe discovered that several officers were spitting blood. Three weeks later, all the officers and soldiers were sick, trembling, the skin of their faces flaking off. Wolfe was convinced that Glasgow's hostile climate could not be the only cause. He reminded everyone of the importance of hygiene. Above all, he fulminated against prostitution, that "ignominy." Soldiers suffered, died of venereal disease, and the king's troops were weakened.

During the summer, the 20th Regiment returned to the Highlands. On the back of an old horse—Wolfe complained to his parents that he didn't have enough money for a better animal—he went west of Loch Lomond. This "beautifully rough and wild" land was teeming with game, and its rivers overflowed with fish. A cousin had made him the gift of a pointer, and a rod and reel. His mother sent him flies.

But it was with no regrets that he finally left Scotland, where people were "excessively dirty and lazy," to return to England, where they were "clean and industrious." At the end of September, the 20th Regiment marched through Cumberland, Westmoreland, and Lancashire. On hearing that the Duke of Cumberland would be passing his regiment in review, Wolfe imposed five-hour training sessions on his men. At the beginning of November, Cumberland was able to appreciate the discipline of Wolfe's infantry: they kept in line, avoided confusion, and were silent during manoeuvres. However, they were less rapid than the soldiers of the 13th Regiment. Lord Bury, the colonel, ordered Wolfe to drill them in the same firing exercises as were used by the 13th.

The long summer march ended at Dover, just as the weather was cooling. Wolfe was lodged in the tower of a castle perched on a white cliff, above a network of subterranean tunnels dug in the Middle Ages. The ruins of a lighthouse built by the Romans looked out over the sea. The port of Dover was the crossing point for French deserters fleeing to England and for the British who wanted to enlist in the French army. Wolfe instituted a reward to encourage soldiers to root out traitors, who were given the lash.

Dover was miserable in winter. It was said that if you marched there, you could break your legs, and if you went on horseback, you could break your neck. To fend off depression, Wolfe drank green tea. He had a lot of time to read. Often, he rode his horse for some "very pleasant recreation." He hunted woodcock and quail, and bagged some pheasant and partridge as well.

After the winter in Dover and its "vile dungeon," Wolfe, on leave for six months, stayed with his parents. In July 1754, he was invited to the country house of Sir John Mordaunt, major-general in the army. Although of different ranks, they had participated in the same expeditions in the Low Countries. They had fought against the French at Falkirk and against Bonnie Prince Charlie at

Culloden. Then, after the victory, they had hunted down Jacobites. Wolfe noticed, on the dining room wall, a portrait of Elizabeth Lawson. She was John Mordaunt's niece. After this shock, Wolfe suffered from gastric disorders for three days.

At the end of his leave, he rejoined his regiment at Exeter. The town was a bastion of Jacobism: its people could not accept that the English throne was occupied by George II, whose father, George I, didn't speak English and preferred to live in Germany. Wolfe succeeded in changing their attitude. To celebrate the king's birthday, October 30, 1754, he invited the town's polite society to a regimental ball. Several women and just one man accepted the invitation. The lieutenant-colonel instructed his officers to turn on the charm and to gain the favour of the Jacobite ladies. Wolfe himself showed off the art of dancing the minuet that he had mastered in Paris. After making a strong impression on the ladies, he worked at winning friends among the clergy.

Despite his youth, he inspired confidence. The wife of a Sergeant White, for example, wrote him to complain that her husband, good and faithful up until the middle of November, was no longer behaving properly toward her and her children. Would the "Collonel" be able to put him back on the right track?

Meanwhile, James Wolfe received a request to select a hundred men from his regiment to prepare to go to the American colonies. The French had invaded British territory. In the Ohio Valley, a young officer from Virginia, George Washington, had been forced to cede Fort Necessity to French brigands. The American colonies had their provincial militias, but they needed more disciplined redcoats.

Wolfe proposed to his superiors that two or three regiments of Scots Highlanders also be recruited by the British Army. Those fighters were intrepid and used to rough country, and it would be "no great mischief if they fall."

11

"Blast the enemy!"

On horseback, James Wolfe went to spend Christmas at Bath, where his parents were already installed. The members of polite society appreciated the therapeutic virtues of this town, but they went there also to dance, to gamble, and perhaps to arrange a marriage. Wolfe was astonished at how well his parents seemed, given that his winters in Scotland and Dover had brought him his "old age and infirmity."

His father did not approve of the military's decision to send reinforcements to the American colonies. He felt that England needed all its strength in Europe to deal with problems in Ireland and Scotland. What is more, France was preparing an invasion of Great Britain. James responded: "I am determined never to give myself a moment's concern about the nature of the duty which his Majesty is pleased to order us upon."

Lord Albemarle, British ambassador to Paris, had just died. Lord Bury, his son, had inherited his title of count. He was certainly seeking a more prestigious command than that of the 20th Regiment. At the age of twenty-eight, having been a lieutenant-colonel for five years, James Wolfe hoped to succeed Lord Bury. He saw to it that relatives and friends in their circles, in the army, and in the government, lauded his good services. He confided to his mother, "I am perhaps something nearer to my end than others of my time."

Back with his regiment at the end of January 1755, now at Bristol, Wolfe trained his soldiers. Meticulous in the assimilation of new recruits, he was convinced that training was the best approach. It taught them to control their nerves when they began to tremble while loading their weapons in combat. He put all his men through exercises in firing muskets and attacking with the bayonet. Drawing his inspiration from the methods of the Prussian Army, he divided his troops into eighteen units and had them fire uninterruptedly in such a way that no section would be exposed to the enemy with its guns unloaded.

In April 1755, the members of the 20th Regiment, now at Winchester, learned who their colonel would be. It was not James Wolfe, but Philip Honywood, a wealthy man. Wolfe was more than upset. He bared his soul to Major-General John Mordaunt, whom he visited often at the village of Freefolk. At the beginning of summer 1755, after passing the 20th Regiment in review, Mordaunt observed that the men showed an "extremely comely appearance under arms." To Wolfe, he expressed "his satisfaction in the strongest of terms," and promised to report as much to the Duke of Cumberland and to the king as well.

Wolfe read the dispatches. The previous June, in Canada, near Cape Breton Island, Admiral Edward Boscawen had seen three ships flying the French flag, emerging from the fog, within range of his cannons. "Are we at peace or at war?" he asked one of the French captains. "We are at peace," replied the captain of the *Dunkerke*, who immediately gave the order to fire. The battle was short. Several French officers and soldiers were taken prisoner. Some officers predicted that this incident would give France another pretext to invade England. The "most beautiful" fleet in

Great Britain, according to Wolfe, was anchored at Spithead, ready to hoist its sails and make for America under the orders of Vice-Admiral Edward Hawke.

On July 2, the Duke of Cumberland was the guest of honour at a military ceremony. Lord George Anson, first lord of the Admiralty, was a guest much remarked upon. Since his expedition attacking the Spanish colonies on the west coast of South America, he had been a popular hero. His circumnavigation lasted from 1740 to 1744. It cost the lives of two thousand men, but the explorer returned with a treasure of 400,000 pounds. The Duke of Cumberland noted the presence of James Wolfe, greeted him, and introduced him to Lord Anson, who invited him to dinner. This recognition by two superior officers was a balm to the wound that had been inflicted by the naming of the new colonel for the 20th Regiment.

It was at this point in his life that Wolfe decided no longer to wear a wig, though it was the custom for men of his rank. But a wig was a haven for lice. Henceforth, he would expose his red hair, he told his mother, who was suffering from an attack of sciatic gout, while he himself was suffering from stones in the urinary system. According to Dr. Webster, he had all the symptoms of renal tuberculosis. His life would likely be short . . .

At the end of August 1755, a dispatch brought the news of an English defeat a month earlier in America, at Fort Duquesne (Pittsburgh), on the Ohio River. Two-thirds of General Edward Braddock's army, made up of regular troops (including a hundred men recruited from Wolfe's regiment) and militias from the colonies, had been massacred by bands of French, Odawas, Ojibways and Potawatomis lying in ambush in the forest. General Braddock had been killed.

Wolfe had little sympathy: "I have a very poor opinion of the infantry in general," he wrote. "In their confusion, they kill each other." He had seen that at Dettingen. Denouncing "the extreme ignorance of the officers," he warned his superiors, "our military education is by far the worst in Europe." He recommended that military training be overhauled for the war in America. If the infantry succumbed so easily to disorder on European battlefields, one could only imagine the chaos when it was assailed by "a horde of savages ambush'd behind timber in an unknown trackless country."

The information gleaned from spies seemed to confirm the rumour: the French were threatening to invade England. In October 1755, the 20th Infantry Regiment was sent southwest to Canterbury. The region commander was General "Hangman" Hawley. James Wolfe, who had been his aide-de-camp ten years earlier, did not shrink from speaking his mind to his superiors: if the French landed on English soil, he said, they would face the most incompetent general in the Royal Army. Convinced that England was facing certain danger, Wolfe advised his father to sell his government treasury bonds and put his money instead into buying land.

Wolfe prepared his troops to encounter the French. Positioned on a height, they fired downward. Then he reversed the angle. He laid out the rules: if a soldier abandoned his weapon, he would be court-martialled; a sergeant who left his post or did not replace a fallen officer would be hanged; if a soldier took to his heels, he would be brought down immediately by an officer; the same punishment would be inflicted on a soldier who fired before receiving the order; marksmen would load their muskets with one or two extra balls—the jolt to the shoulder would be stronger, but they had to be ready to suffer for the king; when the enemy came within twenty yards, soldiers would fix their bayonets and be ready to offer "bloody resistance!" The order of the day was "Blast the enemy!"

In Canterbury, despite the looming French threat, winter was peaceful. It made Wolfe reflect: "The officers of the army in general are persons of so little application to business, and have been so ill educated . . . that I, your son, who have, I know, but a very moderate capacity, and some degree of diligence a little above the ordinary run, should be thought, as I generally am, one of the best officers of my rank in the service."

12

"A good letter to keep . . . in the event of misfortune"

Since the peace treaty of Aix-la-Chapelle, signed in 1748, Colonel Louis-Joseph de Montcalm, having retired to the country, had watched his olive and almond trees as they grew. He fulfilled his duties as a colonel, donning his uniform to visit his regiment and pass it in review. In the autumn of 1755, he was summoned to Paris by Monsieur d'Argenson, the secretary of state for war.

He listened to him explain the situation in the colonies and the French posts in distant territories, where France had to contend with outsized English ambitions. In the East Indies, ports, trading posts, and ships were harassed by the English. In America, Governor Robert Dinwiddie of Virginia had in 1753 ordered the French to abandon their forts, their trading posts, and their lands in Belle-Rivière (Ohio). The next year, the English began to build a fort in French territory, on the Belle-Rivière (the Ohio River). The French went to halt this work, which they subsequently completed themselves. The fort became French—Fort Duquesne (today near Pittsburgh). Governor Dinwiddie wanted to retake it. Along with a few hundred of his militia, he went to attack the fort. In May 1754, Joseph Coulon de Villiers, Sieur de Jumonville, and thirty or so men, confronted them and ordered them to leave French territory. Jumonville and a third of his militia were killed.

The French got even. In July 1753, Louis Coulon de Villiers, Jumonville's brother, captured another English fort—Necessity—built on French territory.

The English colonists of Boston had first taken refuge in Acadia, then crossed the Appalachian Mountains and descended toward the west, into the Belle-Rivière valley. English ships intercepted a French fleet not far from Newfoundland. Their cannonballs left the bridges of the French vessels strewn with dead bodies. The brother of Governor Pierre de Rigaud de Vaudreuil was taken prisoner along with more than four hundred members of the Reine and Languedoc regiments. These assaults on the French in America contravened the Aix-la-Chapelle agreement.

France and England were at peace, but while the English ambassador was paying court to Louis XV, the English Admiralty ordered its ships to pursue all French vessels. France and England were at peace, but at the opening of Parliament in London, the Speech from the Throne was so warlike in respect to France that the French ambassador to London had been recalled.

In June of the year 1755, two thousand militiamen from Massachusetts went to Acadia to besiege Fort Beauséjour. The small garrison surrendered, as did Fort Gaspareaux. And the English deported the French population.

France, as always, favoured peace, but the secretary of state for war thought that it would be hard to avoid a conflict with England. France, he promised, would resist an English invasion of its American colonies!

At the beginning of September 1755, Baron Jean-Armand Dieskau, commander of the King's Army in Canada, set out to repel the English and their native allies, who were making their way toward Montreal. When Dieskau arrived at Fort Lydius (Edward), on the Hudson River, with 220 French soldiers and 680 *Canadiens*,

English cannons and rifles awaited them. The six hundred Iroquois who had accompanied the French refused to attack a fort that was situated on English territory. Dieskau, soon "thrown to the ground by three shots," as he wrote to the secretary of state for war, leaned back against a tree. He refused to be carried off to dress his wounds, saying "the bed where he found himself was as good to die in as the one they wanted to give him." The English made him prisoner, took him to New York, then London, and finally to Bath, where they thought the water of the springs might heal him.

"I must replace Baron Dieskau," concluded the secretary of state for war. "You, Monsieur de Montcalm, are the king's officer I have chosen to defend France in America."

Make war in America? France was divided over the issue. Shouldn't they be attacking Hanover, as some suggested? The King of England would then have to send back to the continent the resources he'd committed to America. Some, like the minister Jean-Baptiste de Machault, dreamed of restoring to the French navy, the marine, "that soul and that life it once possessed" under Louis XIV. For them, the colonies would be better protected by a powerful navy that ruled the seas. Others, pessimistic, like Marshal Adrien de Noailles, were of the opinion that "it would be less shameful for France to abandon America to the English after an unfortunate war than to let it be invaded in time of peace without trying to defend it."

After enjoying peace for eight years, did Montcalm, now forty-three, really want to return to the battlefield? His wife begged him not to be tempted by the adventure. His mother was "overcome by sorrow" at the thought that she would be separated from her son, who would be off with the English and the savages, but she was proud that the king appreciated his qualities. She encouraged him to accept this responsibility.

On January 31, 1756, in a letter from the secretary of state for war, the king charged Louis-Joseph de Montcalm "with the command of his troops in the north of America." With this new mission, he would rise to the rank of major-general. The king granted him one favour: Louis-Jean, Montcalm's eldest son, would succeed his father at the head of his regiment, with the rank of *mestre de camp*. The seventeen-year-old adolescent, very thin, delicate, "prodigiously" tall, became the equal of a colonel!

Having accepted this commission that he had "neither desired nor sought," as he insisted, Montcalm first did his duty as head of his family. He lavished advice on his son, who at such a young age would carry a heavy burden: reply to the officers who write you, say you appreciate their compliments, ask them to help you with their advice. He was concerned: did his daughter write often enough to her grandmother, who lived at the Abbey at Port-Royal? He wrote notes to pay the tailor for his uniforms and those of his son. He transferred a sum of three thousand *livres* to his wife, to be drawn from the funds that the king had bestowed on him. In his absence, she would be responsible for his correspondence. He wrote down what debts should be paid and what loans reimbursed. He also entrusted her with the king's letter that guaranteed him, on his return from Canada, an annual pension of four thousand *livres*, plus the two-thousand-*livre* pension he already received: "It's a good letter to keep … in the event of misfortune." Finally, he gave her a draft of his will.

On February 6, his mind at rest, he boarded ship to sail up the Rhone: the priest in Vauvert had promised to say one mass a week for him. During his slow progress up the river, he read the *History of New France* by the Jesuit father Pierre-François-Xavier Charlevoix, where he found "an agreeable description of Quebec."

On February 13, Montcalm was received at Versailles by the

secretary of state for war, who granted him another favour: he would entrust a company to his second son, Déodat. The father suggested that at twelve and a half, the child should be concentrating on his studies. Montcalm was introduced to Monsieur de Machault, minister for the marine and the colonies. The next day, he was received by the king.

Having received the honour of presenting his eldest son to the royal family as well as to Madame de Pompadour, Louis XV's favourite, Montcalm left Versailles. Four days later, at Rennes, the parliamentary president in Brittany honoured him on behalf of the city.

On March 21, Montcalm arrived in Brest, from where he would set sail. He first met his personnel: a cook, an aide, a valet, two footmen, two liveried servants, and a surgeon.

Then he met his brigadier, the Chevalier François-Gaston de Lévis. He was already aware of the brigadier's impressive track record. Lévis was twenty-six years old. He had fought at the Battle of Dettingen and had played a role in several campaigns on the Rhine, from 1743 to 1748. He had led a detachment during the battle on the Main River, in Germany. In Prague, he had been injured in a bomb explosion. During the Italian campaign, he had participated in the sieges of Montalban, Valence, Villefranche, and Vintimille. At Montalban, Lévis had been taken prisoner by a band of Piedmontese. At Plaisance, his horse had been shot out from under him. He had been wounded in the head by a ball while on a reconnaissance mission near Bigli.

Montcalm then had a long interview with his principal aide-de-camp, Colonel Louis-Antoine de Bougainville, from the world of the sciences. He was a connoisseur of the literary arts, but above all of geometry. His writings had gained him a certain notoriety. He was also a theoretician of integral calculus. A member of the Royal Society of London, he was well versed in the English language. He also aspired to become a member of the Paris Academy of Sciences. Bougainville wanted to see America. He had been recommended by Madame de Pompadour, by the widow of a police lieutenant named Hérault, and by the widow's father, who was the inspector general for sciences.

Montcalm then met his other aides-de-camp. The second, the Sieur de La Rochebaucourt, was a "man of quality from Poitou." The third, "aide-de-camp, workman, and secretary," was a sub-officer from the Flanders Regiment.

Montcalm went on to review the battalions of the La Sarre and Royal-Roussillon regiments: some twelve hundred men and officers. Before their departure, Major-General Montcalm was honoured with "all sorts of kind words from the gentlemen of the marine," a body composed almost entirely of "persons of quality." Several were of "distinguished birth." He was invited to meet the Sieur Gilles Hocquart, who had been "intendant in Canada for twenty years without having inflated his fortune, unlike the common run of intendants in the colonies who, it is said, profit unduly at the expense of the colony." Montcalm had heard rumours about certain of the king's representatives in Canada whose behaviour was suspect.

For fear of accidents, pirates, and enemies, Montcalm divided his leadership among several ships. On March 23, when his troops boarded the *Héros*, the *Léopard*, and the *Illustre*, Montcalm was struck by their "air of satisfaction" and their "gaiety." He embarked with Bougainville on March 26, on the *Licorne*. Not being familiar with the sea, the major-general was reassured to have on board a captain from Quebec who knew the waters, considered dangerous, of the St. Lawrence River.

The ships would sail together, but if they were separated by enemies, storms, or fog, they were to continue on their way without

searching for each other. On March 28, while waiting for favourable winds, Montcalm wrote to his mother-in-law: "I hope that
God will preserve us both." On April 1, the ships had not yet left
Brest, "which angers me," he complained. "When one has a job, one
wants to get it done." The country gentleman had reconnected with
his soldierly soul.

On April 3, the *Licorne* finally cast off, along with the *Héros*.
For ten days, they were borne along by fresh winds. From afar, a
small vessel seemed to be observing them. The English? It disappeared and was not seen again. During the week before Easter,
raging winds threw up mountains of water that plunged down and
re-formed, twice as high as the quarterdeck. The rudders were
useless. The ships hove to. Passengers, thrown to the deck by the
shocks, broke limbs. A sailor was thrown overboard. Dozens of
men were sick. The *Licorne* was blown more than 150 kilometres
off course. A missionary insisted on saying mass. A sturdy man
held the chalice so the wine would not spill. A large warship, not
French, was also trying to ride out the storm's fury. The English?
On April 18, the ocean calmed "for Easter day," noted Montcalm,
who "had little taste" for the sea.

Ten days later, the *Licorne* reached the calm waters of
Newfoundland's Grand Banks. The crew amused itself fishing for
cod. Montcalm had to agree with the historian Charlevoix: indeed,
cod liver, along with the tongue and the head, made for a "natural
and exquisite sauce." When Montcalm saw that they were nearing
gigantic icebergs, the Quebec captain told him not to worry. On
May 5, the *Licorne* entered the St. Lawrence estuary. Five days later,
the wind turned. Stalled in front of Cap Tourmente, Montcalm
refused to be held up by the wind! He had himself taken to shore
in a rowboat. From there, he planned to proceed to Quebec in a
carriage. But none could be found that was suitable. And the track

along the river was not encouraging. He reboarded the *Licorne*. The tide brought him three leagues closer to Quebec. Montcalm again went ashore. This time, he found a carriage like "our cabriolets," he said. The road was good. Parishes appeared "every two leagues." The peasants lived like small gentlemen in France, on their properties two or three acres wide and thirty acres deep. When they talked, they used many seagoing expressions. Montcalm slept at the home of the priest of Château-Richer. He stopped to gaze on the great Montmorency Falls.

After "the rain, the fatigue, and the expense," when Montcalm reached Quebec at last on May 13, there was the *Licorne*, which had already dropped anchor! He was saluted by cannons from the ramparts and the ships in port, "an honour I never received in France." The commander of the French troops in northern America was touched. He had arrived, he said, in "the most beautiful land in the world."

13

"Seeds of discontent"

Despite the Treaty of Aix-la-Chapelle, signed in 1748, Great Britain and France were clashing on many fronts. Each country was trying to extend its possessions, widen its sphere of influence, and enrich itself, both on the European continent and in distant colonies. Frederick II of Prussia, an ally of France, was now making overtures to England. In January 1756, he signed the Treaty of Westminster with George II, with the goal of preventing any foreign army from entering Prussia and Germany. As for Louis XV, he had already concluded a secret agreement with Austria, a traditional enemy since 1498, an agreement that would stem Prussia's growing power and thwart England's ambitious designs. This pact came into being on May 1, 1756, when the King of France and Maria Theresa of Austria signed the Treaty of Jouy-en-Josas.

Immediately, on May 18, 1756, England declared war on France, beginning a seven-year conflict.

Would Lieutenant-Colonel Wolfe be sent to fight in Germany? In India? Four days after the declaration of hostilities, he was posted, along with the 20th Regiment, to Wiltshire in the southwest of England. Disappointed with this mission, he thought of leaving the army, but in a time of war he would be disgraced. He had to do his duty. While Prime Minister Thomas Pelham-Holles, Duke of

Newcastle, demanded increased recruitment, the War Office, short of funds, could not even supply blankets to its soldiers. Wolfe collected donations so that his men could sleep in warm beds.

George II put out a call for help to the armies of Hanover and Hesse. James Wolfe found this recourse to fifteen thousand mercenaries humiliating: it was a dishonour to have to appeal to foreigners to defend one's country.

In spring 1756, the apple trees were in bloom, and Wolfe was waiting, in Canterbury, for a French invasion. British spies had reported intense activity in the port of Dunkirk, which the French were doing nothing to hide. It was all a diversion, as during this time, in the south, the fleet of Vice-Admiral Louis François Armand de Vignerot du Plessis left the port of Toulon with fifteen thousand men to take the island of Minorca. This strategic location had enabled the British to protect their ports in the Levant by monitoring the sea traffic in the Mediterranean. On May 18, a few days after Montcalm's landing in Quebec, the French landed in Minorca. Meeting no opposition, they marched to the fort.

The English Admiralty finally sent out Vice-Admiral John Byng and his squadron, which, on May 20, launched an attack on the French fleet. The French balls and bombs took a heavy toll on his ships. Byng had to retreat to Gibraltar. The loss of Minorca provoked shame and rage in England. Vice-Admiral Byng was recalled. Many patriots wanted him put to death.

Wolfe fretted. In August in Dorset County, one of his battalions, along with two small infantry and cavalry units, passed in review, "to the great pleasure of the ignorant spectators." Not long before, Charles Lennox, Duke of Richmond, had held the rank of major in the 20th Regiment. Lieutenant-Colonel Wolfe, his superior, was during that time most attentive to this officer, who bore a prestigious name and title. The Duke of Richmond had subsequently become lieutenant-colonel of the 33rd Infantry Regiment. To thank Wolfe for his consideration, the duke invited him, in September, to the vicinity of Winchester, for manoeuvres of the infantry and artillery from Hesse. Having seen with his own eyes "their Prussian discipline," Wolfe was very impressed. The application of the men, their consistency, each individual's exact command of his role: these were the virtues Wolfe wanted to cultivate in his own soldiers.

There was no more trade between enemy nations. Torrential rains in some parts of England had spoiled the crops. The price of food had risen dramatically. Anger was growing among the people. Crowds protested. Thousands of soldiers were deployed to contain the uprisings in several regions. In the autumn of 1756, the revolt reached Gloucestershire, known for its clothing manufacture. Wolfe, at the head of six companies, was called on "to help the civil powers to put down the revolt." His companies marched through this land of green hills, woods, streams, and small white houses: he was given enough men, he said with irony, to crush all the revolts in England taken together.

Wolfe saw "seeds of discontent" everywhere. Several weavers were reduced to begging. Some, desperate, had destroyed their comrades' looms. He warned Lord William Barrington, secretary of state for war, that the weavers would commit "some extravagance." The civil magistrates instructed the battalions to point their weapons at the insurgents. Wolfe suggested, however, that this misery could represent a rich terrain for recruitment: those who were impoverished might become soldiers in exchange for food and clothing.

England had been at war for six months. Wolfe and his soldiers were busy policing while the army had to recruit retirees who couldn't shoulder a musket. He didn't shy away from expressing his opinion that the British army was in danger of being "torn to pieces" by the French. Wolfe wanted to play a role in the war. To him, campaigning against "poor devils" dying of hunger was dishonourable.

Public opinion could not digest the loss of Minorca to the French. It rejected the excuses offered by the government for Vice-Admiral Byng's defeat. Toxic press reaction led to the resignation of Henry Fox, secretary of state for the department of the south. William Pitt, the new secretary of state, was called to the rescue. First, Pitt sent George II's mercenaries back to Hanover and Hesse. To the gratification of English patriots, they would be replaced by a militia of thirty thousand men.

Minorca was not Great Britain's only military catastrophe. In India, tension between the East India Company and the indigenous chief of Bengal had led to violence: the company's employees had been crowded into a cell so small that fifty of them had suffocated in one night.

In December 1756, James Wolfe spent Christmas with his regiment at Cirencester. Then came another winter of boredom. He hated playing cards and did not like chess. He thought again of leaving the army. He wandered off, on foot or horseback. He hunted, but took no great pleasure in it. Fortunately, he liked his dogs. He slept a lot. One night, thunder woke his men but did not disturb his own sleep. That worried him, because "a deep sleep is the sign of an inactive mind."

14

"Who would govern the governor?"

After the disastrous Dieskau campaign, the governor general of New France, Pierre de Rigaud de Vaudreuil de Cavagnial, warned the minister of colonies in October 1755: however courageous the commander arrived from France may be, he does not know Canada. Wars in America are different from those he has known in Europe. This officer will reject the advice of the *Canadiens* and will rather listen to the other French officers as "ill informed" as himself. And the French will suffer another defeat like that of Dieskau. When the commander makes mistakes, men are lost. "There are not many of us, and our losses will be felt." Vaudreuil wanted a *Canadien* to lead the king's army: "I will not hide from you, Monseigneur, that the *Canadiens* and the natives will not march with the same confidence under the orders of a commander of French troops as they would under those of this colony's officers."

Montcalm saw before him the city of Quebec. The Château Saint-Louis dominated the cliff rising over the immense St. Lawrence River. At the foot of the governor's residence, the houses in the lower town were lined up along the port, where the ships were at anchor. A few steeples pointed to the sky. As soon as he arrived, he began to explore the city's narrow streets. He paused before the ruins of the Hôtel-Dieu, destroyed by fire the previous year. He felt comfortable in Quebec, but "be sure," he wrote to his mother, "I will always be happy to come home."

In the absence of the governor general, Montcalm was invited to the château of the intendant, François Bigot, responsible for commerce, finance, justice, and civil administration. Forty places were set at a long table, lit by many chandeliers. The major-general was impressed: a "Parisian would have been astounded at the abundance of good things of all sorts." The bishop, Monseigneur Henri-Marie du Breil de Pontbriand, also offered a dinner in his honour.

In the course of the conversation, the Chevalier Pierre-André Gohin de Montreuil gave him some advice: "Do not rely on French troops alone for an expedition; it is the *Canadiens* and the natives who will unsettle the enemy." Montreuil also warned Montcalm that "the officers of the colony do not like French officers."

Because of the rains that held him back for a week, Montcalm could not go to Montreal to present himself to the governor general. Instead, he focussed his attention on his nine companies. He asked them to behave amicably toward the population and the troops of the colony. He forbade them to drink with the natives or to barter alcohol with them. At the first offence, the guilty would be thrown in prison. The second time, they would be flogged. The garrison troops would have to perform an hour and a half of exercise each day. He reminded the battalion commanders that, "to conform to the wise judgment of His Majesty, who wants to increase the number of inhabitants," they must encourage their soldiers to marry young women in Canada.

On May 23, 1756, Montcalm at last went off on the river in a canoe, with ten soldiers "glued to the oars," tormented by mosquitoes and with no pausing to rest. He admired the natural world, astonished at the abundance of fish. Then he climbed into a "carriage of that country." They didn't stop to camp. Three days later,

Montcalm was in Montreal, a "very large fort" with "most attract-ive people." The houses were of wood. Merchandise was extremely expensive. "Here one is prideful, though poor." Montcalm remem-bered reading in Father Charlevoix's history: "There reigns in New England and in the other provinces on the American continent that are under the sway of the British, an opulence one doesn't seem able to make the most of."

Governor General de Vaudreuil, born in Quebec in 1698, had a solid record of service. He had fought at sea; he had been governor of Louisiana. As the representative of the king, he could choose between peace and war. What is more, he supervised the develop-ment of the colony, its commerce, and its fur trade, and he con-trolled the parcelling out of land.

Vaudreuil greeted Montcalm courteously, although he was of the opinion that the *Canadien* troops, who were already subject to the governor and the intendant, did not need a third superior from France. He warned Montcalm that the militia had been so abused and downtrodden by French officers that they might revolt if not treated "gently."

In his directives to Montcalm on March 15, 1756, the king had spelled out the line of authority: "The Sieur Marquis de Montcalm can only exercise the command His Majesty has entrusted to him under the authority of the Governor to whom he is subject in all." Montcalm's commission, signed by the king on March 17, 1756, stated: "The Sieur Marquis de Montcalm will have only to execute and have executed by the troops under his command what will be ordered by the governor general and that is all His Majesty himself has to require of him in this regard."

However, when Montcalm had passed through Versailles, the advisors of the secretary of state for the marine insinuated that, where Vaudreuil was concerned, "the present circumstances and the

current task are somewhat beyond his capacities." The new commander, the advisors hoped, "would govern the governor." A letter from the minister to Montcalm delicately confirmed this view:
"While you will be subordinate in every respect to Monsieur de
Vaudreuil, the opportunities and the means will be there for you to
make manifest your zeal, your talents, and your experience, and to
render them useful in service to the King and glory in battle."

After his meeting with Vaudreuil, Montcalm wrote to Sieur
Jean-Baptiste Machault d'Arnouville, minister of the marine and
the colonies. He recognized that Vaudreuil "is to determine the
path we take, and it is for me to facilitate that task, and to oversee
the details concerning our troops, their discipline, and the execu-
tion of our plans." However, Sieur de Vaudreuil was "a bit weak," in
Montcalm's opinion. "He has good intentions, but he is very indeci-
sive." Finally, he reported that he had not received from Vaudreuil
"his confidence, which he never accords to anyone from France."

Vaudreuil and Montcalm assessed their strength. First, the
marine troops numbered two thousand men. Their soldiers and
officers were recruited from military personnel who came from
France but who settled in Canada. They knew the country; they
had travelled, fought, often learned the indigenous languages. They
had more in common with the militia than with the regular army.
Then, the preceding year, a contingent of 2,100 men arrived with
the unfortunate Major-General Dieskau. Of them, only 1,652
remained. Finally, that spring, Montcalm arrived in Quebec with
1,500 men, to be joined by the Languedoc, Béarn, La Sarre, and
Royal-Roussillon detachments, along with recruits and volunteers:
in all, some 3,700 men.

In addition, the governor general appealed to the entire able-
bodied male population from sixteen to sixty years old. If members
of the militia were unpaid, they nevertheless were fed at the king's

expense and, like the natives, had rights to a share of the booty that was seized. Accustomed to the rigours of life in the bush, often tattooed like the natives, they fought in the same way. Vaudreuil had thrown these militiamen, along with the natives, into battle against the English in Nova Scotia, New England, Pennsylvania, and as far away as Virginia. They had burned houses, taken scalps, sown anguish and terror. However, on account of the tasks that occupied them in the fields or forests, it was always impossible to predict how many militiamen would turn up at any given time.

Vaudreuil outlined to Montcalm the plan that Governor Shirley of Massachusetts had devised for an attack against Forts Niagara and Frontenac on Lake Ontario, and Carillon (Ticonderoga) at the south end of Lake Champlain. The French had discovered this plan in General Braddock's attaché case at the time of his defeat at Fort Duquesne.

In front of his maps, Vaudreuil showed Montcalm how the English could attack Canada from three directions: the St. Lawrence to the east, Lake Champlain to the south, and the Great Lakes to the west. Above all, he asserted, French supremacy must be maintained on Lake Ontario in order to keep communication lines open to Fort Niagara, which controlled the passage to Lake Erie and the chain of French forts on the Allegheny River and the Belle-Rivière—the Presqu'île, Le Boeuf, Machault, and Duquesne—as well as the posts that had been established in the *pays d'en haut*—the Upper Country, a vast territory reaching around the Great Lakes and expanding with every exploration toward the south of the continent or to the west.

According to Vaudreuil, the most effective way to fight the English was to increase the number of raids on their trading posts and isolated farms and the frequency of skirmishes with English scouting parties and merchants. The preceding winter, a small

{68}

detachment of Canadian militiamen and natives from the Upper Country had made forays that "devastated" villages in Pennsylvania and Virginia. In the deep of winter, three hundred *Canadiens* and natives, and sixty volunteer French soldiers, after covering two hundred leagues through the woods, had surprised the enemy not far from Chouaguen (Oswego, New York).

Vaudreuil also said he was happy that at this time of the year no significant movement on the part of the English had been reported in the vicinity of Fort Duquesne. Captain Jean-Daniel Dumas had led diversionary operations while the French were preparing an attack on Fort Chouaguen. In the west, the native peoples of the Upper Country seemed friendlier since the French had shown themselves to be stronger. Montcalm listened to Vaudreuil.

On June 3, 1756, the Iroquois of Long Sault came to pay their respects to the new chief of the Great King's army. They were accompanied by "ladies of the council." Montcalm was astonished to learn that these native women "always take part in government." The Iroquois offered him a wampum of shells. Montcalm had been told that their colours and designs carried a message. Even if he thought the Iroquois were "unsavoury characters," Montcalm promised to go and visit them in their village.

"Since I've arrived," he complained to his wife, "it's just been visits, harangues, and deputations on the part of those gentlemen who daub themselves with various colours, perch feathers on their heads, stick pendants in their ears and noses, and have their earlobes stretched until they reach their shoulders: a sign of great beauty among them." The natives, fortunately, were becoming increasingly civilized: he was told that burning prisoners was "almost a thing of the past," although they had "burned some at Belle-Rivière, so the practice would not be lost."

Delegates from the Nipissing nation came in their turn to pay their respects to Montcalm. The chief offered him the mother of an English family, who had been captured. Montcalm had to negotiate a price for the woman and to express his thanks to the chief for having so well served the chief of the French armies in Canada. He had been advised always to hear the natives out, even if they knew no loyalty. They allied themselves with the French or the English according to their interests at the time. Often, they served both masters simultaneously and never seemed loath to cheat or betray.

In England, public opinion demanded that Vice-Admiral Byng's defeat in Minorca be avenged, as well as the defeat in America of General Braddock. Responding to the popular will, the government, in mid-June 1756, increased the budget for the defence of the English colonies in America. The War Office sent additional supplies, munitions, artillery, arms, and tools. Prisoners claimed that John Campbell, Count of Loudoun, governor of Virginia, and general-in-chief of the English Colonial Armies, was going to send ten thousand militiamen to take Fort Saint-Frédéric, and that they would then continue on to Montreal. Six thousand men would occupy Fort Niagara. Three thousand would march on Fort Duquesne. Finally, two thousand would attack Quebec from the Chaudière River. Loudoun would have 25,000 men at his disposal, about three times as many as Montcalm.

It was probably a bit late to initiate this plan of attack. According to some Mohawks of Sault Saint-Louis who had returned from an expedition near Orange (Albany, New York), the British and colonial forces together had instead put in an appearance around Lake Saint-Sacrement (Lake George) with the idea of taking Fort Carillon (Ticonderoga). *Canadien* scouts confirmed the information.

Given all that, Vaudreuil decided to block the route to Canada south of Lake Champlain. Militiamen and natives would set off to intimidate the settlers north of Orange, in the west of Massachusetts, and to the north of Connecticut. At Fort Carillon, work would be done on the earthworks and masonry, barricades would be thrown up, the garrison would be expanded, and the thirty cannons would be supplemented. The same would be done at Fort Saint-Frédéric, a bit farther north than Carillon, on the west shore of Lake Champlain. On Lake Ontario, Fort Frontenac was in very bad shape. The storehouses had no roofs and needed to be covered. The trenches that had caved in would have to be redug. This was all urgent. Intendant Bigot, who had just reduced by a third the wages of soldiers assigned to construction, asked the engineer Jean-Nicolas Desandrouins to come down hard on "idlers." At Fort Niagara on Lake Ontario, the soldiers from the Béarn militia, along with friendly natives, dug ditches, built up earth banks, carried stones, mixed mortar, fitted joints, and chopped down, dragged, and piled up trees to impede the progress of the enemy.

Montcalm and the Chevalier de Lévis went to Fort Carillon with a Royal-Roussillon battalion, plus some *Canadien* militiamen and natives. The troops' *aide-major* wrote in his diary, "Monsieur de Montcalm does not seem eager to attack the enemy." Given the roads, barely discernible and damaged by rain, and given the lack of carts, horses, and boats, the transport of provisions, munitions, arms, and tools caused "infinite pains and delays." On June 27, 1756, people living on the shores of the Richelieu saw a procession of boats and canoes full of soldiers and natives, and loaded with supplies being propelled by sails and oars, or even, through the rapids, hauled by ropes. The convoy made short stops at the forts of Chambly, Saint-Jean, and Saint-Frédéric. Montcalm, Lévis, and their men disembarked at Fort Carillon on July 3, 1756.

Montcalm familiarized himself with the geography of this uneven terrain, and he assessed the strengths and weaknesses of the fort's position. Scouts went to spy on the enemy's every movement. Lévis and a small detachment marched three days through the woods to see whether, between Lake Saint-Sacrement and the Trout River, it would be possible for the English to make their way along the Indians' trail, bordering the rapids of the La Chute River. The strengthening of the fort was taking too long. A lot of men were sick. The bread was so bad that many, even if they were starving, threw it to the crows. Montcalm discovered that the cooks were using spoiled flour because Intendant Bigot insisted that the king would tolerate "no waste." The major-general decreed that in future good flour had to be added to the spoiled.

He soon observed the inability of the *Canadien* militia to march in formation, their reluctance to respond to orders, their awkwardness in performing traditional military tasks. The lax habits and discipline of the marine troops inspired in the regular soldiers "a spirit of independence." He tried to improve their overall discipline through military exercises.

Montcalm was busy. The councils of war with his officers lasted five or six hours. His "boring" war councils with the natives went on forever. He had "adopted their ways." He smoked with them. "They love me," he boasted. In addition, every day there were dinners for twenty or so people. He was so occupied that he slept only four hours a night. He told his wife that he suffered from "extreme fatigue" because it required "a great deal of patience and application to wage a war with *Canadiens* and savages."

15

"The direct cause of all our troubles in the colonies"

On July 13, 1756, Governor General de Vaudreuil summoned Montcalm to Montreal. The major-general handed over command of his two thousand men to Brigadier de Lévis and, after travelling day and night by canoe, arrived exhausted in Montreal three days later. Intendant Bigot, a little red-haired man who sprayed himself with perfume because he suffered from ozena, warned him that Vaudreuil would be sending him on a difficult mission.

Vaudreuil explained to Montcalm that the English had in 1722 set up a trading post at Chouaguen, a place they called Oswego, on the southwest shore of Lake Ontario. It encroached on French territory. From this base, the English were bit by bit taking control of the fur trade. The post had since been transformed into a fort, and armed English boats were now patrolling Lake Ontario. The local natives had become their allies. It was at Chouaguen that the English "had determined to slaughter the French." Chouaguen, the governor general continued, was "the direct cause of all our troubles in the colonies, and of the enormous expense that has meant for the king." He concluded: the time has come to destroy Fort Chouaguen.

Bigot feared that it was too late. The fort was already defended by a strong garrison, and the English had doubtless added to their numbers. What did the marquis think? Montcalm remembered the difficulties he'd had putting together supplies and munitions for the Carillon expedition. His departure for Chouaguen would be delayed for the same reasons. The French boats would have to make their way past the enemy fleet. Were there enough men for the mission? Montcalm shared Bigot's concerns. "God or the devil!" swore Vaudreuil. "We must risk a battle."

And so Montcalm would go to Chouaguen. In order to speed up the journey, he ordered a reduction in the baggage to be transported. There would be fewer officers. They would sleep two by two on a bearskin, under a tarpaulin. There would be no chickens for eggs. He allowed only one portmanteau per officer, and no more than twelve shirts. They would not have their usual kitchen utensils. They would receive the same rations as the soldiers: "salt pork, peas and biscuits." Montcalm took care to forbid the king's troops to enter "into disputes with the *Canadiens*."

He set out in his canoe on July 21, 1756. Rapids on the St. Lawrence forced the convoy to take long portages. Six days later, the army arrived at La Présentation (Ogdensburg, New York), a small square fort made from stakes dug into the earth, neighbouring a village where a hundred Oneida and Onondaga families lived with their cows, horses, pigs, and chickens. Corn swayed in the fields. Montcalm held a council with the natives. Their loyalty seemed suspect. Other allies, the Menominee, had decided to return to their village after a disagreement with the Iroquois. Montcalm insisted they stay, and gave them pork, wine, tobacco, and porcelain necklaces. Finally, the Menominee agreed to join with the Iroquois in a war dance.

On July 29, the expedition arrived at Fort Frontenac. The 150 transport boats, which were to take on the men and their baggage, were not there. A thousand *Canadien* militiamen had just arrived. They had no experience, no commander, no arms: they were "almost naked." They were questioned, one by one. Units were formed—leaders were chosen from the most capable. When the boats arrived at last from Fort Niagara, they had to be caulked. Having studied the report of an engineer who had been on a reconnaissance mission, Montcalm chose the most promising spot to assemble his troops. They came together at the Bay of Niaouré (Sackett's Harbor), fifteen leagues downstream from Chouaguen. An advance guard commanded by François-Pierre de Rigaud, Governor General de Vaudreuil's brother, would prepare the terrain. Montcalm asked him to build ovens for the kitchen and shelters for storing arms, munitions, and food. He also ordered that two armed boats with twenty-eight cannons cross near Chouaguen to discourage the English from trying to head toward Fort Niagara.

On August 4, Montcalm got back into his canoe with two engineers and some natives. Arriving at the Bay of Niaouré on August 6, he held a council of war. As the officers couldn't agree, Montcalm asked the two engineers to determine the best place to land. In the afternoon, he held another war council with 250 Iroquois, Abenakis, Nipissings, and Algonquins. In their orations, the chiefs swore to exterminate the English, on condition that they could fight in the woods, in the manner of their ancestors.

Having listened to the engineers' report, Montcalm chose the cove that offered the shortest route to Chouaguen. His time was limited because he had only so much food. And to transport provisions, there were only twenty or so "rather bad" horses. Decision: they would land at Anse aux Cabanes (Wigwam Cove), three leagues from Chouaguen. From there, a path led to the fort.

One after the other, the divisions advanced: four hundred men of the Guyenne Battalion, six hundred *Canadien* militiamen, the La Sarre battalions, natives, five hundred other militiamen, the Béarn Battalion, and another four hundred *Canadien* militiamen. As the

English lookouts were keeping close watch, the boats stayed in the coves, hidden under tree branches, waiting for nightfall before moving out.

Montcalm went down to Anse aux Cabanes a bit before dawn on August 10. When the transport vessels set off, their keels scraped bottom fairly far from shore. How to get the heavy guns in? How to transfer the powder without its becoming wet? And the cove was not big enough to handle all the boats. After coming so close to Chouaguen without being spotted, they were not going to seek another haven. Let the artillery captain, François-Marc-Antoine Le Mercier, have the four cannons transported! Let the munitions be unloaded! They would set up camp there, on the height! If the enemy showed itself, Le Mercier's cannons would cover the landing.

Before dawn, on August 11, the engineers De Combles and Desandrouins, escorted by a squad of *Canadiens* and natives, made their way from tree to tree, sometimes crawling through ferns. The engineer Jean-Claude-Henri de Lombard de Combles drew near to Fort Chouaguen, where everyone was sleeping. He cautiously made his way back to his companions through the bushes. One of the natives thought he saw an Englishman. A report. The echo resounded over the lake. At the fort, a cannon shot sounded the alarm.

Montcalm had wanted to surprise the enemy. Now things were different. He went back to the sketch Desandrouins had made of Chouaguen. The post was defended by three forts. At the mouth of the Oswego River on the east shore, Fort Ontario, on a high plateau, was a square enclosure whose embankment gave it the shape of a star. The palisade, nine feet high and pierced with slits, was made of squared-off tree trunks on two sides, driven into the ground and bound one to the other. Inside, a raised gallery for marksmen ran the length of the palisade. The fort was surrounded by a moat eighteen feet wide. On the west bank of the Oswego

River, Fort Pepperell was a machicolated redoubt with stone walls a metre thick, pierced with slits from the ground to the first floor. A crenellated rampart surrounded the redoubt. This rampart was itself surrounded by a trench. Eighteen cannons as well as fifteen mortars and howitzers lay in wait for the French. Finally, on the same west bank, 550 metres away, Fort George held the height. This third fort was in poor repair, and the palisade's stakes, rotten, sometimes dropped to the ground. The total garrison at the three forts amounted to 1,700 men, to which were added servants, some surgeons, merchants, employees, and a few black slaves.

Toward noon, while all was peaceful, three large armed English boats emerged from the river and advanced purposefully toward the French camp. "Warmly welcomed" by Captain Le Mercier's artillery, they turned about before suffering too much damage.

On August 12, Montcalm's grenadiers and militia dug trenches in front of Fort Ontario. Other crews put together fascines to support artillery pieces, blinds to underpin parapets, canvas tubes filled with gunpowder to top off the trenches. Positioned around Chouaguen, soldiers prevented messengers from escaping to alert the English troops. They also stood in the way of any help that might arrive. The *Canadien* militia and the natives, hidden behind trees and bushes, directed an onslaught of gunfire at Fort Ontario. The next day, the grenadiers advanced along the trench they had dug.

Colonel James Francis Mercer, commander of the fort, sent for help. Rigaud intercepted the messenger. Mercer was asking Colonel Daniel Webb, commander of the troops on the northern frontier, to come quickly: the Chouaguen garrison would not be able to ward off the French. Montcalm had a new battery of guns set up.

On the morning of August 13, sensing certain victory, the French troops ran to the trench, anxious to strike the deciding blow. An aggressive cannonade made it clear that the garrison was far from ready to surrender! Suddenly, at the end of the afternoon, the cannons went silent. Colonel Mercer had decided to evacuate Fort Ontario and to fall back on Fort Pepperell. He had his cannons put out of commission and his powder doused with water, before his troops abandoned the fort.

It remained to dislodge the English from Fort Pepperell. The boats brought twenty or so cannons, plus munitions, from the other side of the river. Then, by main force, the militia transported everything they needed in front of the ramparts. They built barbettes onto which they hoisted the cannons. From there, balls and bombs would be projected over the ramparts.

The next day, August 14, at six in the morning, the French battery unleashed a storm on Fort Pepperell, while Rigaud, the Béarn Battalion, and a hundred *Canadiens* went in a boat out onto the lake with three cannons, to take Fort George. At first, Fort Pepperell's own cannons boomed out aggressively. But launched by cannons raised onto barbettes, French projectiles plunged into the enclosure, and the garrison troops were forced to take refuge behind barrels of salt pork.

At the end of the day, rain soaked the cannon and musket fuses, and the powder became wet. Water gathered in the trenches. The ground went soft. With every jolt of the cannons, their wheels sank deeper into the mud, and the barbette foundations wobbled. Montcalm wanted to order Mercer to surrender. The engineer Desandrouins persuaded him, however, to continue the bombardment until the enemy was paralyzed!

The English saw natives and militiamen swimming in the river toward Fort Pepperell. Terrified, they counted more than they saw. Lieutenant-Colonel Baker John Littlehales had replaced Mercer, whose body had been torn apart by a ball. At ten o'clock at night, he had flags run up for a truce. The surrender was signed at eleven o'clock. The garrison, including the workers, servants, and some black slaves, all prisoners of war, were taken to Montreal. A messenger from Montcalm delivered to Vaudreuil the standards of five English regiments, plus a trunk, taken from the enemy, that contained nearly twenty thousand pounds sterling. Some asserted that this treasure was not so large, because as it was being surrendered, the English officers had dipped into it.

The plunder from the operation was considerable: two hundred barges, a two-masted merchant vessel, a brigantine, a schooner, a small boat, more than two hundred cannons, smaller cannons, mortars, howitzers, hundreds of barrels of powder, eight cases of balls, 2,890 cannonballs, 450 bombs, 1,800 rifles, 1,476 grenades, 352 barrels of biscuits, 1,386 barrels of lard or salt beef, 712 barrels of flour, 32 cattle on the hoof, lofts full of peas, flour, barrels of salt, sugar, coffee, chocolate—supplies for two years. "All that cost us only thirty men," Montcalm congratulated himself.

The natives were waiting for him to hand some prisoners over to them for their rituals. The major-general disapproved of their cruel practices and refused to present them with victims. The natives then stormed the hospital, clubbed the wounded on their pallets, and cut their throats. They pillaged, got drunk, danced, and roamed around looking for heads to scalp. Montcalm resigned himself: "It's extremely difficult to prevent 300 savages and 1500 *Canadiens* from claiming their spoils."

Chouaguen's three forts were demolished. What the axe could not take down was blown up, everything that would burn was set afire, the moats were filled in, the glacis flattened. On August 20, in front of the ruins, the troops and the prisoners were brought together for a ceremony in the course of which Father François Piquet thanked God for having been on the side of the French. He blessed the booty that had been seized. He also blessed the cross that Montcalm had planted, bearing the Latin inscription *In hoc signo vincunt* (In virtue of this sign, they prevailed).

Colonel Webb, who had arrived with reinforcements four leagues away from Chouaguen, on the Oswego River, learned that an army of six thousand French and Indians were at Oswego. He turned about, destroyed a few posts on the river on his way, blew up a cache of arms and munitions, and then felled trees into the water to serve as obstacles to the passage of enemy boats and canoes.

Montcalm was delighted with his victory: once more masters of navigation on Lake Ontario, the French would also control the fur trade with the natives in that part of the world. And the way would be clear to Belle-Rivière.

16

A different nation, the same enemy

In Montreal, the faithful were singing a *Te Deum* that shook the walls of the church. Colonel Bougainville presented the priest with two English flags seized at Chouaguen. This offering, said the priest, was pleasing to the "God of armies: it is He who strengthened your arms; it is to Him that your leader owes the intelligence and resources with which he confounded the enemies of justice and peace." In Quebec, Bishop Pontbriand asked his flock to thank God for this victory.

On August 24, Vaudreuil informed the minister of the marine: "There is not a great deal that I have the honour of telling you about the land forces. . . . They did not greatly distinguish themselves. . . . It was only a portion of the colony's troops, the *Canadiens* and the natives, who attacked the forts."

Instead of relishing his victory, Montcalm was concerned: Would this harm his career? Should he reproach himself for having adopted native strategies for making war? He felt the need to justify his conduct to the minister of war. On August 28, he wrote: "The measures I took involving eighteen hundred men were such a departure from standard practices that the daring manifest in this enterprise must seem like rashness in Europe." If the king still wanted the major-general to serve in Europe, he promised: "I would base my conduct on different principles."

Montcalm had little respect for the *Canadien* soldiers. On August 30, he described his comrades-in-arms to his wife: Artillery Captain Le Mercier is "ignorant and a weak individual." Montigny, a scout, was "an idiot"; another was a "braggart and a blabbermouth." "All the rest," he wrote, "are not worth mentioning, even my first lieutenant, General Rigaud," brother of the governor general.

However, as Vaudreuil was increasingly claiming credit for the victory, Montcalm reminded the minister of war that the "success" at Chouaguen, decisive for the colony, "was due to an officer general whose selection was determined entirely by yourself." He even suggested that his written account of the campaign be published, "in order to highlight an event of the greatest glory and with the most significant consequences for the north of America."

The tension between the French and the *Canadiens* did not escape Bougainville: "The *Canadiens* and the French, although sharing the same origins, the same interests, the same religious and governmental principles, and a present danger, cannot agree." He concluded: "It seems that we are a different nation, even hostile."

On Vaudreuil's orders, Montcalm returned to Fort Carillon. On August 31, escorted by fifteen *Canadien* militiamen and thirty Odawas, on foot, on horseback, and by carriage, Montcalm crossed La Prairie, south of the St. Lawrence River. They were cautious. The day before, a party of natives had been seen on the plain. Montcalm stopped at Fort Saint-Jean, "a square enclosure with four bastions," on the Richelieu River. Bougainville remarked: "It's very poorly constructed, even though it cost ninety-six thousand francs."

During this time, on September 1, 1756, Vaudreuil completed a report for the minister in which he reproached the French officers for the "haughty fashion" in which they treated the *Canadiens*, who "are obliged to bear these gentlemen on their shoulders through cold water, tearing their feet on rocks, and if by chance they stumble they're treated shamefully." Vaudreuil accused Montcalm of having "such a volatile temperament that he will go so far as to strike the *Canadiens.*" The governor general had asked Montcalm to warn his officers against this "bad practice." But "how can he contain the officers, if he cannot himself control his temper?"

Montcalm, in a canoe, travelled up the Richelieu, crossed Lake Champlain, and made a stop at Fort Saint-Frédéric, where to his mind the terrain favoured the attackers more than those being besieged. By September 10, he was at Carillon. With the arrival of reinforcements transferred by Vaudreuil from Lake Ontario, the army at Carillon was five thousand strong, natives included. Even with twice as many troops, General Loudoun seemed reluctant to attack. If no English were seen before September 20, none would be seen before winter. Under those circumstances, the French could harass their enemies. And the natives, Montcalm thought, would appreciate a bit of plunder before returning to their villages for the winter.

Montcalm convened a council: the ground troops, the marine troops, and the *Canadien* militia formed a square. Inside, the natives were seated in a circle. In the centre, amid the smoke from fires cooking meat in cauldrons, Montcalm outlined the next mission. Paul Marin de La Malgue, a *coureur de bois* who had navigated all the rivers and who spoke several native languages, would be the commander. He would leave the following day with his detachment for Lake Saint-Sacrament, where the English had set up trading posts and two forts. Part of his detachment would descend Lake Saint-Sacrement to its southern end, where Fort George stood. The other part would continue farther, toward Fort Lydius (Edward), on the Hudson River.

The natives greeted this news with cries of joy. Later in the day, the Iroquois returned with seven deer they had hunted. The feasting, the songs, the dances, the drinking went on until dawn. In the morning, no one was in any condition to leave.

A day later, on September 15, the Odawas, the Menominee, the Ojibways, other warriors from the Upper Country, and a hundred *Canadiens* settled into their canoes. They travelled only at night. Marin forbade them to light fires. The natives obeyed him when it was convenient for them. The next day, four leagues from Fort George, Marin chose 110 natives with the "best legs," thirty of the "nimblest" *Canadiens*, and twenty cadets from the colony to approach the fort. A league and a half from the enclosure, fifty or so English farmers were busy in their fields. Suddenly, bands of natives, howling like wolves, burst out of the nearby woods, surrounded them, and battered them to death with their tomahawks. Four or five farmers were able to escape to the fort and to alert the garrison.

Marin was killed during this skirmish. His detachment had taken seventeen prisoners. Bougainville noted: "The cruelty and the shamelessness of those barbarians fill one with horror and blacken the soul. It's an abominable way to make war."

At the same time, other campaigns were taking place. A short time earlier, an English party had attacked a village between Fort Duquesne and Fort Machault, inhabited by the Loup, friends to the French. To avenge this aggression, Captain Dumas loosed a "pack" on the border villages of Pennsylvania and Virginia. In the Belle-Rivière valley, houses and stables were burned, families massacred, the wounded scalped, prisoners captured, crops burned, animals slaughtered. Louis Coulon de Villiers and fifty-five men fell upon Fort Granville, twenty-five leagues from Philadelphia. Despite the artillery, they penetrated the enclosure and, swords in hand, killed part of the garrison. The survivors were handed over to the natives. Villiers set the fort on fire.

At Carillon, the mornings had become chilly. Winter was approaching. The enemy did not show itself. Most of the natives went back to their villages with their booty, their prisoners, and the eau-de-vie they'd traded for scalps. Montcalm worked at parcelling out the troops to their winter quarters. Families were obliged to house them, keep them warm, feed them in their modest houses, often with only one room. They were paid in playing card money, which Intendant Bigot would exchange for produce off French vessels the following spring. This forced hospitality was not without its problems. The prescribed punishment of twelve blows from a cane for indecent assault on a young girl did not always stem the ardour of the idle soldiers during the long months when the land was covered in snow.

The Odawas taught Montcalm how to fish. He also, with them, hunted duck, teal, passenger pigeons, and even deer. However, he left Carillon on October 26, with his health, he wrote, "much disturbed." When he arrived at Fort Saint-Jean three days later, he found that the governor general, without having consulted him, had portioned out his troops. Montcalm accused him of having "done all that with his eyes closed," of not having taken into consideration the enemy threat. He denounced this cavalier behaviour to d'Argenson, the minister of war. Under the aegis of the governor general, Montcalm was responsible to the intendant for his supplies, and also responsible to two ministers: the minister of war for the command of the troops, their discipline, their behaviour, their promotions, transfers, and leaves; and to the minister of the marine and the colonies, who delegated to the governor general the managing of operations. Overlaps, contradictions, encroachments, friction, and frustration were inevitable.

Passing later through the La Prairie countryside, Montcalm noted, under the night-time frost, that the fields were being neglected. There had been no harvest. Called up by the militia, the men had not been left enough time to attend to it. Montcalm thought back on his property in France, under the southern sun...

On November 23, before being trapped in the ice, the last ships cast off for France. Montcalm sent his wife marten tails for a muff: "All my prayers will be answered when I can be with you again in October 1757." Despite their differences, Montcalm played back-gammon and whist with Vaudreuil.

If he was bored with "this sad government of Montreal," he found that his victory at Chouaguen had inspired an outpouring of friendship from the indigenous nations. A hundred and fifty Onondagas and Goyoguins, with wives and children, came to dem-onstrate as much in front of the governor's château. Then came the Seneca and the Oneidas. Five cannon shots greeted their arrival. Their chief had planned for a sojourn of four days in Montreal, but deeply touched by the welcome, he and his warriors stayed for four moons "with a good father who would not let them lack for anything." There followed, up to December 29, the Iroquois, Mohawks from Sault Saint-Louis, the Nipissings, the Abenakis, the Algonquins, the Potawatomis, the Odawas. Summoned to a war council, each delegation arrived in its ceremonial dress. At the end, medals bearing the effigy of the English king, now enemy to all, were trampled underfoot.

Vaudreuil's news for the minister of the marine and the col-onies was that the Abenakis, the Nipissing, the Algonquins, and other natives were ready to go wherever they might be sent, as long as they were not "subject to the orders of Monsieur de Montcalm."

17

"If I was to serve two or three years in America"

In Europe, in March 1757, the French philosopher Voltaire wrote to his friend François-Augustin de Paradis de Moncrif, author of *The Story of Cats*: "One pities that poor human race that slits its throat on our continent over a few acres of ice in Canada." In London, the intellectual Samuel Johnson was no more enthusiastic about the American colonies: "The new world must have many vegetables and animals." After the defeat at Chouaguen, William Pitt, secretary of state, nevertheless sent more help to the colonies. He was, in fact, prepared to recruit two thousand rough and brave Scots Highlanders who, not long before, had rebelled against King George II. James Wolfe dreamed of commanding those two battalions. Did he not already know the Highlands and their inhabitants? Did he not, like many of them, have red hair? "I have very much the look of a Highlander," he remarked to the Duke of Richmond.

In January of that year, the weavers of Gloucestershire had intercepted barges loaded with provisions on the River Severn. The magistrate called for the army to intervene. Wolfe carefully explained to his soldiers that their mission was not to kill the artisans but to calm them, and he warned the soldiers that they would be insulted by the population. He asked them to receive those insults "with a soldierlike contempt." Informed of the approach taken by this young lieutenant-colonel to defuse the crisis, William Barrington, secretary of state for war, pronounced himself impressed.

That winter, Wolfe spent time reading ancient authors: Vegetius, who had described Roman military tactics, Caesar of Nostradamus, Xenophon. He read the history of Turkey and that of the wars of religion in France. He read the biographies of Gustavus Adolphus and Charles XII, kings of Sweden and great warriors. He read *The Rules of the King of Prussia for his Cavalry and Infantry.* For Wolfe, Frederick II was "the first soldier of this age and our Master in the Art of War." He also read Montesquieu's *Spirit of the Laws.*

His officers did not always feel at ease with this lieutenant-colonel who was too tall, too pale, too serious, too young, and whose advancements had come too early. They feared Wolfe's repartee and his being "so intent upon having everything done in its proper way." When it was not, irrepressible fits of pique drove him to reprimand, to punish. He was conscious of it: "If I was to serve two or three years in America, I make no doubt that I should be distinguished by a peculiar fierceness of temper suited to the nature of war." For the moment, Wolfe did not have to win the war, but he had to keep the peace with the weavers of Cirencester. And he knew that the inactivity that had been imposed on him would delay his promotion to the rank of colonel.

According to the Treaty of Westminster, Prussia, Hanover, and England had agreed to support each other. When the 110,000 French of Marshal Louis Charles César Le Tellier, Comte d'Estrées, marched on Germany, the Duke of Cumberland—obese, asthmatic, and limping from a war wound—commanded an army made up of English, Hanoverians, Hessians, Brunswickers, and Germans. Lieutenant-Colonel Wolfe, who wanted a military role, asked Lord Albemarle if he would arrange a meeting with the Duke of Cumberland, to whom Wolfe wished to offer his services.

Then Wolfe received a letter. John Russell, Duke of Bedford, a longtime friend of his father's, proposed to him two postings in Ireland: barrack master-general or quartermaster general. Everything required for the troops passed through these offices. In the past, those positions had been very profitable. Lord Bedford even advised James Wolfe to occupy both at once. Then the king would doubtless make him a colonel. But the offer didn't fill Wolfe with enthusiasm: "I had rather see the King of Prussia's operations the next campaign, than accept this appointment with all its advantages," he wrote to his father. George II, however, thought that Wolfe had not yet served long enough to merit the rank of colonel. On March 29, 1757, at St. James's Palace, overcoming his disappointment, Wolfe kissed the royal hand and accepted his new responsibilities in Ireland. Regretting having done so, and before assuming his new duties, he returned to the 20th Regiment.

Yielding to the will of the people, George II ordered that Vice-Admiral Byng, defeated at Minorca, be executed on March 17 on the bridge of his ship in Portsmouth harbour. Wolfe wholeheartedly approved of this punishment for an officer who had not been equal to his duty.

England's problems multiplied. In June 1757, the reputedly invincible army of its ally Frederick II was defeated by the Austrians at Kolín, near Prague. The French advanced to the west, the Austrians to the south, and the Russians to the east. No longer able to count on the Prussians, Cumberland had to retreat.

England was demoralized. Its government had been idle since the fall of the Devonshire-Pitt administration in April. William Pitt had won over public opinion through his decisive action: sending away foreign mercenaries, reorganizing the army, stimulating recruitment, creating Scottish regiments, increasing the manpower in the American colonies. But his virtues did not shield him from the intrigues of Thomas Pelham-Holles, Duke of Newcastle, his rival. The country lived under threat of a French invasion, but the land and sea armies no longer had a minister to represent them in Parliament. George II needed Pitt and Newcastle in the government, despite their mutual detestation. Pitt was indispensable in time of war. Newcastle, for his part, had a keen sense of finance and was adept at pulling strings; he could keep the administration going. For the good of England, the two political adversaries accepted their appointments on June 29, 1757. Newcastle would be prime minister. Pitt, secretary of state, would manage external affairs and the business of war. Not long before, James Wolfe had advised his father to be cautious in his investments. Now he urged him to lend three or four thousand pounds to the government.

To William Pitt, who wanted a less timorous England, Lieutenant-General John (Jean-Louis) Ligonier proposed taking Rochefort in France, south of La Rochelle. First, Rochefort was not far from English territorial waters. Second, the operation would create a diversion: French troops would have to reduce their participation in the coalition with Austria to deal with this attack. Rochefort was protected by an unfinished rampart and a dry moat. The wall could be scaled with ladders. At little cost, it would be possible to destroy a number of French ships of the merchant marine and the Royal Navy that were moored there, plus shipyards, warehouses, and a huge quantity of arms, munitions, and supplies stored at the arsenal. In mid-July, Pitt received George II's approval for Ligonier's proposition.

James Wolfe, once more stationed at Dorset with his regiment, had not yet taken up his duties in Ireland. In his heart, he would have preferred to renounce them, but he did not want to irritate the Duke of Bedford, who had offered them to him.

On July 26, Cumberland's troops suffered a humiliating defeat at Hastenbeck: the French now occupied Hanover, so dear to George II and his family. The Rochefort operation seemed all the more justified. To raze this city of carved stone, the king sent about eight thousand men. A sizable squadron of ships would take orders from Vice-Admiral Edward Hawke. William Pitt, to avoid long debates, honoured the sacred principle of seniority and appointed Lieutenant-General Mordaunt to command the mission. He would be assisted by Major-General Edward Cornwallis, a former colonel under whom Wolfe had served. Sir John Mordaunt was one of James Wolfe's protectors. It was not a coincidence that the young lieutenant-colonel was summoned to London. Mordaunt chose him to be his quartermaster general, responsible for food supply, a crucial task in an operation involving both sea and land troops. Wolfe was aware of the rivalry between the navy and the infantry. Their refusal to co-operate was at the root of the disaster at Cartagena. His father, haunted by those tragic events, had never stopped telling the story.

When Lord Anson, first lord of the admiralty, announced that the transport would not be ready on the required day, William Pitt threatened him with a discharge if it was not there on time. The admiral became more zealous in his efforts. Thousands of sailors were enlisted, often by force. Six months' worth of supplies were put on the ships, distributed in such a way that the soldiers could land swiftly and go on the attack. Sliding ladders were built to scale the ramparts.

On August 10, 1757, James Wolfe waited on the Isle of Wight, just as he'd waited at the age of thirteen to leave, with his father, for Cartagena. As then, precious time was lost. Ten infantry regiments were assembled on the island, but the ships would not be ready before September.

There was other bad news. In America, the French general Montcalm, who had destroyed Fort Oswego the year before, had burned Fort Henry on August 6. The Indian allies of the French had subjected the garrison to inhuman torture. Elsewhere, in the northeast, Admiral Francis Holburne's fleet was about to attack the imposing fortress at Louisbourg on Cape Breton Island (Île Royale), with twelve thousand men. But on August 21, the French fleet was waiting in the port, armed with 1,360 cannons. Holburne went back to Chibouctou (Halifax).

In Europe, at Klosterzeven, the French occupied Hanover and western Germany on September 7. George II lost Hanover, with which his family had historical ties.

On the same day, before the news of this latest disaster had arrived, seven thousand soldiers boarded ship, and the English fleet got underway: sixteen warships, six frigates, two fire-fighting ketches, two fire ships, two hospital ships, six supply cutters. Destination: Rochefort. Objective: to invade the city, destroy ships, docks, warehouses, arsenals, and shipyards. Usually, the voyage took four days. This time, the ships entered the Bay of Biscay ten days later. From the outset, Wolfe suffered from seasickness: "I am the worst mariner in the whole ship."

On September 21, the fleet headed into the channel between two islands, the Île de Ré and the Île d'Oléron, but the wind was pushing out to sea. Powerless in the face of nature, Vice-Admiral Hawke had to wait until September 22 before being able to drop anchor between the two islands. The English ships had of course been seen from Rochefort.

The English officers were aware that the west coast of France was defended by fewer than ten thousand men. And they knew their army was vastly superior in numbers to the garrison at the single city of Rochefort. What is more, they hoped that the Rochefort populace, largely Huguenot, would have a natural inclination to support its Protestant brothers.

The next day, September 23, while the fleet was anchored in two places, a local pilot, a Huguenot, was steering the *Magnanime*, a French vessel captured by the British in 1748. Seeing the ship approach from the Island of Aix, the French opened fire. The *Magnanime* was not damaged. Captain Howe, in a daring move, dropped anchor near the fort, which his twenty-four cannons proceeded to bombard. The French response was sluggish. An hour later, the flag of surrender was raised over the fortress.

"Drunkenness will be harshly punished; it is forbidden under the most severe pains for soldiers to behave in an inhuman, barbarous or brutal manner toward the inhabitants of a country." Despite strict orders from their officers, the soldiers and sailors celebrated this easy victory. They became "furiously" drunk. They insulted and manhandled the people. They pillaged the church, they "disturbed" the Catholic priest's library. Pages ripped from books flew around the room. They tore away his cassock, which one of the soldiers donned. This drunken English "priest," blessing everything left and right, got many laughs.

Lieutenant-Colonel Wolfe, at the top of the tower where the British flag was now flying, scanned the surroundings with his telescope. Six kilometres to the east, he saw, on a promontory, the square keep of Fouras, surrounded by thick ramparts. They would have to take this fort before moving on to Rochefort. The Bay of Châtelaillon seemed propitious for dropping anchor and landing. Wolfe reported his observations to Mordaunt and Hawke. They all agreed: the fort of Fouras would be attacked the next day.

The French pilot assured them that a landing in front of Fouras was possible, but the scouts declared that sandbanks would keep the ships far from shore. And on the beach, the attackers would be faced with dunes behind which the enemy could hide. Mordaunt began to waver. The vice-admiral conferred with the generals. No decision was taken that night. The war council began early the next morning. It was learned that a ship had sunk on the way to Fouras. They would not attack.

But Rochefort was still very vulnerable. They could put ladders in place and scale the ramparts. Inside the walls, they would find fellow believers. An officer objected that the moat around the walls could be filled with water in the event of a threat. That was what he'd learned from a prisoner. Exasperated by so much hesitation, Vice-Admiral Hawke threatened to head back to England. On September 27, everyone agreed on one point: they could not go home without attempting an assault. Everyone was thinking about Vice-Admiral Byng, executed for his failure in Minorca. The next day, after heated debate, a decision was taken: they would attack not Rochefort, but Fouras.

At midnight, the men silently boarded the boats and awaited the order to leave. Three hours later, they were still in the same place. Finally, an order was given: they would attack not Fouras, but Châtelaillon. Shivering in the autumn dawn, the men waited for the signal. A strong wind came up, blowing out from shore. The officers thought it would favour the enemy. Let the men reboard their ships!

On September 29, on a reconnaissance of Châtelaillon, James Wolfe saw that there was no trench, there was no battery, and there were no redoubts to ward off an attack. However, enemy snipers could hide behind dunes. In any case, it was all for naught. Vice-Admiral Hawke, weary of Mordaunt's indecision, was taking his squadron back to England. Wolfe wrote to his father: "We lost the lucky moment in war."

When James Wolfe returned to Blackheath, his parents had already left their home for Bath. Alone in the house, he was pensive. He was deeply disappointed by the Rochefort campaign, and his pride as an officer was wounded: while a promotion to the rank of colonel had been refused him because he was too young, that distinction had been granted to an officer who was no older. Wolfe, smarting, declared to the secretary of state for war, Lord Barrington, that he was giving up his posting as quartermaster general in Ireland. Lord Barrington advised Lieutenant-Colonel Wolfe to show a bit of patience.

William Pitt was exasperated by this new defeat. Since Anglo-Saxon times, all able-bodied men from sixteen to sixty years old had been called up to fight. After the civil war in 1642, that practice had ceased. William Pitt revived it. The Militia Act received royal assent on June 26, 1757, and the English army hunted down those who tried to slip away. Wolfe participated in these unedifying exercises in the villages between Bath and Stratford-upon-Avon, where he saw that the Rochefort fiasco had become a pretext for insulting soldiers.

During the Rochefort campaign, James Wolfe's ardour had not gone unnoticed. On October 21, he was promoted to the rank of colonel. He withdrew his notice of resignation and accepted the posting to Ireland.

After the huge fiasco at Rochefort, the pamphlets, the speeches, the newspapers deepened the popular dissatisfaction. How could such a failure occur? Lieutenant-General Mordaunt offered all the excuses he could think of for not taking action. Colonel Wolfe was called to testify. With shrewdness and some humanity, he did not allow himself to criticize Mordaunt, his protector, but he did indicate that at the war councils, he had recommended a landing, after having calculated the risks. The inquest report, published on November 21, 1757, rejected Mordaunt's excuses and concluded that Wolfe's plan would have led to victory. John Mordaunt was brought before a court martial.

Privately, Wolfe expressed his indignation more directly: "As to the expedition, it has been so ill that I am ashamed to have been of the party." He claimed that the navy officers "do not care to be engaged in any business of this sort where little is to be had but blows." He accused the infantry officers of being "profoundly ignorant."

After his testimony before the court martial, James Wolfe was invited, in December, to meet the Prince of Wales. The future George III wanted him to tell the tale of the Rochefort campaign, and wanted Wolfe to describe how he had disciplined his 20th Regiment so successfully.

In the end, the year 1757 had not been a complete loss, thought Colonel James Wolfe in the coach that was taking him to Bath, where he would celebrate Christmas with his parents. That day, he had heard a rumour: he would be one of the officers selected to be sent to America.

18

"A sort of general"

To reduce the exorbitant costs of providing for New France, Louis XV handed over its management to private enterprise. On January 1, 1757, Sieur Joseph-Michel Cadet, a friend of Intendant Bigot, became the general munitions supplier. Montcalm was not fond of this "overnight moneybags." Cadet supplied the king's troops, the colony's troops, the militias, the native allies, the garrisons of Quebec, Montreal, and Trois-Rivières, and the camps on the coasts, as well as all the forts, from the Upper Country all the way to Acadia. To launch the operations, the intendant lent Cadet a million *livres*. Jean Corpron, who had already been fired by merchants for "roguery," became his first lieutenant. Cadet's representative in Montreal would be Sieur Louis Pennisseault, who'd had to flee France because of his suspect business practices.

When Montcalm returned to Quebec on the night of January 5, 1757, there was little bread for the city's twelve thousand inhabitants. Wheat flour had to be supplemented with ground oats or peas. Every day, people were squabbling at the bakery doors. Bougainville, Montcalm's aide-de-camp, hoped that the English prisoners would not see this distressing spectacle.

The presence of both Vaudreuil and Montcalm in Quebec offered an ideal opportunity to celebrate the victory at Chouaguen.

In the courtyard of Intendant Bigot's château, greeted by lackeys in livery, the guests, wrapped in their fur coats, stepped down from their sleighs. The ladies, young and old, were "very pleasant and well attired." At these "very beautiful" balls, the guests dined on beef, pork, mutton, goose, turkey, game, fish, stews, fricassees. They drank bottles of Bordeaux and danced all night.

As snow flurries obscured his view of the river, Montcalm, in his first winter in Canada, was drafting a proposal for the king: would it not be preferable for the soldiers to be able to marry during their service, rather than waiting for the moment when they'd be returning to France? Married, instead of being idle all winter, they would clear their land, practise a trade, make children. He also prepared two reports for the governor general: one, on the advantages of using sliding ladders to scale ramparts or board a boat, the other on the need to arm the boats that gave chase to the English on Lake Saint-Sacrament with more powerful cannons.

On January 26, Vaudreuil went back to Montreal. At the gate of Château Saint-Louis, the people of Quebec came to wish him bon voyage. He was accompanied on his journey by officers and their wives. He was served by a steward, coachmen, grooms, cooks, servants. All along the way, soldiers ordered the settlers, on pain of imprisonment, to level the road, clear the snowdrifts, and harden the snow by having their cattle walk over it. A militia captain made certain in advance that there would be fresh horses at the ready to replace exhausted animals. A convoy of twenty or so sleds carried the trunks, food, table services, utensils, and toilet cases. In Trois-Rivières, Vaudreuil became so sick that his death seemed imminent.

Montcalm, for his part, returned to Montreal bundled in furs, in a sled drawn by two horses. Here and there was a house with smoke rising out of its chimney. When the horses bogged down in snow that was too deep, the coachman took to the river. Montcalm prayed God that the ice would support them.

Had the barber-surgeon in Trois-Rivières accomplished a miracle? Had God heard Bishop Pontbriand's prayers? The governor general's pleurisy was suddenly cured. Just as Vaudreuil was setting out en route again, a messenger brought him some news: on January 21, fifteen militiamen from Fort Carillon had been returning from Fort Saint-Frédéric, their sleds loaded with provisions. Suddenly, the English, on snowshoes, had pounced on them! Rangers from New Hampshire. They carried off seven militiamen. The others escaped and sounded the alarm at Fort Carillon. A hundred soldiers from the ground forces and the marine troops, some militiamen, and a band of Odawas hid themselves on either side of the ravine through which the rangers would have to pass to get back to Lake Saint-Sacrament (Lake George). In the middle of the afternoon, the rangers appeared. The commander of the Carillon detachment cried, "Surrender or you will be taken and scalped by our savages!" The English resisted until the Carillon detachment ran out of ammunition. The rangers then escaped, leaving behind them thirty or so dead and a dozen prisoners. It was certain that the English would plan revenge.

Vaudreuil was back in Montreal. Not very generously, Montcalm made the following assessment: he was "in as good a condition to work as before, that is, to do next to nothing." Vaudreuil did not want to let the incident of the rangers go unpunished. Montcalm reminded him that it was impossible for an army to set out on a campaign in winter. The governor general would be satisfied with a detachment that burned houses, barns, and storehouses. Any damage done to the English would discourage them from descending on Carillon in the spring. Fort George must be attacked!

Montcalm then proposed that he take charge of this "little war."

Vaudreuil made his move: with the exception of the captain of the grenadiers, François-Médard de Poulariez, all the officers would be *Canadiens*. Montcalm advised him not to discount the experience of his officers. The commander of the detachment, Vaudreuil decided, would be Rigaud, his brother.

Montcalm foresaw the difficulties of marching, transporting, and sleeping in the cold and the snow. He felt that, "in circumstances where it will be in short supply," food must be rationed. For him, seven to eight hundred men could carry out the mission. Vaudreuil wanted 1,800 men. This overly nebulous and overly costly campaign, Montcalm warned, could lead to the colony being lost if the English forces were to "gather themselves together soon enough." He was concerned: how long could they count on the good fortune "that up to now has saved Canada despite the errors we continue to make?"

After the exchange, the commander of the French troops in North America was kept at a distance. Bougainville remarked, "They do not do him the honour of consulting him." Despite his frustration, Montcalm chose from the battalions the best candidates for the French units that would take part in the expedition. He exhorted them not to err on the side of "timidity."

On February 20, after a meal washed down with plenty of wine, Montcalm admitted to Vaudreuil that the latter's knowledge of Canada gave him an advantage. But was it not he, Montcalm, who had long experience on the battlefield? He ought to be able "to assist him with the details and the means." Vaudreuil replied that he was keeping Montcalm in reserve for a great expedition, and invited him to come back in two days to taste some moose nose.

Montcalm lived "honourably." Three times a week, he had dinner in the company of ladies. Rather prudish and pious, they dressed in the latest Paris fashions and were avid gamblers. He honoured with his presence three balls given by the extremely sociable Chevalier de Lévis, who invited sixty-five ladies! These parties went on until two in the morning, or even later. At times, the revellers were not in bed until seven.

Did the subject ever come up, at these dinners, that in the countryside the farmers feared having insufficient wheat for the next season's seeding? Intendant Bigot considered drawing on the army's stores for thirty thousand kilos of grain to be given out for the spring planting. Did Bigot mention the beef he sold to the poor in Quebec, one pound a day, at half the price the bourgeois paid? Three thousand people took advantage of this charity, which required more than eighty head of cattle each week. Realizing that at that pace the herd would soon cease to exist, the intendant considered reducing the consumption to half a pound per person.

Montcalm found the evenings tedious, but what else could he do during those "unbearable days of drifting snow"? Happily, there was conversation with Madame Catherine Madeleine de Beaubassin. But in truth, he preferred his dinners with the Sulpician Fathers. He longed for Lent, to "throw himself into devotion." If he had become "a sort of general, although in no uncertain terms subordinate to the governor general," he congratulated himself for having approved the marriages of twenty-four soldiers and two officers. He also denied marriage to two young officers "with a prospect of paternity" who had "only consulted their passions." And he authorized a Chevalier du Languedoc to marry a fifteen-year-old young lady "with an honest fortune." The marriage of officers was another source of disagreement between Vaudreuil and Montcalm: how could this *Canadien* "surrounded by relatives of low birth" understand?

During the last two weeks of February 1757, the participants in the expedition against Fort George came together at Fort Saint-Jean:

50 grenadiers and 200 volunteers from French regiments, 280 soldiers from the colonial troops, 600 *Canadien* militiamen, and 350 resident Abenakis and Iroquois. In all, 1,480 fighters. Rigaud sent for the canoes. They set off. But the cold returned. Ice re-formed on the river and on the northern part of Lake Champlain. Rigaud asked for sleds. The men marched on ice. They had sixty leagues to cover. Horses pulled sleds loaded with barrels of provisions. Men and dogs hauled toboggans piled high with baggage. The French took note of what the *Canadiens* did. Before going to sleep, they cut branches of fir that they laid out on the snow to serve as mattresses. They planted their snowshoes upright in the snow on the side of the mattress from which the wind was blowing, and they draped their tarpaulins over the snowshoes to act as screens. After the meal, they rolled themselves up in bear or moose skin. They huddled together for warmth, their feet toward the fire, which they took turns tending.

They hid in the forest during the day. At nightfall, they marched in silence. They didn't want the dogs to bark or the horses to neigh. It was forbidden to light a fire; they ate ice-cold food. If a partridge, a rabbit, or a deer appeared, they couldn't shoot—orders the natives could never remember.

On March 18, the French were a league and a half from Fort George. Scouts described the fort to Commander Rigaud: one side of the rampart gave onto a swamp, and it was less high. The swamp was frozen; it was possible to walk on the surface. Rigaud decided to attack from that side! Poulariez, the only French officer, told Rigaud that doing so would lead to defeat. During the night, the scouts tested the thickness of the ice on the swamp. English sentinels heard the noise made by their picks and shot at the scouts' shadows. And so Rigaud lost the advantage of surprise. If they all ran to that side with their ladders, that was where the English would mass their defence. Rigaud nevertheless gave the order to attack from that direction immediately.

A few moments later, he changed his mind and commanded instead that they set fire to the palisade, the small fort, the houses, the storehouses, and the stables. But a spring rain soon drenched the wood. Nothing burned. The following night, Rigaud's men returned with fuel, setting alight three hundred flat-bottomed boats they'd found under the melting snow, armed boats, and other boats under construction. The hospital, the sawmill, the small fort, the sheds, the houses, the stables, the storehouses, and the firewood all went up in flames.

The next day, March 20, Rigaud paraded his closely formed regular troops, his militiamen, and the natives in front of Fort George out of range of the cannons. When ordered to surrender, Major William Eyre swore that his men would resist.

On March 23, snow covered the cindered remains of the store-houses and boats around Fort George. The garrison watched from the ramparts. Rigaud's detachment headed back to Carillon. The English would be weaker that summer.

In a letter to the minister of war, Montcalm said that in the eyes of the *Canadiens*, the French soldiers and officers at Fort George "were every bit their equal in a war and a kind of marching to which they were not accustomed." He reiterated that it had not been necessary to commit so many men. The same goal could have been achieved with seven or eight hundred men, as he had recommended. Besides, had not the governor general admitted to him that it was "shameful to have set fifteen hundred men marching, and to have wasted so much food"?

19

Victory is painful even to the victors

After the victory at Chouaguen the previous year, the governor general sent emissaries into the native villages in the autumn and over the winter. They distributed gifts to the chiefs, they told the story of the great French victory, and they repeated Vaudreuil's message: "I left Fort Chouaguen in flames, the English retreated before me. Why are you harbouring those snakes in your breast? They only want to enslave you."

The ice had drifted down the lakes, it had melted in the rivers, it had been carried off by the currents in the St. Lawrence. On April 20, 1757, there arrived in Montreal, by canoe, groups of natives from the Upper Country and south of Lake Saint-Sacrament, Odawas, Mohicans from the Hudson River, Oneidas from Wisconsin, Sakis from la Baie des Puants (Green Bay), Abenakis, Illinois, Miamis from south of Lake Michigan, Mi'kmaq from Maine, Menominee and Iowas, Shawnees from the south of Virginia, Cherokees, and Chactaws.

They were everywhere in town. Tall, "naked except for a cod-piece," their bodies painted, their heads adorned with feathers, they moved about with impressive dignity. They wanted to see Montcalm with their own eyes, he who had struck at the enemy like lightning at Chouaguen. They were amazed that he was such a small man: "We thought his head would be lost in the clouds," said the chief of three hundred Odawa from Michilimackinac, who was a master of language and flattery. "We see in his eyes the majesty of the pines and the flight of the eagle."

Montcalm was deluged with orations vaunting the greatness of the King of France, their "Father from the other side of the Great Lake." A chief offered him his young warriors: "We have young people . . . they must be taught how to use the blade and to bury it in the heart of the English." The natives danced to the beat of the *chichikoué* (a gourd containing dried kernels of corn) and became drunk as if they had already won the war. Although the settlers were short of food, the allied tribes all had to be fed. It was said that the allies would even have devoured a plump English prisoner. A missionary tried to reassure Montcalm: "These barbarians" would abandon their bad practices "once they were brought to prayer."

As defined by Vaudreuil, the goal of the summer's military campaign was to destroy Fort George, which served as a base for English expeditions.

Montcalm had not received any news from France since the autumn. While waiting for the ships to arrive in the spring, he wrote to his wife and swore that he would have had no time to involve himself with women even if he'd wanted to. However, when he spoke about one of them to François-Charles Bourlamaque, he was not so dispassionate: "I find in her too much wit and too many charms for my peace of mind."

At the beginning of May, the French ships had still not arrived. And every delay favoured the enemy. Vaudreuil sent the Bourlamaque Battalion on its way to Fort Carillon on May 8. Two other battalions would build a road between Forts Chambly and Saint-Jean.

It wasn't until June 9 that the first two French ships came up the river, carrying 170 foreign mercenaries in addition to supplies. They also brought news from France, where there was great unrest among the people, who reproached the court for its sumptuous feasts, its entourage, its reckless spending. On January 5, a man by the name of Robert-François Damiens, mingling with the crowd at the Palace of Versailles, managed to get close to Louis XV and stab him with a knife. The king was saved by his heavy winter clothing. Damiens was condemned to be executed on March 28, 1757, on the Place de Grève in Paris, where a huge crowd gathered. First, the hand that had held the knife was burned with sulphur. Then, after Damiens's limbs and chest had been cut open, molten lead was poured into the wounds. Finally, four horses, attached to each of his limbs, tore them from his trunk, which was thrown into a fire. So it went, in the civilized world . . .

Montcalm insisted that no one mention to the natives "the horrible attempt on the life of the sacred person of the king." Nor was anyone permitted to speak of Damiens: that could "lessen the esteem they have for us, if they were to see that we are capable of producing such monsters."

Montcalm had more news. Louis XV had dismissed d'Argenson, the minister of war, for having made indiscreet mention of the king and Madame de Pompadour in a letter that had been intercepted. Montcalm was saddened because a large part of his career as an officer had coincided with the tenure of d'Argenson, who had been minister since 1743. It was d'Argenson who had chosen Montcalm to command the troops in America. The new minister of war, Marquis Antoine-René de Voyer de Paulmy d'Argenson, was the other d'Argenson's nephew. Would he be as solicitous as his uncle? Machault, the secretary of state for the marine and the colonies, had also been let go. The new minister, Sieur François Marie Peyrenc de Moras, was the brother-in-law of Madame Marie Hélène Moreau de Séchelles Hérault, a protector of Bougainville. She was the second wife of Police Lieutenant René Hérault, whose first wife had been the aunt of Montcalm's father-in-law. The major-general was reassured.

On its way to Quebec, the *Saint-Antoine* had captured two English ships, on which were found instructions relating to England's intentions in America: first to conquer Louisbourg, then to take Quebec. If it were attacked, Quebec could not resist: its population was starving, and even Intendant Bigot asked Vaudreuil to cancel the expedition to Lake Saint-Sacrament in order to concentrate his forces in Quebec.

Vaudreuil did not fear an imminent attack on Quebec. According to the scouts, enemy movement was more in evidence in the direction of Fort Carillon.

Montcalm scanned with some discomfort a letter from Moras, the new minister of the colonies, concerning the *Canadiens*: "It appears that some infantry officers have been treating them too harshly." Montcalm went on reading: "We can reliably count on the *Canadiens'* valour and even their zeal and goodwill, when we treat them in such a way as not to offend them." Who had made the minister think that French officers were behaving in such a way as to offend the *Canadiens*? The minister gave Montcalm some advice: when a good relationship has been established between two superior officers, "there will be no fear of division or any altercation between the ground troops and those of the colony."

Writing to the Marquis de Paulmy, minister of war, Montcalm affirmed his "unconditional devotion and loyalty." The minister should know, however, that his remuneration was inadequate for a commander of French troops. He had to keep up appearances. Each day, he had at least sixteen mouths to feed: "I must respect myself, no one here will do so; rather they begrudge me any esteem." As a consequence, he had already "eaten up" more than his salary. He did not want to "deplete the small inheritance of [his] six children."

In addition, Montcalm asked Madame Hérault to personally send to the minister of the marine and the colonies, Monsieur de Moras, another letter, not to be seen by his officials, in which the major-general accused Governor General Vaudreuil of having "no character of his own," and of surrounding himself with "people seeking to dispossess him of any confidence he might have in the general of the ground forces." He even allowed himself to propose to Minister de Moras a solution to this power struggle: "By writing in such a way as to inspire confidence, to openly accord me some respect, and to express the wish that one pay some heed to my opinions when it comes to military operations."

On July 9, 1757, Vaudreuil sent Montcalm instructions concerning the campaign against Fort George. If the superiority of the English forces prevented the taking of this fort, Montcalm would fall back on Carillon and prepare for its defence. If Fort George fell into the hands of the French, Montcalm would leave a garrison there and quickly move on to besiege Fort Lydius. If this fort was too strongly defended, Montcalm must not compromise his army. Vaudreuil warned Montcalm that "he must not fail, at the end of the month of August, to send the nations of the Upper Country and most of the *Canadiens* home to take in their harvest."

That day, Montcalm was not in Montreal. Along with some *Canadien* officers, he was at Lake of Two Mountains visiting his Iroquois, Algonquin, and Nipissing allies. At night, around the fire, the natives danced and chanted warlike incantations: "We will trample the English underfoot!" The day ended with a feast laid on by Montcalm, who calculated the cost of those "three oxen gobbled up!"

Back in Montreal on July 11, after reading Vaudreuil's instructions, Montcalm expressed his discomfort in a letter to Madame

Hérault, which she would hasten, he hoped, to pass on to Minister de Moras. When he left on his mission to Canada, he recalled, Monsieur d'Argenson had "wisely" advised him to avoid launching himself into a fever of conquest, but rather to employ the less glorious strategy of a war of attrition. Vaudreuil "wants always to act and throws caution to the winds." He had little confidence in the French troops and relied too much on the natives, who to him resembled "the infernal militias in Milton's *Paradise Lost*, when Satan, 'inflam'd with rage,'" descends to earth.

Despite Montcalm's hesitancy and "timid objections," which he reported to the minister, Vaudreuil was convinced that his expedition would succeed "if Monsieur de Montcalm follows the instructions I gave him."

In the La Chute River flowing from Lake Champlain into Lake Saint-Sacrement, there was a difference in level of seventy metres, which created rapids, falls, and unnavigable cascades over a distance of five kilometres. And so a portage was necessary to reach Lake Saint-Sacrement. From Fort Carillon, a road had to be opened up. Under the orders of Lévis, three French battalions and *Canadien* militia were given this task. Officers as well as soldiers in the ranks picked up hatchets, picks, and shovels. Men bathed in sweat, in the humid heat of the woods, tormented by clouds of bloodthirsty mosquitoes, chopped down trees, levelled mounds, broke stones, filled in ponds. Horses and oxen hauled boats, cannons, wagons. Men pulled, pushed, or held in place cannons and boats on carts or blocks of wood. Or else they walked, bent over under the weight of sacks full of tools, munitions, and supplies. After two weeks of effort, 250 boats, two hundred canoes, a long trail of cannons, munitions, and supplies that would last eight thousand men for a month were lined up on the shore of Lake Saint-Sacrement, under close watch.

Montcalm arrived at Carillon on July 18. After inspecting the work that had been done between the two lakes, he had grave doubts whether the troops could still surprise the English. He conferred with Lévis on the urgency of imposing discipline on their indispensable native allies: on their departure, they had received provisions for a week, and three days later the provisions were gone. The natives were superstitious. When one of them saw, in a nightmare, Lake Saint-Sacrament covered with thousands of English boats, all the natives wanted to leave. And they were thieves. They pilfered from the officers' trunks, they stole eau-de-vie, even muskets. When they arrived at Carillon, they had a feast! Not far from the fort, some cattle wandered through their enclosure. They killed twenty!

A detachment of three hundred natives and eighty *Canadiens*, scouting out the Rivière aux Chicots on the way to Fort Lydius, ran into two parties of English soldiers who were also on a reconnaissance mission. The detachment came back to Carillon with a prisoner and thirty scalps. A few days later, a band of Mohawks, allies of the English, came across a French camp along the La Chute River. The grenadiers defended themselves, but the Mohawks left with two scalps. On July 24, a detachment of four hundred natives and fifty *Canadien* militiamen spotted a flotilla of English barges in the channels between the islands in Lake Saint-Sacrament: they were 350 militiamen from New Jersey who, having left Fort George the day before, had heaved to for the night. Natives and *Canadiens* hid on one of the islands and at dawn surrounded the English, who were quietly going back to their boats. The English responded, tried to resist. The attackers boarded and overturned the boats. The natives flailed at their victims with their tomahawks as the English floundered in the water reddened by their blood. Two hundred prisoners were captured. After the skirmish, the natives staged a cruel and drunken celebration. Pierre-Joseph-Antoine Roubaud, a Jesuit, saw a native gnawing on a man's head. The missionary went up to him to teach him some humanity. The native shot back: "You have the taste of a Frenchman, me of an Indian; this meat good for me."

On July 26, at the La Chute River, Montcalm held another council with the natives. They were Christian and pagan, from the east and west: Iroquois from Sault Saint-Louis, Hurons from Lorette, Nipissings, Abenakis from Pentagouet, Algonquins from Trois-Rivières, Mi'kmaq, Abenakis and Malecites from Acadia and Maine, Odawa, Ojibways from Lake Superior, Mississaugas from Lake Erie, Potawatomis from Lake Michigan, Sakis, Fox, Winnebagos from Wisconsin, Miamis from Illinois, Iowas from the Des Moines River. While Montcalm was talking, a very tall pine that a soldier was cutting down fell at his feet. Montcalm gave a start, then took advantage of the situation: "This is how the English will be overturned, this is how the walls of Fort George will fall."

The next day, he invited the natives to unite their forces. They were nearly two thousand, from thirty nations. They were tall, tattooed with the symbols of their nations; they had heads adorned with feathers or shaved, faces painted with coloured tallow. Some had previously been fighting against the French. Others, they were seeing for the first time. They formed a wide circle around Montcalm, his officers, his missionaries, and his interpreters. Many couldn't even see Montcalm. In all the brouhaha, they heard neither his voice nor that of his interpreter. They became restless, shoved at each other to get closer. The chief of the Nipissings spoke: "We thank you for having come to help us defend our lands against the English, who want to usurp them." Amid the approving hum, Montcalm replied: "As long as our union lasts, the English will not be able to resist us." At that moment, he held up a wampum of six thousand beads of porcelain: "With this necklace, a sacred pledge of the Great King's word . . . I bind you one to the other, so that none of you can be separated before the defeat of the English and the destruction of Fort George." Two hundred Mississaugas, Odawas, and Miamis left, preferring to seek other hunting grounds.

Since there were not enough boats to transport all the troops, Montcalm divided them into two columns: one would head for Fort George by water, the other by land. In this terrain of dense forest, rutted farmland, and raging rivers, Montcalm limited the baggage. The officers would sleep two to a tent, the servants eight. Cages of chickens were forbidden. Each officer could take only fifteen jars of wine. The battalions that travelled by boat carried the baggage of the soldiers who went on foot. Montcalm had made the inventory of his forces: 2,500 ground troops, 3,461 colonial troops and militia, 180 cannoneers, 1,599 natives. In total, 7,740 men.

The First Division, 2,970 men commanded by Lévis, set out on foot on July 29. All along Lake Saint-Sacrament, the forest was dense. The ground was sludgy. The sweltering shade under the branches was infested with mosquitoes. The division had to travel ten leagues before arriving at the Bay of Ganaouaké (Northwest Bay, New York), where Montcalm and the Second Division joined up with it, five leagues from Fort George.

While the First Division was making its painful progress, the rest of the army, at the La Chute River, loaded supplies, munitions, and other luggage into the boats. The natives were uneasy being confined in a camp. Those who stayed in the camp, not knowing what to do, went to the missionaries to make confession and attended mass. The "pagans" also had their ritual ceremonies: they made offerings of tobacco to the head of an animal stuck onto a stake planted in the ground. Others got drunk. Still others fished, swam naked in the river, or hunted rattlesnakes.

Finally, leaving a slim garrison of two hundred men at Fort

Carillon and the La Chute redoubt, Montcalm and his Second Division climbed into their 250 barges on August 1, at two in the afternoon. Leading the convoy were a 12-pounder cannon and two catapults for stones. To increase their range, the engineer Desandrouins had yoked the boats and built platforms across them to which the artillery pieces were secured. There followed the boats with supplies, munitions, the hospital, and the rear-guard defence. Lake Saint-Sacrament, a league wide, was set among mountains at the foot of which were tree-lined bays. At five o'clock, it was raining. A bay opened out before Montcalm's flotilla. Someone saw a signal: three fires in the form of a triangle. It was the camp set up by Lévis at Ganaouaké. The orders were clear: no drum, no cannon fire, no gunshots.

On August 2, after a few hours of sleep, the troops resumed their march at eleven o'clock: Lévis's army by ground and Montcalm's by boat. The two armies advanced in parallel, each ready to intervene if the other was attacked by the enemy. At five o'clock, they were a league from Fort George. Lévis prepared the camp. Montcalm's fleet glided into a cove.

By moonlight, some natives on reconnaissance spotted two barges. Suddenly, the bleating of a sheep intruded on the night. There were sheep in those boats! The natives jumped into their canoes and went to board the barges. They came back with some sheep and three English prisoners, from whom the French learned that more than a thousand men had just arrived to reinforce Fort George, along with four cannons and 150 supply wagons.

During the boarding, the Nipissing chief had been killed. The three English prisoners were turned over to members of his family, who inflicted on them the punishments they deserved. The chief's remains were then dressed in his ceremonial dress and adorned with porcelain necklaces, silver bracelets, pendants hanging from his ears and nose, and his military decorations. His musket was placed on his arm, his spear in his other hand. A peace pipe was slipped into his mouth. Gathered around the mound where the chief lay, seated in the grass, his warriors chanted and danced to the sound of a drum.

On August 3, at five in the morning, having placed the barges and boats under close guard, Montcalm set his troops in motion in the direction of Fort George, which gradually came into view. Montcalm thought to himself that if he and his men had arrived a few weeks earlier, they would have had to face only five hundred adversaries. With its four bastions, the fort rose up in a slight depression between the lake and the mountains. It was square. Each side was 110 metres long. On the northeast, the wall faced the lake. On the southeast, the wall was inaccessible because of the swamp. On the other two sides, the walls were protected by a moat six metres deep. Behind a gravel embankment, the palisades were made up of two parallel rows of thick pine stakes driven into the ground and propped up by other stakes tied to them crossways. The space between the two lines of stakes was filled with sand, forming a five-metre terreplein. All around the fort, to a distance of 135 metres, the English had created a "desert."

At ten o'clock, Lévis's advance party took up its position on the road linking Fort George to Fort Lydius, as it was from there that reinforcements might arrive. The two forts were separated by some twenty-five kilometres. Most of the Fort George troops were at their posts in a camp entrenched behind an abatis of tree trunks on the heights dominating the fort, and defended by cannons. The natives rushed toward the entrenched camp. Assailed by a hail of balls, the English took shelter, but they could not save their animals in the fields. The natives killed 150 cattle and proudly led twenty-five, alive, to Grand Chief Montcalm's tent, hoping to be pardoned for having killed the animals at Carillon.

At three o'clock, Montcalm had a surrender order delivered to Lieutenant-Colonel George Monroe, commander of the fort. He listed the reasons why the English should yield. The French army was larger. Its artillery was more powerful. The French army had the support of "a great many natives." Monroe ought to fear "their cruelty." If natives were killed while the English put off surrendering, "I would not be able to control them," threatened Montcalm. If he persisted in fighting, Lieutenant-Colonel Monroe "would needlessly expose an unfortunate garrison that cannot be saved."

During the truce that was called for negotiation, the natives, very curious, went to examine the abatis. Behind it, New England militiamen were terrified by that "frightening contingent." Many of their villages had suffered cruelly from bands that had set fires, cut throats, scalped the populations. In one village, rangers had taken a very unchristian revenge: they had dismembered fourteen warriors in what they thought was the Indian manner and had thrown their torsos to the pigs. These militiamen knew that the Indians had long memories.

Lieutenant-Colonel Monroe's messenger brought Montcalm his answer: "Monsieur . . . I have little fear of barbarity. I also have under my command soldiers who are determined like myself to perish or to prevail." Montcalm would have to take the fort by force. Despite all the precautions taken by the French to intercept any communication between Fort George and Fort Lydius, the following day, August 4, three rangers from Fort George were able to deliver to Fort Lydius a note from Monroe calling on General Webb for help.

Montcalm had not for a moment forgotten that this was where General Dieskau, whom he had replaced, had suffered a humiliating defeat in 1755. He had read the reports of Dieskan's expedition. Accompanied by the artillery captain and the engineer

Desandrouins, Montcalm went again to survey the battlefield. On his return, he had brushwood gathered for his fascines, to fill in marshy ground, and prepared his saucissons, with their gunpowder rolled into canvas. That night, his cannons, large and small, his mortars, munitions, and supplies, were all unloaded from the boats. On the night of August 4, 365 metres from the ramparts where cannons were belching out thunder and lightning, hundreds of men dug trenches.

In the jacket lining of a prisoner captured on the road from Fort Lydius, a letter was found from General Webb to Lieutenant-Colonel Monroe. Montcalm listened to Bougainville's translation: Webb could not come to Monroe's aid before receiving reinforcements for his militia that he had requested from the governor of New York. According to a confession made by a *Canadien* prisoner, the French army, with its native allies, numbered at least eleven thousand men. Webb advised Monroe to surrender. This letter provided Montcalm with a weapon he could never have hoped for.

While the workers in the trenches wielded picks and shovels, the natives sniped impatiently at the fort. Once the trench was finished, gun batteries were installed overnight. On August 6, the French artillery spat fire. The natives greeted every detonation with cries. Bombs exploded, and heavy black smoke drifted into the compound, where the garrison was trying to put out fires. The French artillery installed more howitzers and mortars. The workmen again began to dig.

On August 7, Montcalm decided that the time had come to read Monroe the letter from General Webb found in the prisoner's jacket. At nine o'clock, he had the flag for negotiation hoisted and sent Bougainville, his eyes blindfolded by the English, into their camp. He delivered Webb's letter to Monroe, advising him to surrender. Monroe refused. In the middle of the afternoon, his men, in a desperate initiative, came out of the camp, only to be pushed back by Villiers's militia and natives, after having lost fifty or so men.

On that day, Montcalm was brought a message from Versailles. Not only had Louis XV bestowed on the major-general the prestigious honour of Commander of the Order of Saint-Louis, where "virtue, merit, and services rendered are the only qualifications for admittance," but His Majesty also tendered gifts to his army's brave soldiers. The fighters became all the more courageous!

On August 9, forty cannon mouths bombarded Fort George. Balls fell onto the infirmary. In a bastion, a barrel of powder exploded. The English had already lost three hundred men, killed or wounded. At seven o'clock, they ran up the flag of truce. Lieutenant-Colonel John Young came to negotiate the terms of surrender. At a time when supplies were low, the French could not take prisoners and feed 2,400 extra mouths. Montcalm could offer only a "generous outcome." The English would come out of Fort George bearing their arms, drums, and flags. They would be escorted to Fort Lydius by a French detachment. They would have to desist from fighting the French and their allies for a period of eighteen months. All the French taken as prisoners in North America since the beginning of the war would be returned to a French fort. The artillery, boats, war *matériel*, and food at Fort George would become the property of the King of France, except for the cannon Montcalm ceded to Monroe as a tribute to his intrepid resistance.

Before finalizing the agreement, Montcalm brought the native chiefs together to explain the conditions granted to the enemy. He asked them to make sure that their warriors respected the agreement. Bougainville, along with some of his men, left to take the news of the French victory at Fort George to the governor general in Montreal.

When the English garrison withdrew from Fort George to join

the rest of the army in the fortified camp, the natives jostled each other to get into the enclosure, because their "father," Montcalm, had promised them "many good things." They laid hold of whatever was there, sacks left behind, abandoned objects. They searched for jugs of rum. In the end, they were unhappy at the lean pickings.

That night, at the fortified camp of the English, the natives eluded the sentries, roamed around, burst into tents with knives in hand, raided the officers' trunks and chests of drawers. Montcalm urged their chiefs to intervene. But what authority did he have over them? To appease his allies, Montcalm suggested that the English open a barrel of rum. Around nine o'clock, order seemed restored, but at dawn intoxicated natives burst into a hut where seventeen sick and wounded were lying. They battered them to death with tomahawks and scalped them in full view of the surgeon, Miles Whitworth. The Jesuit Roubaud saw a native parading around holding up a head "streaming with blood."

There was panic in the fortified camp. The soldiers wanted to march to Fort Lydius without waiting for the escort of two hundred French soldiers promised in the terms of surrender. The *Canadiens* suggested appeasing the looters by giving them a few bottles. Commander Monroe accused the French of not respecting the agreement. Finally, the escort was ready, made up of the Reine and Languedoc detachments, along with *Canadien* militiamen.

The column of vanquished soldiers began to move. The English were drawn up into very tight formation. Natives came to harass the fringes of the column. They snatched hats, grabbed muskets. The English tossed them various possessions to appease them, offering them rum. Drawn by the rum, more natives appeared. Some pulled women and children out of the column. Others laid hold of blacks and mulattoes. A group of Abenakis threw themselves on the New Hampshire rangers: they wanted to avenge their brothers killed the previous year in front of Fort Pentagouet. They stripped the men of their clothes, took scalps. The English troops had their muskets but no reserves of ammunition. How could they defend themselves against 1,500 natives? Lévis and Bourlamaque tried to limit the carnage. Captain Jonathan Carver begged for help from the French officers who were marching along and chatting. "English dog" was the answer he received. Three or four natives seized Carver. An English officer without clothing came to his aid. The natives turned away from Carver to deliver tomahawk blows to the back of the naked officer. Carver slipped away. A twelve-year-old child who had lost his parents followed him. The child was caught, then killed.

Around nine o'clock at night, Lévis and Bourlamaque tried to persuade the natives to return some of their prisoners to the officers. The natives preferred to kill them. Arriving at the chaotic scene, Montcalm threw himself in front of the natives, opened his shirt, bared his chest, his arms spread wide: "Since you do not want to obey your father, kill him!"

Astonished that this theatrical gesture had calmed the natives, Montcalm offered his hospitality to Lieutenant-Colonel Monroe, who asked him why he had not provided a stronger escort. Montcalm assured him that he had given him protection as defined in the agreement's protocol. However, he had been betrayed by the natives, who had, after all, ratified the terms of surrender. Besides, he could not commit more soldiers to escort the vanquished, because he had to protect his artillery, munitions, and supplies. And it was always possible that reinforcements would arrive from Fort Lydius.

Brigadier Lévis told Monroe that he didn't understand how 2,300 English soldiers could allow themselves to be stripped and looted by natives who had only spears and tomahawks. And the engineer Desandrouins asserted that even though they were armed with muskets, cartridges, and bayonets, the English did not even "pretend to defend themselves." The *aide-major* Jean-Guillaume-Charles de Plantavit, Chevalier of La Pause, had seen them: "They let themselves be taken like sheep." Lévis insisted that "without the help they received from the French officers, they would all have been killed."

When Lieutenant-Colonel Monroe and his officers withdrew from the table, where they had paid in humiliation for the hospitality of the victors, the French officers continued the discussion late into the night. Emptying several bottles, they all blamed the *Canadien* militiamen and the interpreters for not persuading the natives to respect an agreement concluded in the name of the king.

The troops of the marine and the *Canadien* militia were talking also. Montcalm, his officers, and the French officials were all passing through Canada, then going back to France. The *Canadiens* had their families here, their farms, their shops. They would stay on in this country. Some had been here for generations. Canada was at war, and France sent meagre assistance to its colony. To conquer a little town in Europe, they rolled out a hundred thousand men. In protecting Canada, France pinched pennies. Perhaps the natives were the *Canadiens'* only true allies . . . Let them massacre their enemies . . .

Every bureaucrat knows that following a catastrophe, the first thing to be done is to blame the victims. Montcalm sent a letter to his counterpart, Lord Loudoun, commander-in-chief of the British troops in America. If Monroe's soldiers, he wrote, had moved out in greater order, they would have been better able to defend themselves. If Monroe had agreed to give rum to the natives, his soldiers would not have been the victims of "disturbances." If Monroe's soldiers had not shown so much fear, the natives would not have been motivated to massacre them. Montcalm sought an understanding grounded in their shared experience: "You know what it's like to control three thousand natives from thirty-three different nations." Finally, Montcalm asserted that he had shown great humanity. "I rescued more than four hundred prisoners from the savages."

On August 14, as promised, an escort of 250 men led these prisoners bought off by Montcalm to Fort Lydius.

His men reloaded the boats with the supplies, munitions, artillery, baggage, and tools they had brought with them. In the flat-bottomed boats taken from the English, they stowed the booty, arms, and munitions they had taken. They filled in the moats, burned the blockhouses, storage buildings, and stables, tore down the ramparts, razed the fortifications. On August 15, Fort George was but a vast conflagration.

The next day, Montcalm passed his army in review and handed over command to the Chevalier de Lévis, who immediately assigned small detachments to watch over Lake Champlain, Lake Saint-Sacrement, and the Rivière aux Chicots, in case of a surprise attack from General Webb's army. Montcalm and his men climbed back into their boats. The *Canadiens* hoped to be back on their land in time for the harvest.

Some natives presented themselves at the governor general's château in Montreal with two hundred English prisoners. They also had fifty or so scalps that they hoped to sell at a good price. They'd found a way to make two scalps out of one and double their profit. Why had the natives not respected the terms of surrender? Vaudreuil was certain that the British government would never recognize this capitulation. On the other hand, he didn't want to embark on pointless arguments with the natives. For every prisoner, he offered two barrels of eau-de-vie. That was not enough to satisfy the natives. Bougainville saw them take hold of a prisoner, kill him, dismember his body, and throw the pieces into a cauldron of boiling water. When the flesh was cooked, they forced the other prisoners, horrified, to eat it.

Learning of these events, Intendant Bigot offered the natives guns, canoes, cloth, necklaces, eau-de-vie. Whatever the cost, he wanted them to be happy when they returned to their villages.

"Poor king..."

Governor General de Vaudreuil made his dissatisfaction known to Montcalm. The victory at Fort George should have been a triumph, but the task was not complete. However, on August 18, 1757, Vaudreuil was proud to announce to the minister of the colonies that Fort George had been destroyed. The better to glorify himself, he doubled the number of his enemies: "By bringing my forces together at Carillon, I was able to keep General Loudoun in check, even if he had at his disposal twenty thousand men." He did go on to express his regret that Commander Montcalm had not seen fit to follow his orders to take Fort Lydius "even if the *Canadiens* would not have been back in time for their harvest." He insisted that "to destroy that fort would have been an easy task. The surrender of the first fort would certainly have led to that of the second." As for the massacre of the English garrison by the natives, Vaudreuil affirmed that it "would not have happened" if Montcalm "had only given Monsieur de Rigaud, the missionaries, the officers, and interpreters the responsibility to contain the natives with whom they were associated . . . but he had confidence only in himself."

In his report to the minister, the engineer Desandrouins itemized the reasons Montcalm did not lay siege to Fort Lydius. The soldiers were exhausted by the siege at Fort George. There did not remain enough "war *matériel* or food." One cannot imagine, in France, said the engineer, how hard it was to transport artillery, munitions, and food supplies in the wilds. There were no oxen or horses. A portage using only manpower, over a distance of "six leagues" between two forts, was an impossible task, which would have been made even more impossible by the departure of the *Canadiens*. And "it was of the greatest importance to send all the *Canadien* militias back for the harvest."

In a letter to Montcalm, Intendant Bigot was of the same opinion: "I very much fear that the government of Montreal's harvest would have been lost, had you kept the population away for a longer time." He said that he understood one of the reasons Montcalm did not go to besiege Fort Lydius: "You did not have enough supplies at Carillon for this enterprise . . . in a year when we are to all intents and purposes without bread."

These words may have comforted Montcalm, but the same Bigot wrote to the minister of the colonies on August 25: "We are of the general opinion that Monsieur de Montcalm ought to have laid siege to Fort Lydius after taking Fort George."

It was in this recriminatory climate that Montcalm and Vaudreuil prepared the troops' return to their winter quarters. Given the danger represented for Canada by the English and their colonies' militias, they agreed this time to locate the forces in places where they would control the waterways in the vicinity of Quebec, Trois-Rivières, and Montreal.

The minister of war, Monsieur de Paulmy, and the minister of the marine and the colonies, Monsieur de Moras, were concerned about the relations between the French and *Canadien* troops. Did they need any proof that the commander of the French troops in America was addressing himself to this issue? "On the fourteenth of last month [August]," Montcalm wrote, "I had a corporal of the Sarre hanged for being disrespectful of an officer of the colony."

Montcalm requested that the minister of war confer promotions on Brigadier Lévis and Colonel Bourlamaque. After this gesture on behalf of his subordinates, he made his own case. Had he not served the king for thirty-six years? Since his arrival in Canada, had he not in two campaigns won two victories? Montcalm suggested that the minister accord Vaudreuil a Great Cross of the Order of Saint-Louis. That honour would ease the hierarchical friction between the governor general and the commander of the French troops.

Montcalm didn't want the minister to conclude that he was merely ambitious: "Whether or not I am made a lieutenant-general," he promised to display the "same zeal for service, the same attachment to my minister." The minister would certainly hear him being criticized by "people as poorly educated as they are ill-intentioned." Fortunately, he wrote, "Vaudreuil and Bigot have assured me that they would both undeceive you." Was Montcalm extremely naïve or extremely adroit?

On September 11, 1757, he was in Quebec to pass in review two battalions from Berry, initially intended for India but then redirected to Canada. During their crossing, which lasted three months, they were ravaged by an epidemic. More than two hundred soldiers died. The "bad air" of the ship, in port, poisoned the air of the city. Both Quebec hospitals were crowded with seven hundred sick patients. Beds were set up in churches and convents.

Surgeons, nurses, and nuns were not spared. Montcalm lamented the fate of the unfortunate Acadians who had sought refuge in Quebec after having been dispossessed of their land by the English: "Our Acadians are dying of poverty, of smallpox."

This ship also brought bad news from Louisbourg: an English

fleet of twenty warships (that of Admiral Holburne) was coming and going at the entrance to its port. The ships were going to attack the fortress. Montcalm described to Lévis the climate prevailing in Quebec: "All here are s—ing in their pants for Louisbourg; as I am not naturally fearful, I will wait serenely for events to unfold."

A few days later, it was learned that God, once more, had fought on the side of the French . . . A "perfect storm" in the Atlantic, two leagues from Louisbourg, had scattered the English fleet, wrecking nine of its ships on the rocks.

Despite the "sad situation due to the scarcity of bread," Monsieur and Madame de La Naudière gave a party in honour of Montcalm, victor at Chouaguen and Fort George, and godfather of the surgeon André Arnoux's newborn. Madame de La Naudière, Louise-Geneviève Deschamps de Boishébert, was the godmother. Quebec was "full of business and suspect speculation." It was the time of year when, usually, merchants, fur traders, officials, artisans, and individuals could receive in currency the nominal value of their playing card money. Up to that time, playing card money had been reimbursable annually. Bigot had imposed a new rule: a quarter of its value would be paid the following year, in 1758, half in 1759, and the last quarter in 1760.

Montcalm was anxious to complete his letters, reports, and memoranda before the last ships left for France. His secretaries were being overworked. For each of his texts, they had to make two or three copies that were sent off on different ships in the event of shipwrecks, enemies, pirates... "Overwhelmed by all sorts of affairs and writings," he also had to endure a variety of idle visitors. He had a sore throat. He had a boil on his cheek because his "blood was on fire from fatigue." His hemorrhoids were "torturing" him. To his wife, he complained: "I'm going into debt here, damn it! I want to live!" Would she confirm with his business agents in Paris that the payments that were his due as a colonel no longer in service were being received? He entrusted to his mother a very special mission. Thanks to the Order of Saint-Louis, with which he had been honoured, he had the right to wear a red scarf. The major-general had a "great desire" to wear, rather, the blue scarf of the Order of Saint-Esprit, whose president, Mathieu-François Molé, was his wife's cousin. Montcalm asked his mother to ask his wife's mother to intervene on his behalf with the president. Montcalm made her a list of the products he needed: two hundred bottles of muscat wine, three hundred bottles of liqueur, sachets of scented herbs from Portugal, lavender and a "small box of aromatic pomade," and so on. After describing Vaudreuil's brother, Rigaud, and "those that follow him," to the minister of war's sister-in-law, Madame Hérault, as "good people, but lacking in wisdom," Montcalm asked her to suggest that Monsieur de Moras write him a letter "where it appears . . . that I have said many good things about the *Canadiens*": a letter that "would be useful to him."

In light of the lack of respect accorded him by Vaudreuil, and not wanting to offend the intendant, who supplied his troops with transportation, supplies, and arms, Montcalm was cautious . . . Of Bigot, he said to Madame Hérault that he "takes good care of his friends and their fortunes. I think he will return to France rich, but he serves the king well." He took the precaution of adding, "Burn my letter."

Mysteriously, he wrote to his wife on September 16: "Ah, if I wanted not to indebt myself here, I could. I would perhaps be better loved. . . . I would rather that Monsieur de Moras or a land sale pay my debts than be in high society."

The 1757 harvest was pitiful. In July, a fierce sun scorched the grain. One morning in August, the fields were white with frost. Now it had been raining for two weeks. Montcalm feared that they would be "very poor in bread." On September 26, he warned Lévis at Carillon: "Circumstances require that we and our soldiers commit ourselves to a considerable rationing of provisions." Bigot felt sorry for himself: "All who live in Quebec" are reduced "to a quarter pound, including me."

On October 10, Montcalm, Bougainville, and Fiacre-François Potot de Montbeillard, an officer in the Royal Artillery Corps, left for a reconnaissance east of Île d'Orléans with Gabriel Pellegrin, a *Canadien*, as their guide. The best way to defend Quebec would be to stop the English from getting too close. Near Cap Tourmente, about eight leagues from Quebec, Montbeillard, the artilleryman, imagined, on top of the 150-metre cliff, a battery that would bombard the enemy fleet along the string of little islands that narrowed the passage: the English would not be able to escape the barrage for "a good fifteen minutes." Returning to Quebec, Pellegrin observed that there was no place that lent itself to a landing. The cliff of Sault Montmorency, eighty-five metres high, was an unscalable wall. Beginning at this river, which flowed into the St. Lawrence, Montcalm wanted to build a line of small forts as far as Quebec. When they got back to the city, Montcalm, Bougainville, and Montbeillard went to inspect the stone rampart that protected Quebec. It was in very bad shape.

On October 13, the governor general arrived in Quebec. For that occasion, Montcalm offered his "last great meal." It was a dinner "splendid in flavour, in abundance, and in its double service of dessert." He had invited "our powerful men and five ladies." They were all there, the Péans, Maurins, Pennisseaults, and Corprons . . . Intendant Bigot sat with Joseph Cadet, the colony's munitions supplier.

Despite the perfume and the pomade, Montcalm smelled corruption. Little by little, he had schooled himself in the ploys of high society. For example, the Bordeaux merchants, Gradis & Sons, "a bit bankers and a bit shipowners," sent merchandise to Canada. Jacques-Michel Bréard, an associate of Bigot and responsible for finances, declared at customs that his supplies had been sent by the king, who didn't have to pay duty. Once it was landed, this merchandise was sold by an intermediary to Bigot, who then resold it to Cadet. Of course, the price rose at each stage.

By bribing the officers of the forts and trading posts, Cadet had provided himself with attestations confirming that the merchandise delivered corresponded to the orders. Bigot always had an associate or an employee ready to append his signature to the bottom of a phony order, a phony bill, a phony receipt. A fort's order provided an excellent opportunity to make a profit. Vaudreuil had named his future son-in-law, Louis Le Verrier de Rousson, commander of the fort at Michilimackinac. In three years, the young officer put together enough money to start a household. In the end, it was the king who was on the hook for these disproportionate expenses.

Every autumn, when the intendant drew up for the ministry of the marine and the colonies the inventory of his supply requirements for the following year, he deliberately underestimated them, thus creating a shortage of products in the king's stores. Under false names, Bigot had opened a business in Quebec City. And he proposed to soon open another in Montreal. Through the involvement of Gradis & Sons, Bigot bought what he had not ordered from the ministry, and the high society store was able to sell its merchandise, at great profit, even to the king. The people called Bigot's store *La Friponne,* or "The Swindler."

Bigot and his associates had other things going. The furs destined for the French market had to be brought to the intendant, who was responsible for commerce. Bigot sold them first to his associates, who sold them back to him. The profits were shared.

Bigot was also responsible for troop transport. He rented at low cost, under false names, boats that he sub-rented at a high price to the king's troops. He needed rowers, boatmen, coachmen, carriers, ferrymen, cowherds, grooms. Militiamen were exempted from combat to assume these tasks, and one of Bigot's aliases charged their salaries to the king's account, money that in theory was not to be paid to the militia.

To feed the Acadian refugees in Quebec, the intendant and his associates bought, in the name of the king and at a high price, spoiled cod and other unmarketable food. Far-seeing farmers had accumulated reserves of wheat. Bigot circulated an order stipulating that this wheat had to be sold at a fixed price, set by him, to the king's munitions dealer, Cadet. Bigot had seals put on mill doors, so the inhabitants who still had reserves of grain could not have it milled in secret. As a result, Cadet enjoyed a monopoly: he resold the commodity, which was becoming ever scarcer, at a high price to the king for his troops and militia, and then for seeding to the very farmers from whom he had extracted it at low cost. On October 14, Montcalm wrote to Lévis: "People are crying out against the intendant and high society, and between us, I believe they are not wrong to do so. As for me, I remain silent."

Vaudreuil called a council that included Intendant Bigot, Montcalm, the arms supplier Cadet, and Major Michel-Jean-Hugues Péan. Montcalm let it be known that the governor general and the intendant had to set an example where frugality was concerned, and impose on themselves a "tightening of belts." In this city where the populace lacked for food, "all through winter there had to be no balls, no violins, no feasts, no gatherings." He proposed scattering the troops, for winter, to a greater number of villages, in order to lighten pressure on the reserves of food. Decisions were made. As of November 1, the soldiers' rations would be reduced.

In December, horses would be slaughtered so there would be meat for January and February. During this time, they would let the pigs fatten up.

Montcalm sent his instructions to Lévis, the commander at Fort Carillon. To encourage moderation, he recommended that Lévis follow his own example: his guests would receive only a frugal repast, "a soup, four large entrées, a veal shoulder, a portion of cold dessert, all served together, the boiled meat flavouring the soup." Montcalm warned his men: the shortage of food would place them in an increasingly difficult situation. As the harvest was poor, grain would be even harder to come by. If the animals were not fed, meat would become as hard to find as bread. "He who . . . consumes the least," he said, "will show the surest sign of love for his country, and for service to the king."

Montcalm refused to participate in a war council, on October 24, 1757, when two fort commanders from Acadia were to be judged, accused of having capitulated to the English army in 1755 without having waged an honest battle. He did not think justice would be done. Two hundred and seventy soldiers of England's Royal Army and two thousand militiamen of the English colonies had marched for two days, escaping notice, to Fort Beauséjour. When they appeared before the fort, Commander Louis Du Pont Duchambon de Vergor, assigned to this post by Bigot, had offered no resistance. "The idiot commander surrendered," wrote Thomas Pichon, a French spy in Acadia in the service of the English. Later, Benjamin Rouer de Villeray, commander of Fort Gaspareaux, three and a half leagues from Fort Beauséjour, also surrendered, even before being attacked. Following the council, Montcalm wrote to Lévis: "This morning Vergor and all the officers of Beauséjour were exonerated. . . . Villeray . . . will be absolved tomorrow."

In a letter on November 4, 1757, Montcalm spelled out to the minister of war the sources of "our suffering" in New France. The munitions supplier Cadet, who had not foreseen the poor harvest and the shortage of grain, had imported from France more wine than flour because he made a better profit from wine. What is more, new battalions had increased the numbers of the regular troops. More *Canadien* militiamen had also been called up to form a larger contingent. Hordes of allied natives had arrived to join the army. Finally, the Acadians, who had lost everything, had sought refuge in Quebec. The number of mouths to feed had doubled: the munitions supplier had neither anticipated nor calculated this increase in consumption.

On November 6, the last four ships left the colony for France. One of them had been given the name *Chouaguen*, after Montcalm's first victory in America. A week later, during the night, a hundred marine fusiliers and *Canadien* militia, along with two hundred resident Iroquois, surrounded the sleeping village of German Flatts, sixteen leagues from Corlear (Schenectady), where there lived some German émigrés from the Palatinate. At dawn, the invaders broke down doors, smashed windows, killed or kidnapped men, women, and children, pillaged, sacked, set afire, then slit the throats of sheep, pigs, and horses. They left with 150 prisoners and so much plunder that they had trouble carrying it. The English who thought of settling on French land would now fear the punishment that lay in wait for them.

Montcalm lived, he said, "too well and too richly domiciled," in one of two apartments in the house of Descheneaux, Bigot's secretary. He read, he wrote in his diary, he reflected on the letters and memoranda he received, he assessed officers' requests, he calculated his expenses, he planned for the defence of Quebec. To distract himself, he frequently visited Monsieur and Madame de La Naudière. In his view, this lady, a Boishébert, was one of the most beautiful women in Quebec. At their home on the rue du Parloir, he met Madame de Beaubassin, a cousin of Madame de La Naudière, and Madame Péan, whom many called "the reigning sultana" on account of her special relationship with Intendant Bigot. He also dined at the home of Monsieur Pierre-Roch de Saint-Ours, a captain in the colony who had married Charlotte Deschamps de Boishébert, sister to Madame de La Naudière. Montcalm still visited the Pennisseaults and the Péans. The families of Quebec high society formed a tapestry whose warp was made up of blood relations and whose woof consisted of their functions, their businesses, and their intersecting interests. Montcalm, on December 2, 1757, confided to Lévis: "I see blatant chicanery everywhere . . . the poor king."

Intendant Bigot declared that he was substituting horsemeat for beef in order not to destroy the herd. On December 1, 1757, the governor general's château was besieged by angry women who were repelled by the idea of eating horses, their workmates. The Catholic religion, they cried, prohibited killing that animal! They would die of hunger rather than eat it. They demanded bread, even if it was, according to a certain Mother Lagrange, "as black as our dresses." The governor general answered that he would not tolerate such impertinence. If they went on protesting, they would go to prison! And he would have half of them hanged!

When the soldiers at Fort Carillon refused to eat horsemeat, Lévis brought the garrison together, had pieces of horsemeat brought in, and told the grenadiers to share them. They refused. The commander ordered them to bite into the meat. Whoever didn't obey would be hanged.

Bigot, for his part, explained to the people that they had too many horses. In the interests of the colony, they had to reduce this number. He'd calculated that they could consume three thousand. To sell the king one, two, or three horses meant money for the populace, not to be disdained. But when there were no more horses, they would want to kill their calves. Bigot prohibited the people from slaughtering these young animals. Montcalm doubted the efficacy of such an injunction, "because we have accustomed this people to having a great spirit of independence, respecting neither rules nor regulations." Protests broke out in the streets. The soldiers joined with the people who were giving them shelter. The marine troops refused to show up for the distribution of provisions.

On December 16, 1757, at the intendant's château in Quebec, in a brightly lit salon, three long tables were set with eighty places. Visitors arrived in sleighs, wrapped in fur. Their clothes were elegant, they wore lace ruffles, embroidered cuffs, powdered wigs, and they were scented with musk. The ladies were dressed as at Versailles. On the French officers' uniforms, medals gleamed. The music was joyous. People danced. They played at lansquenet, betting on cards. Bigot, master of the house, was "magnificent in every way," observed Montcalm. So as not to interrupt such a successful party, dinner, which was to have been served at nine o'clock, was put off until midnight. Montcalm was dumbfounded at the amount of gambling, "so far beyond the means of the individuals." He wrote: "I thought I was looking at madmen, or more accurately, at people burning with fever." After a "large bet," there were "serious skirmishes." Some citizens had been granted the privilege of being invited up to the gallery, from which they could admire high society at play in the hall below.

21

"*The enterprise of Louisbourg will cost a multitude of men*"

At the end of the year 1757, William Pitt shored up England's support for his ally Frederick II of Prussia. He provided the East India Company with a modest naval force and saw to it that the attacks against French ships and trading posts continued on the West African coast; but above all, he put England's power behind its American colonies.

First, William Pitt replaced Lord Loudoun. It was said that Loudoun had been unlucky, but shouldn't an army general be able to outwit chance? Major-General James Abercromby became commander-in-chief of the British forces in America. Then Pitt urged the English colonies to make common front against the French. Up to then, they had paid out of their own pockets for the recruitment of troops and had been responsible for their clothing and pay. In future, Pitt would reimburse those expenses. A patriotism that did not entail any increase in taxes—that would be readily welcomed by the colonial assemblies. According to a royal order in 1756, the colonial generals were demoted to the rank of captain as soon as a British major appeared on the scene. Pitt promised to have another look at the parity of ranks between colonial officers and those of the mother country.

Marshal John Ligonier, the commander-in-chief who had replaced the Duke of Cumberland, translated William Pitt's vision for America, one approved of by the king, into a winning strategy. An army of twenty thousand regular soldiers, backed up by twenty thousand colonial militiamen, would be divided up and given three objectives. The first expedition would target Louisbourg on Cape Breton Island. A second would invade Canada through Lakes Saint-Sacrement and Champlain. It would raze to the ground the principal obstacle, Fort Carillon. A third expedition would make up for Braddock's mistakes and would take Fort Duquesne, at the forks of the Belle-Rivière (the Ohio River).

To start, the largest part of the force would be directed at Louisbourg on Cape Breton. This imposing fortress was the bulwark for the last French communities holding out against the English in Nova Scotia.

Louisbourg was located near Cabot Strait, through which all ships going to or coming from New France had to pass. From this fortress, the French could also keep an eye on navigation in the Gulf of St. Lawrence and around Newfoundland. Louisbourg was the busiest port on the Atlantic after Boston, New York, and Philadelphia. It was close to the fishing banks; every year, more than fifteen thousand fishermen came there to spread their nets. Its port was well protected by the cannons of the impressive fortress. Its little town was both Acadia's seat of government and its military hub. Its four thousand or so inhabitants were fishermen, but they also raised pigs, and they were armed. In the summer, Louisbourg was very lively, thanks to sailors and merchants from France, Quebec, Boston, and Martinique. Its commerce thrived at the expense of that of New England and Newfoundland. The French sold or exchanged merchandise from the West Indies and Europe with crews that stopped over at their port. They even did a lot of trade with New England, despite the fact that such activity was prohibited by both England and France. At times, half the ships at anchor in the port of Louisbourg belonged to merchants from the English colonies. However, it was from Louisbourg and the island called Royale by the French that pirates took off in pursuit of New England's ships. And it was from there, often, that raids on the New England population were launched.

It was well known that the ramparts were in poor condition. The French builders, avid for profit, had put insufficient cement in with the sand ... Serious damage done to the Louisbourg fortifications during the 1745 siege had not been repaired. The King of France, extremely attentive to his mistresses, had not taken the trouble to maintain his colony's defences. Everyone knew that the French treasury was depleted. The king had even considered pulling out of any enterprise whose expenses exceeded its revenue.

England could relieve France of the burden of Louisbourg! The English navy had already taken it in 1745. When it signed the Treaty of Aix-la-Chapelle in 1748, England had given the fortress back to France, but for all that, the English had never lost interest in Louisbourg. In 1755, Vice-Admiral Boscawen had cut off its navigation with a squadron of fifteen ships, but the Louisbourg garrison and its population had resisted, and when winter arrived, Boscawen had had to withdraw. The following year, Commodore Charles Holmes had tried to renew the blockade, but he had been surprised by the unexpected appearance of a French squadron returning from Quebec. Holmes went to seek reinforcements in Halifax. When he returned, the French fleet had disappeared. Holmes put the blockade back in place. The Louisbourg garrison and its people had little to eat, but there was no surrender. In 1757, a storm scattered Holburne and Loudoun's fleet. Now, in this summer of 1758, Marshal Ligonier was determined that England would not fail again at Louisbourg.

After all of England's recent defeats, it had become clear that the experience of elderly generals was not enough to win battles. Marshal Ligonier, sixty-seven years old, convinced George II to entrust the next campaigns in America to the vitality of new blood. The old marshal knew the young generation well; he frequented young actresses and young singers, and he supported four or five mistresses who were not yet twenty years old.

Colonel Jeffrey Amherst, forty-two years old, an officer referred to as a "bulldog," was promoted to the rank of major-general and would command the expedition against Louisbourg. Amherst would be seconded by three new brigadiers: Charles Lawrence, Edward Whitmore, and James Wolfe. At thirty-one years old, Wolfe, the youngest in age and experience, was jubilant; the American colonies would no longer be in the hands of "decrepit old generals"!

Ligonier allotted to Amherst the largest portion of the redcoats who would be sailing, or fourteen battalions. He assigned him a partner with experience and practical good sense: Vice-Admiral Boscawen. Like Wolfe's father, Boscawen had witnessed the disaster at Cartegena. He had participated in the combined operations of the navy and land forces. He had even been in charge of such operations, including one in India, against the French post of Pondicherry. He knew Louisbourg and its surroundings, both land and sea.

On January 7, 1758, after having spent another Christmas holiday with his parents at Bath, James Wolfe returned to his 20th Regiment. He had barely arrived at Exeter, bruised by the jolting of the coach and the tossing of the post horse, when a letter from London informed him of the imminent departure of the fleet for America. Wolfe asked his servant François to prepare the horses for an immediate return to London. They rode all night. The entire way, François held a candle ready to replace the one that had melted inside the lantern. They made no stops. The brigadier and his servant were in London by the next day, after a twenty-hour ride. Wolfe wrote to Captain William Rickson, a friend who was in Nova Scotia in 1750 and 1751, and who knew Louisbourg, for any information that might be useful concerning that country, its inhabitants, and the fortress.

James Wolfe arrived in Portsmouth on February 2, 1758. On seeing the ocean, he didn't conceal his terror: "I know that the very passage threatens my life." At the port, while the refitting was being completed, he threw himself into his correspondence to put the sea out of his mind. He got back in touch with Lord Sackville, his regiment's former colonel, who was now commander-in-chief of the British artillery and was also master of his lodge of Freemasons. Wolfe commented on recent events in India: Bengal, Bihar, and Orissa had passed under British domination because sixty thousand undisciplined men, badly trained and plagued by conflicts among their leaders, had lost their battle against Lord Clive's three thousand soldiers. Was that not clear evidence of the need for training and discipline among the troops? He asked Lord Sackville whether the recent guidelines from high command for improving the training of English troops were strict enough.

James Wolfe hated "the diabolical citizens of Portsmouth." He had no more respect for the city's garrison: "vagabonds that stroll about in dirty red clothes from one gin shop to another." His judgment of the twelve thousand soldiers and four thousand sailors who were preparing to board ship with him was even harsher: "dirty, drunken, insolent rascals, improved by the hellish nature of the place."

Wolfe entered his ship's cabin as if it were a torture chamber, and on February 15, 1758, Vice-Admiral Boscawen's fleet left Spithead, on Portsmouth's great bay. A week later, it was barely farther out in Plymouth Sound, where a bad wind had driven the

Invincible onto a sandbank. For sailors who read the future in wind and waves, this was a bad omen for the expedition.

Contrary to what the government in London assumed, France had not abandoned Louisbourg. English spies had surprised a flotilla that was preparing to leave Toulon, on the Mediterranean, heading for the fortress. Admiral Henry Osborn, with the *Monmouth* and its sixty-four cannons, arrived to intercept the flotilla on its way out of the Strait of Gibraltar. Osborn brought a trophy back to England—the *Foudroyant* and its eighty-four cannons. At the same moment, at Rochefort, a French fleet was taking to the sea in the direction of Louisbourg, when the sailors spotted one of Edward Hawke's frigates preparing to blockade the port. Without being observed, the French were able to cut the cables of many English ships, which ended up foundering in the mud. To free them, the sailors had to throw cannons, provisions, and munitions overboard.

Finally, on February 19, favourable winds filled the sails. Wolfe was on board the flagship, the *Princess Amelia*. A storm blew up and did not die down. According to the old sailors, this was the worst crossing of their lives. Wolfe, closeted in his cabin, brought up everything he ate. If he tried to get up, he was dizzy. The redcoats were stacked one on top of the other in their hammocks, in steerage. The air was foul, the smell nauseating. The sailors, in the wind, the fog, the rain, and the snow, had to clamber up the ice-covered rigging to work on the yards, but the soldiers could not go out on the bridge for fear of breaking their bones. Three months later, on May 9, 1758, the Boscawen fleet arrived in the port of Halifax. The men disembarked, haggard, hollow-eyed. They could barely stand erect on solid land. They needed rest, and the ships needed repair.

James Wolfe could not forgive the storms for having robbed him of eleven weeks, as any delay aided the French. He discovered that the expedition could not count on all the men inscribed on the roster:

more than three thousand were missing. They had deserted, or were sick, wounded, or dead. On the troops that were left to him, Wolfe imposed a very exact training program. At Louisbourg, the ground and sea troops would have to combine their expertise to vanquish the enemy. This collaboration was not natural to them. Brigadier Wolfe had them rehearse the landing procedures together. His instructions were clear: in front of Louisbourg, so as not to waste ammunition, no one could open fire from the boats. To avoid accidents, soldiers would also be forbidden to fix bayonets to guns before stepping on shore. As soon as the men were out of the boats, they would form up in ranks and march, eliminating whatever obstacles they faced, to ease the progress of those who came behind.

Wolfe did not have a very high opinion of his soldiers: "I believe no nation paid so many soldiers at so high a rate." The rangers from the colonies did not impress him either: they were "little better than *canailles*." He was unhappy with the men's equipment. They didn't have enough picks, and too many muskets were defective. Their uniforms were not suited to the climate: "Even our shoes and stockings are all improper for this country." The food was bad: Our "army is undone and ruin'd by the constant use of salt meat and rum." James Wolfe said what he thought, but whatever the conditions for the king's army, he would insist on victory from his soldiers.

To encourage them to know each other better, Brigadier Wolfe invited forty-six army and navy officers to a Halifax inn on May 24, 1758. Ten musicians accompanied the traditional songs of their regiments, their companies, their branches of service. At dinner, they emptied seventy bottles of Madeira, fifty bottles of Bordeaux, and twenty-five bottles of brandy . . .

Wolfe had informed himself of the failed Louisbourg expedition the previous year. The ships of Admiral Holburne and Lord Loudoun were to have joined up at Halifax. But confused policies in England, preparations that lagged, and unfavourable winds had held Holburne back. Loudoun and his troops were waiting for him in New York. To keep twelve thousand men busy, Loudoun had them planting vegetables. After one of his officers dared compare him to Lord Byng, executed for his defeat at Minorca, Loudoun, with no news from Holburne, decided to risk taking action. On June 30, his fleet entered the port of Halifax. Disguised as fishermen, rangers on a reconnaissance mission reported that Louisbourg was defended by powerful artillery on its ramparts and, in the port, by twenty-four warships, five frigates, 1,360 cannons, and seven thousand men. This was Admiral de la Motte's fleet. Holburne's ship didn't arrive until July 10. Audaciously, Holburne tried to provoke the French, hoping they would chase after him. La Motte didn't take the challenge. Ultimately, Loudoun headed for New York, and Holburne's fleet was scattered and almost destroyed by a hurricane.

Brigadier Wolfe, still waiting in Halifax for Major-General Amherst while overseeing exercises or bending over maps or sketches of Louisbourg, wanted the king's army to have a greater will to win, less indecision, more effectiveness, and better communication.

In June and July, Cape Breton Island melted into a fog that, knowledgeable officers explained, was caused by the exhalations of serpents, fish, and other sea dwellers. These noxious vapours, they knew, could make you blind. Bad weather was perhaps Louisbourg's best protection, but Wolfe thought that with adequate dominion over the sea, enough artillery, and reasonable zeal on the part of the men, Louisbourg could be taken in a few weeks.

On the other side of the Louisbourg ramparts, everyone was certain the English would be back this year. Since the beginning of spring, enemy sailing ships had been seen lurking on the horizon. Governor Augustin de Boschenry de Drucour was concerned.

The death of a French officer in a quarrel with an officer of the colony had created animosity and divided the garrison. He also suspected that Swiss and German mercenaries wanted to go over to the enemy. He wasn't sure that his Mi'kmaq allies would remain loyal to the French. What is more, smallpox was rampant.

The month of May would soon be over. Vice-Admiral Boscawen could no longer await the arrival of Major-General Amherst, commander of the ground troops. If a contingent was delayed, his instructions were to attack Louisbourg, assuming he had eight thousand men at his disposal.

When the English had conquered Louisbourg in 1745, they had attacked the fortress by the Bay of Gabarus, Boscawen remembered, and what had succeeded once ought to succeed a second time. The Bay of Gabarus was an easy approach. Brigadier Lawrence shared his opinion. Wolfe contended that the French had already lost Louisbourg because of their weak defences on the Bay of Gabarus, and so they expected to be attacked from that side. If they were not irresponsible, they would have dealt with that weakness; they would have put in place stronger artillery. Boscawen insisted: they would attack from the Bay of Gabarus. On the morning of May 28, 1758, he headed his ships toward Louisbourg.

They were still just a short distance from Halifax when the *Dublin*, Major-General Amherst's ship, appeared. The commander of the ground forces boarded the *Namur*. Scouts confirmed that the French had reinforced the ramparts on the side of the Bay of Gabarus and that they had added cannons. Wolfe then suggested attacking by the Bay of Mira, in the northeast. It was big enough to accommodate the entire fleet, and the distance the troops would have to cover to reach the ramparts would be the same as if they had started from Gabarus. Amherst feared those sixteen kilometres of unknown territory, with woods, bogs, and bush. Like Boscawen, he favoured the approach from the Bay of Gabarus. The fleet sailed up the rugged, jagged coast toward Cape Breton Island, where the sea had carved out the rocks in its own image.

"*I foresee by my good fortune that the campaign will turn out well*"

On Twelfth Night, January 6, 1758, at Intendant Bigot's table in Quebec, Montcalm found, "as one might expect," the bean in his cake. Madame de Beaubassin was his queen. "The gaiety at the end of the meal" had taken on "the aspect of a tavern." He retired at one in the morning, "fed up with so much gambling and prevarication." A few days later, he went to visit Lorette, the Huron village near Quebec. He relished the *sagamité*, a corn flour stew with pieces of different kinds of game, fish, beans, and squash. He loved the people's dances, he communed with them, smoked the peace pipe. He found that, thanks to the Jesuits, the village "was beginning to reflect French manners and a French feeling."

Montcalm was nevertheless shaken by the slander that followed on his victories. On February 20, 1758, Bougainville wrote to his protector, Madame Hérault, to plead in favour of Montcalm, who was "disparaged in secret" by "writers of low status, or perhaps the leaders of this land." Montcalm, he assured her, had won the respect of the "*Canadien* people," who "prefer marching with him and the French than with their own officers." Bougainville was counting on her passing on the message to her brother-in-law, Minister de Moras.

Given the English threat, many thought about leaving the colony. The chief administrator of the marine, Monsieur Jean-Victor Varin de La Marre, member of high society and friend to Bigot, was getting ready, so it was said, to return to France. Some put his fortune at four million *livres*. Bréard, another member of polite society, had already left to live in a manor he had purchased in Poitou.

For Montcalm, it was time to "cover sixty leagues on ice," to return to Montreal. As soon as he arrived, on February 22, he wrote to his wife. His health was reasonable, he told her, but he'd had to undertake a purge. He told her about his visit to the Hurons: "I find in them more truth and candour, often, than in those who think they are expert in civilizing other people." He confessed to her: "The shortages are greater than we could have believed." He talked to her about his next campaign against the English: "If we only present a defence, as long as it stops the enemy, that will not be without merit." Mentioning his correspondence with "my lord" Loudoun on the subject of the massacre of the English troops after their surrender at Fort George the previous year, Montcalm raged: "It's a trial conducted with strokes of the pen, while waiting to deal with an incident with blows from the sword, from the gun." He bemoaned the fact that his duties as commander required him to spend as much as the governor general or intendant: "Surrounded by people who will leave the colonies, enriched . . . I cannot live on 25,000 francs." He had to borrow twelve thousand francs from Bigot. "The longer I go on, the more I will owe him," he lamented. Persuaded that his letters to Minister de Moras were being intercepted by the chief clerk, Monsieur Arnaud de La Porte, who was devoted to Intendant Bigot, Montcalm asked his wife to advise Madame Hérault of his financial concerns, so that she might intervene in his favour with her brother-in-law, the minister . . .

Given the threat from the English army, Montcalm, on February 23, 1758, openly shared his distress with Monsieur de Paulmy, minister of war: "Whatever success we may have, peace should be the goal for New France or Canada, which in the long term must succumb, given the number of English and how difficult it is to transport supplies and reinforcements." But the minister had other worries. The Franco-Imperial Army of the Prince of Soubise had suffered a disastrous defeat at Rosbach. It was driven out of Hanover by an army half its size.

At the end of March, in Montreal, the dinners were still being put on, with "twenty-three personages, the bigwigs, a thousand ladies . . ." Some of the gentlemen were "pettifogging tattlers, dangerous characters," but Montcalm could not publicly spurn the governor general: even though he complained of having to "keep him company every night," Montcalm acknowledged, "it's good for the service, good for me."

The English, who were spied lurking around Fort Carillon, were clearly preparing for a more consequential visit. At the end of January, an English party had captured two soldiers and stolen fifteen cattle from the stables. They'd had the impertinence to attach a message to the horn of an animal they'd left behind: "I am much obliged, Monsieur, for the repose you have allowed me, and the fresh meat you have sent me. I will take good care of your prisoners. My compliments to the Marquis de Montcalm. [Signed] Major Robert Rogers." In March, this same Major Rogers returned to Carillon with eighty rangers. A band of Abenakis saw them and surrounded them. Rogers escaped with a few of his companions, but the natives took forty-four scalps and captured seven prisoners.

Before the melting of the snows, Governor General and Madame de Vaudreuil took advantage of the still-passable roads to visit some important people who resided along the river. Intendant

Bigot, accompanied by Madame Péan and followed by her "family," her husband's associates, did the rounds of their friends in the village of Lachine. It was bruited about in Quebec that during this time Monsieur Péan was consoling himself with Madame Pennisseault. For high society, the party went on. When Holy Week arrived, and the revellers had to repent of their sins, Montcalm was finally able to stay home and dine alone. He needed some rest. His stomach was disturbed. The surgeon recommended enemas.

Montcalm was also tormented by an extremely important decision he had to make: one soldier wanted to lodge with the goldsmith, and another wanted to lodge with the Loiseaus. Both were protégés of Madame de Beaubassin. Of course, he could not refuse to please Madame de Beaubassin, but it would be to set "a bad example..." Oh! It was not easy to be commander of the French king's army in North America! And then Montcalm was not in a position to make his fortune in Canada; he was still working toward a promotion. Having asked for the support of a Lieutenant-General de Boshy, he scanned the reply with considerable satisfaction: "I thought I could do nothing better than to read your letters to the beautiful lady." The beautiful lady was Madame de Pompadour, Louis XV's mistress. "I will try to convince the Abbé [de Bernis] to put his shoulder to the wheel." Abbé François-Joachim de Pierre de Bernis was the "beautiful lady's" confessor. Montcalm had reason to hope.

As of April, bread was even more severely rationed. Indignant, the women flocked to Intendant Bigot's château: "We have no flour! We have no bread for our children! We have no bran for the animals!" The intendant would hear nothing of these lamentations. And so they went to complain to his secretary, Descheneaux. This son of a cobbler would understand them... Instead, Descheneaux reprimanded them and sent the poor women on their way. They then went to François Daine, civil and criminal lieutenant-general of the Quebec provostship, who had just submitted a report to the minister of the colonies on the penury in Canada. On February 6, he had written that more than three hundred Acadian refugees in Quebec had died of smallpox. During that exceptionally cold winter, they'd had only horsemeat and dried cod to eat. All the grain would soon be used up. Even the animals were badly fed. The butchers had no more beef, no veal, no mutton, no fowl. All that remained were vegetables. Intendant Bigot had calculated that 3,400 wretched individuals could survive on "ten ounces of food per day." In the streets of Quebec, you could see people "falling to the ground from weakness."

On April 13, Montcalm visited the surrounding countryside with La Rochebaucourt in a horse-drawn carriage. Farmers were sowing, carefully, a few grains of seed, when they had any. Some people were reduced to eating grass.

Fortunately, on May 18, eight French ships, escorted by a frigate and followed by a boat captured from the English, arrived at the port of Quebec with 7,500 barrels of flour. They also brought news that confirmed what was already known: the English were preparing "to lay siege to Louisbourg, and at the same time to invade from New York" by Lake Champlain, then the Richelieu, toward Montreal and Quebec. "All parts of the city" were now "very keyed up and full of activity," wrote Montcalm. The French ships also brought him news of the death of his sister. He felt so far from his family! His children were growing up. His mother was getting old. His wife was on the other side of the ocean. On April 20, 1758, he had written her: "When will I embrace my most dear one, a moment I would prefer even to that of defeating Abercrombie."

At Versailles, the minister of war had again been replaced. Montcalm was quick to express his happiness to Marshal Charles Louis Auguste Fouquet de Belle-Isle, that "the foremost representative of our military profession, who combines the talents of a great general, the qualities of a statesman, and the virtues of a citizen, has consented to take the helm of our ministry."

Montcalm's regular troops were fewer in number than the single English garrison at Fort Lydius, and his officers were not happy: "A lieutenant, who in 55–56 had enough to live on with his pay, is now dying of hunger." His regular troops, it was true, had the support of the troops of the marine and the *Canadien* militia. Unfortunately, those individuals knew nothing of military discipline. And could he count on the natives? Their cruelty sowed terror in the enemy, but it caused so much concern . . . The previous spring, the natives asked the governor general for the privilege of making war with the French. This year, few natives were seen in Montreal. The warriors at Fort George were unhappy because the French had stopped them from taking the booty that was coming to them. And many went back to their villages with smallpox. The rumour circulated that the French had poisoned them.

While waiting for reinforcements from France or for peace to be declared in Europe, Montcalm proposed ways of preventing the English from getting to Canada. First, to block the invasion being prepared at the south of Lake Champlain, he would concentrate his forces at Carillon. At Louisbourg, Fort Niagara, and the forts of Belle-Rivière, the garrisons would have to bar the way to the invaders for as long as possible by their own means.

Vaudreuil disapproved of this strategy. That was not how, with the meagre amount of help received from the French troops, the *Canadiens* and their allies had, up to now, been able to resist British ambitions. They had infiltrated enemy territory. They had turned up, unexpectedly, at farms and villages, and had put to the flame, killed, and captured. They had inspired fear of the French. These small detachments launched against many enemy objectives had forced the English to split up their army. The strategy had succeeded. That was what Vaudreuil prescribed. Not able to convince Montcalm, he brought accusations against him in a letter to the minister of war: "I devote my best efforts to defending the soil of our frontiers foot by foot, while Monsieur de Montcalm and the ground troops seek only to preserve their reputation in France."

Vaudreuil launched an operation to draw the enemy away from Carillon. Under Lévis's command, four hundred regular soldiers, four hundred soldiers from the troops of the marine, eight hundred *Canadien* militiamen, and nine hundred natives would enter Lake Ontario and go up the Chouaguen River. They would set up a post on the Iroquois River (Mohawk), and from there burn houses, stables, and mills as far as Corlear (Schenectady).

Montcalm denounced this expedition, which would "perhaps result in the loss of our colony." He proposed instead to assemble a solid army made up of ground troops, troops of the marine, and elite militiamen backed up by natives, for an attack that would strike at the English like lightning and would end the war at the frontier of Lake Champlain. Montcalm accused Vaudreuil of "not wanting a decisive victory for the colony, where the general of the ground forces would be instrumental."

By the middle of May, the city of Quebec no longer had the wherewithal to feed the Queen's Battalion, which was sent to Fort Carillon. On May 22, Colonel Bourlamaque replaced Lévis as commander of this fort. Vaudreuil gave him five thousand men. The militia was keeping everyone waiting. The farmers refused to leave their fields before having seeded them. Because of the food shortage, it was difficult to provide supplies. And transport took forever. Montcalm complained to his mother on June 2, 1758: "Imagine that I cannot be on campaign, with mediocre people, before six weeks." Many of those "mediocre people" would lose their lives following Montcalm's orders, but the marquis deserved a better fate than Canada: "Will I never head an army in Europe?" He poured out his feelings. Had he not "more of a name" than Vaudreuil? He confessed to harbouring for him a "secret hatred that time renders all the more total and strong." But his old mother should not worry. "I will serve the king the best way I can," he said, but conditions being what they were, "do not expect anything spectacular." These confidences of a son to his mother were accompanied by a gift of Canadian balsam, which had antiseptic and healing properties.

Major-General John Abercromby followed the instructions he received from William Pitt on March 7, 1758, for the Canadian campaign. His mission was first to take Fort Carillon. Abercromby sent a request to the governors of the colonies of New York, Connecticut, Massachusetts, New Hampshire, New Jersey, and Rhode Island, asking them to recruit twenty thousand men. Volunteers were not breaking down the doors. Connecticut did not itself feel threatened, protected as it was by its neighbour Massachusetts. However, in the churches, preachers were declaiming sermons resonant with biblical patriotism: this campaign against the French was a crusade against Babylon, the city of all abominations. They evoked the combat between Joshua and Amalek, Israel's enemy. They inveighed against those who were hesitant: "Cowards will not go to heaven." In the end, the English colonies voted for compulsory conscription: 17,840 men marched behind Abercromby against the French.

These troops were concentrated first at Orange (Albany). At the beginning of June, New England militiamen were seen marching in the countryside, fitted out like woodcutters with rifles, powder horns, and bags of ammunition, the colonial regiments in their blue uniforms, the English troops in their red coats, the Scots Highlanders in kilts. They were followed by a convoy of wagons and travois loaded with supplies. Abercromby went to set up his camp at the tip of Lake Saint-Sacrament, on the very site of Fort

George, which Montcalm had razed the year before. This was the rallying point where all the troops would gather after June 19. The ten thousand muskets they were awaiting from England had not yet arrived.

On June 23, Montcalm prepared to leave and take command of his army at Fort Carillon. At ten o'clock, as he was going to bed, Vaudreuil came to give him his instructions for the campaign. Despite the late hour, Montcalm began to read them. In his preamble, Vaudreuil stated that he had consulted the commander of the French troops in North America regarding "all the colony's affairs," and that he had sought "his opinions on everything." Montcalm made his own correction: "He never consulted me on anything." Vaudreuil contended that if the English attacked Louisbourg, it was very unlikely that they would have the strength to march on Carillon. The news had not yet reached Montreal that Louisbourg had been surrounded by the English for two weeks. What is more, Fort Carillon scouts had seen English troops on the march between Orange and Fort Lydius. If, "against all expectations," the English attacked Carillon, Vaudreuil ordered Montcalm only to harass them to slow their advance. He must not risk "a general and decisive affair."

Montcalm was seething. What did these ambiguous instructions mean? Finally, Vaudreuil demanded that the boats be returned as soon as they had transported the troops to Carillon. Montcalm thought it necessary to keep the boats at Carillon in case the troops had to make a retreat.

The major-general felt that he was not compelled to obey instructions "whose vagueness and contradictions would seem to hold me responsible for events that might happen and that we ought to have foreseen." The night was well advanced when he finished his reply to Vaudreuil. He later noted in his diary that Vaudreuil's instructions, "ridiculous, vague, specious . . . were worded in such a way that any unfortunate turn of events would be blamed on me."

Vaudreuil revised his instructions, and Montcalm left Montreal on June 24, 1758, much too late for him to be able to surprise his enemies. While he was on Lake Champlain, a Huron brought him a message from Bourlamaque: the English army had set up camp near the ruins of Fort George.

A thousand boats had transported no fewer than ten battalions of regular troops and five companies of rangers up the Hudson River, with munitions, arms, tents, and supplies. Two hundred Massachusetts whalers had helped transport this baggage, which formed huge mounds on the shore of Lake Saint-Sacrament. The artillery convoy followed. Major-General Abercromby was leading the largest army ever to tread the soil of North America.

23

"By the greatest of good fortune imaginable"

With its four bastions, Louisbourg's ramparts surrounded the Château Saint-Louis—the governor's residence—the Royal Chapel, a convent, the garrison's barracks, storehouses, and seven or eight stone houses, but in particular more modest wooden dwellings and a few inns where one drank well and bet heavily.

On June 1, 1758, the sentinels sounded the alarm. The horizon was white with sails! English sails! James Wolfe was astonished that, in the port, the French fleet sat still.

The next day, Major-General Amherst, as well as Brigadiers Lawrence and Wolfe, on board a sloop, went in search of a favourable place to land. A few small boats went to harass the French cannons: when they fired, they revealed their positions. The scouts took note. On the water, which pounded the rocks and formed white whirlpools, Wolfe moaned that he was going to die if he could not return to dry land.

Boscawen met with Amherst and the officers. With persistent stirrings in his stomach and a ghostly pallor, Wolfe insisted: since they could no longer surprise the French, they had to confuse them.

George II's thirteen thousand men could not calm the sea. And on June 3, the waves ruled out any approach to shore. Wolfe, in his bunk, dizzy, his stomach heaving, retched every time the boat rocked. He wanted to describe his suffering to his mother, but how could he put pen to paper?

On June 4, 1758, Louisbourg was shrouded in fog. Furious gusts seized hold of some cargo ships and threw a frigate against the rocks. On June 6, the fog changed to rain. The old sailors said the sea was getting tired. It calmed during the night. They would land at Louisbourg! The order was given for the soldiers to drop down into the boats to which they had been assigned. The rowers awaited the signal to plunge their oars in the water . . . Suddenly, the sea rose up. Back to the ships!

Two days later, at two o'clock in the morning, the troops were waiting in silence in the boats. The English soldiers had scores to settle. The infantrymen of the 48th Regiment were part of Braddock's expedition in 1755. They had not forgotten their comrades, who had been wounded, tortured, scalped by the Indians. At Fort George, the previous year, the French had not wanted to quell the barbarity of their allies. James Wolfe described these feelings in a note to Amherst: "When the French are in a scrape, they are ready to cry out on behalf of the human species, when fortune favours them—none are more bloody, more inhuman; Montcalm has chang'd the very nature of war, and has forced us in some measure, to a deterring and dreadful vengeance." That night, Wolfe enjoyed seeing his men imbued with a "perfect rage" against the French.

Behind the ramparts, the garrison's own vengeful urges craved satisfaction. The English had usurped Acadian villages, farms, and houses. They had forced onto their ships old people, women separated from their husbands and children, children separated from their parents, and they had taken them off, stripped of everything, to foreign lands. Everyone in Louisbourg had brothers, sisters, parents, friends who had been uprooted in this way. These ships facing Louisbourg had perhaps served to deport their relatives, their friends. These soldiers in boats before Louisbourg had perhaps prodded with bayonets their relatives and friends who resisted going on board . . .

James Wolfe would be at the head of the division that would attack the Cove of Cormorandière (Freshwater Cove or Kennington Cove), where the sea was less rough. The warships would advance into the cove, and the artillery would cover the disembarkation. During that time, Whitmore's and Lawrence's divisions would carry out a diversion at Pointe Blanche (White Point) and Pointe Plate (Flat Point or Simon Point). Twelve companies of grenadiers—more than three thousand men—would march behind the young brigadier. The grenadiers had the reputation of being the most aggressive unit in a regiment. Wolfe could also count on a new corps of elite marksmen. Finally, he would have the support of the Highlanders. Would he be able to exert authority over his companies of rangers from New England, who were undisciplined, wild-looking drinkers?

At the break of day on June 8, frigates and bomb-launching ketches took their positions at various locations in front of their targets. Suddenly, they loosed a storm of cannonballs and other projectiles. The populace awoke: this was no nightmare. To attract the attention of the garrison, the boats of the 28th Regiment paraded slowly in front of the entrance to the port. After a fifteen-minute bombardment, the boats of Wolfe's division, filled with redcoats, glided in close to the shore of the inlet. The rocks, in their eternal stillness, with their ridges and spurs, were more and more intimidating in this sea that never quieted down. The soldiers, numb with cold in their wet uniforms, clutched their muskets to their bodies.

Beyond the beach, which formed an arc over four hundred metres long between two rocks, Lieutenant-Colonel Joseph-Hippolyte de Bouvier, Viscount of Saint-Julien, awaited the invaders. Protected by trees that had been cut down and thrown one on top of the other, his 985 soldiers and his Mi'kmaq allies were supported by eight pivoting cannons placed at two forward points of the inlet, creating a crossfire targeting the enemy. The French let the English come close. When their boats touched land, they were instantly riddled with iron grape-shot and balls from invisible marksmen. A ball shot away the Red Ensign topping the mast of Wolfe's ketch. A boat slowly sank into the water with its grenadiers weighed down by their bags. A few knew how to swim; the others drowned. A young drummer boy, tied to his instrument, floated along with it, and the sea bore him away. Several damaged boats, overturned by the waves, were swallowed up. Others were smashed against rocks. Soldiers drowned. Some lost their muskets while thrashing about in the pounding waves. All was frenzy and confusion.

It was impossible to set foot on land at that spot. Wolfe waved his hat high, his arm outstretched, giving the signal to retreat. Two young lieutenants and an ensign, seeing Wolfe's signal, took it to mean that they were being ordered to heave themselves onto shore. They clambered up a bank slathered with moss and viscous algae. Major George Scott followed them in another boat. Like them, he disembarked, followed by ten men who began to climb with him. Above, French and Indians waited. Scott received three bullets, but they only pierced his clothes. He defended himself. Soldiers came to his aid.

James Wolfe, in his turn, very tall, very thin, unarmed, a staff in hand, climbed the rock. At the top, the light infantry bit by bit regrouped in tight formation. With bayonets at the ready, the sol-diers, in their sopping uniforms, advanced on the nearest French battery. Brigadier Wolfe offered guineas to the two men who had helped him make his way up. More and more redcoats, rangers, and Highlanders made it on shore. And here was Lawrence's division.

Then Amherst's. The French were afraid of being surrounded. They abandoned their battery, turned back toward the town.

The few French and Mi'kmaqs who did not give in to panic were killed. The bloodied body of a Mi'kmaq chief, much scarred from old wounds, had around its neck a medallion bearing the likeness of the King of France. The chief was scalped by a young lieutenant from the English colonies.

With no resistance now but that from the waves and rocks, the support divisions disembarked. The English had lost 109 men and captured seventy of the French. James Wolfe told his former regiment colonel that the landing was "next to miraculous."

The French had lost fifty men. They had already abandoned the Great Battery, which, on the west, guarded access to the port. Before leaving their post, where they were accustomed to installing themselves every spring with family and livestock, the artillerymen set fire to the houses, stables, storehouses, and the landing stage for fishing boats. Under cover of darkness, the French frigate the *Écho* slipped past the ships of the English fleet, threading its way, and escaped to seek help in Quebec. Two days later, the Louisbourg garrison saw the *Écho* returning, with the British flag hoisted on its mast.

Amherst set up his camp at Pointe Plate. The men cut down trees, carved out a road, built fortifications. Scouts kept watch on the Acadians. Sailors unloaded cannons and *matériel*. The operation was made difficult by the treacherous reefs, the heavy, often violent swells, the slippery rocks. Almost a hundred boats had their bottoms smashed on the rocks. On June 12, Swiss and German deserters from the mercenary battalions came to present themselves to Captain Peter Townsend. The following day, the population of Louisbourg saw appear, within the walls, gallows from which were hanging soldiers who had tried to go over to the enemy.

Amherst gave James Wolfe the task of capturing the battery at Pointe à la Croix (Lighthouse Point), which guarded the entrance to the port on the east. Wolfe's 1,200 elite soldiers opened a passage two leagues long along the shore, and transported their cannons, mortars, munitions, and projectiles. The rocky soil did not allow them to dig trenches nor to construct breastwork. To protect themselves, Wolfe's soldiers hauled up tree trunks that had washed up on shore. With alder branches, they made fascines. When the French had evacuated the tower at Pointe à la Croix, they had left behind, without putting them out of commission, thirty-six 24-inch siege guns that shot explosive hollow cannonballs. Wolfe added his own cannons and mortars. On June 19, his artillerymen bombarded the island battery and the ships in the port that were plaguing them with constant volleys of shot. The French ships sought cover at the far end of the port.

A small French frigate, the *Aréthuse*, was particularly combative. Manoeuvring boldly, it came so close with its thirty-six cannons that Wolfe's men fled, seeking shelter. Still, soon afterward, they were able to set up a mortar platform in the hills that, on the morning of May 25, reduced the island battery to silence. With the entrance now open, the port was accessible. To block the passage to Boscawen's fleet, Governor Drucour ordered four large ships sunk, along with some smaller ones.

On July 1, Wolfe and his detachment advanced toward Barachois, a lagoon to the west, behind the town. On high ground, under a bombardment from the *Aréthuse*, which came and went, they built a redoubt and lobbed shells over the Louisbourg ramparts. Tireless, Wolfe's detachment installed at the western end of the port another battery that soon was making things difficult for the ships and their captive crews in the port. The artillerymen damaged the *Aréthuse*. On the side of the sea, five hundred metres from the Princesse bastion, Wolfe's detachment built another redoubt.

On July 9, during the night, surprised in their sleep by seven hundred regular French soldiers, the English grenadiers counterattacked, driving the French off at bayonet point. On both sides, the attackers and the attacked, the losses were great. According to Major-General Amherst's aide-de-camp, the French had been made "beastly drunk" before being loosed beyond the ramparts . . .

Help arrived for Louisbourg. An officer of the troops of the marine, Charles Deschamps de Boishébert, landed at Mira Bay with four hundred Acadians, *Canadiens*, and Mi'kmaqs. They were in a pitiful state, sick, starved, almost without munitions. Instead of ordering his men to defend the fortress, Boishébert sent them along paths where they could find natives and *coureurs de bois* to trade and bargain with. He was one of Intendant Bigot's partners. In Montcalm's estimation, "he pocketed a hundred thousand écus."

Governor de Drucour's wife came to the ramparts every day to visit the garrison. She brought cakes and delicacies. Each day, she insisted on firing three cannon rounds at the invaders. Courtesy was not entirely dead, even in the midst of battle. The French governor advised Major-General Amherst that there was a surgeon at Louisbourg whose skills were unrivalled. If some of his officers had need of his art, the governor would be honoured to offer the surgeon's services. Amherst wrote Drucour a thank you note, which he sent along with letters from French prisoners. To Madame de Drucour, he expressed his sincere regrets for imposing on her this discomfort, and sent her a basket of pineapples from the West Indies. Madame de Drucour replied with a charming thank you note and a basket of bottles of French wine.

The damage done to the *Aréthuse* by the English cannons was repaired. On the night of July 14, the frigate was towed past the sunken vessels blocking the port, and it headed for France with news of the recent events. Only five French ships were left in the port.

In mid-July, behind the ramparts of Louisbourg, the feeling grew that the garrison would not be able to escape the certain end to the siege. Soldiers and the populace wanted to surrender. Deserters revealed to the English that the French, short of projectiles, were reduced to firing broken bottles, nails, pieces of iron.

On the night of July 21, an English bomb exploded on the *Célèbre*, in a store of ammunition. The French ship caught fire. The wind blew. Flames spread to the sails of the *Entreprenant*, then to the ship, and on to the *Capricieux*. The English fed the conflagration with so many shells that the fire lit up the port and the hills around. On the flaming ships drifting toward the Barachois, the French artillerymen did not leave their posts. They continued the roar of their cannons, hoping to strike the English with their projectiles.

An English shell passed through the roof of the king's bastion and fell among the officers staying there. The building caught fire. The fire leaped to the neighbouring chapel. As enemy shells rained down, soldiers, civilians, and sailors, with pails of water, fought the flames. Next to the ramparts, the blockhouses were filled with the wounded and women who had come with their children, seeking shelter. But the flames were moving in that direction, and so the women with their children, and the wounded who could barely stand, left in a state of terror, seeking some protection. Fire consumed the rows of wooden barracks occupied by the soldiers. In the morning, afloat in the port was the charred debris of the French ships.

Major-General Amherst regretted having to hand over to his king a damaged fortress: "Burning the town is spoiling our own nest," he wrote. That night, Captain Townsend noted in his diary that James Wolfe was "ye most indefatigable man I ever heard of."

On July 24, one citizen and one soldier in four at the Louisbourg garrison was in the hospital, wounded or sick. The others were exhausted from sleepless nights, repair work, defence of the town, fire-fighting, and fear of cannonballs and bombs. On the ramparts, the firing from the batteries was so weak, lamented a French officer, that it was "like a funeral cannonade." English muskets had cut down in series almost all the artillerymen. Only four cannons were still functioning. Shaken by the shocks from the French batteries when they fired, and weakened by enemy projectiles, the ramparts were falling apart; the cement was crumbling, stones were coming loose. Governor de Drucour reported: "Since yesterday morning until seven o'clock at night . . . from one to two thousand bombs, large and small, have fallen on the town." There were wounded everywhere. The surgeon was amputating a limb. There was a cry: "Watch out! A bomb!" The surgeon ran for shelter. After the explosion, he returned to his patient, who was howling in pain, and finished his operation.

In the port, there were only two French ships left in combat condition: the *Prudent* and the *Bienveillant*. On the night of July 25, under cover of fog, boats filled with Royal Navy sailors crept into the port and approached the ships. Armed with pistols, cutlasses, and axes, Boscawen's bold sailors climbed on board the *Prudent* and overpowered the crew. Then, peacefully, in the silence of the night, the *Prudent* towed the *Bienveillant*, to Wolfe's delight, in front of his cannons.

At ten o'clock, Louisbourg asked for a truce. A messenger delivered to Major-General Amherst a letter saying that Governor de Drucour would capitulate if *Messieurs les Anglais* accorded him conditions comparable to those the French had granted to Vice-Admiral Byng two years earlier, at Minorca. Amherst replied to Drucour that his adversaries, given their weak defence, did not merit the honours of war. All the French troops stationed on Île Saint-Jean (Prince Edward Island) would be subject to the same conditions. He gave Governor de Drucour one hour to agree.

Immediately, Boscawen and Amherst began to plan a punitive attack, in case the governor refused to surrender. Brigadier James Wolfe would command the elite grenadiers, who would enter the town through the breaches the artillery had opened in the ramparts.

Behind the walls, the officers of the regular French army, with pride, rejected the humiliation of even thinking to cede the fortress to the English. More mundanely, the engineer hoped they would continue the fight because, he promised, the ramparts were untakeable ... Intendant Prévost reproached the military for being inspired only by "the glory of their king" and "the honour of their corps." He was intervening "for the preservation of the king's subjects." He wanted to avoid "horrors dreadful for humanity." He said he was talking in the name of "a cowed people." Governor de Drucour, for his part, begged his officers to look reality in the face.

The lieutenant-colonel of the Battalion of Foreign Volunteers went to announce to Amherst: "We accept! We accept!" He brought the governor back a letter from Amherst concerning the people of Louisbourg: "It is nowise our intention to distress them, but to give them all the aid in our power." Amherst committed himself to respecting property rights, and promised to grant the sick and wounded of the town the same care as his own.

The English took possession of the town on July 27, 1758, at noon. With Louisbourg now under the sway of the British flag, the way to Quebec was open.

24

"To rid them of the idea that the French are weak"

On June 30, 1758, Montcalm arrived at Fort Carillon, "a poor fortress," in his judgment. In his eight battalions, many recruits had no experience. And many more feared the huge English army coming from Fort George with an immense herd of oxen for transport. Montcalm sent a messenger to alert Vaudreuil. A detachment of regular and marine troops, militia, and fourteen natives were to leave for Chouaguen with Brigadier Lévis . . . Vaudreuil had them diverted to Carillon.

Fort Carillon, rectangular in form with its four bastions, was surrounded by moats. The ramparts were made of stone but also, perhaps half of them, of tree trunks planted in the earth. It was built on a cleared peninsula dominated on the west side by a hill. On the east side of the peninsula, Lake Champlain, very narrow, stretched toward the south. Connected by the La Chute River, Lake Saint-Sacrament and the south part of Lake Champlain formed two long parallel ribbons of water separated by a ridge of mountains, including Mount Defiance. To the south of Carillon, Lake Champlain extended seven leagues. Lake Saint-Sacrament stretched nine leagues. At the end stood Fort George. Coming along Lake Saint-Sacrament, the enemy could approach by boat within half a league of Fort Carillon. At that point, on the La Chute River, its passage would be blocked due to falls and rapids created by the difference in levels between the two lakes.

The regular French troops pitched their tents on the cleared plateau, near the fort. The *Canadien* militia had no tents. They made huts from branches. All around was the forest, like a green sea, dark. The English army could burst out of it at any moment. Montcalm considered. If the English took Fort Carillon, they would come to take Montreal, then Quebec . . . He sent another messenger to Vaudreuil, repeating that he needed more supplies and reinforcements.

During the winter, an engineer had studied the position of Fort Carillon. To take it, the enemy would have to control the hill that looked down on it. Therefore the French had to barricade those heights. The engineer recommended ramparts of tree trunks piled up, reinforced by a fortification of small dry trunks planted in the earth, pointed, crossed over each other, and tilted toward the enemy. Then, at a distance of ninety metres in front of the ramparts, an abatis should be constructed of trees thrown one over the other, their branches sharpened with an axe, pointing as well toward the enemy. Not at all sure that this site was the most advantageous for a battle, Montcalm began the work.

On July 1, leaving the guard of the fort and the work on the fortifications to a battalion from Berry, Montcalm went to set up the camp for the main body of his army beside the La Chute River, near a sawmill, some distance from the start of the rapids. He reinforced the garrison of the redoubt between the two camps. Less than half a league farther down, he placed three battalions of regular troops under the command of Bourlamaque. He sent a small detachment to keep an eye on Lake Saint-Sacrament. Bands of natives would be able to smell the enemy's presence on the wind. Montcalm was trying to impress the English, to "rid them of the

idea that the French are weak." But work at the fort was not proceeding fast enough. He was worried: "We lack manpower and perhaps we'll be short of time as well."

On July 4, all the components of Abercromby's army, British
and colonial, arrived at Fort George. There were six thousand
redcoats from Great Britain and ten thousand soldiers and militia from the English colonies in America. The fleet was ready:
transport boats with sides of tarred pine, plus canoes and rafts.
Flat-bottomed boats armed with cannons and propelled by twenty
rowers would defend the fleet if it was attacked.

Brigadier-General George Howe convinced the commander-
in-chief Abercromby that the army was ready, that the hour had
come to march on Carillon! This young, frugal officer was loved
by his soldiers. In his tent, he had no chairs; officers sat on logs.
And he himself cooked the meat he offered them. He was not
ashamed to do his own laundry. He tried to break down the barriers
between the regular troops and the colonial troops. The campaign
commander, Major-General Abercromby, was "an aged gentleman, infirm in body and mind," according to a young militiaman.
Brigadier George Howe, thirty-four years old, bit by bit emerged
as the de facto commander.

In 1757, he had lived with Major Rogers' rangers. He had participated in expeditions against the French, and he had seen how
war was waged in America. Wanting his men lighter, more agile,
more rapid, Howe made sure that they took with them only what
they needed. The officers could bring only a bearskin, a blanket, and
a portmanteau. Every man had to carry almost thirty-five pounds
of food. In that way, the army's march would not be delayed by the
slow progress of supply wagons. Usually, washerwomen followed
the army to do the laundry and provide other necessary services for
the men . . . This time, they stayed at the base camp. Howe had the

men's long hair shaved so that in the forest it would not get caught in branches. There would also be fewer lice. They had to wear gaiters to protect their legs from thorns. Howe had their long coats cut off at the waist so their tails would not be held back by the bushes. He even had the barrels of their guns darkened: that would stop sun flares from revealing the men's positions.

To prevent enemy scouts from seeing the English troops, the baggage, arms, munitions, and food were loaded onto boats during the night. On July 5, dawn signalled a radiant day. In front of Fort George, nine hundred boats, 135 whalers, fifteen rowboats, canoes, rafts, with warships to cover the landing, as well as supply boats, pulled away from shore and slowly took their positions in the convoy on Lake Saint-Sacrement. Everything unfolded in solemn silence. The flags and standards barely stirred in the light breeze. The regular forces in red uniforms occupied the centre of the convoy, while the troops from the colonies, in blue uniforms, were distributed on each side. The oars, in rhythm, dipped into the water.

Canadien scouts saw the vanguard of the English fleet, more than five and a half leagues north of Fort George, in front of Sabbath Day Point. They were pursued, but the 130 scouts escaped in their canoes and returned to their camp to shout out that the English army was on its way.

Once more, Montcalm ordered that work on Carillon's fortifications be hurried along. At five o'clock, he dismantled the camp on the La Chute River. For some days, it had served to mask the defensive work being carried out at Carillon. He left the watchmen to keep guard overnight. On the banks of the La Chute, three squads of snipers would inhibit the enemy's landing. Finally, 130 volunteer militiamen, under the command of Sieur Jean-Baptiste Levrault de Langy, installed themselves on Mount Pelée, at the end of the plain west of Lake Champlain. They would be seconded by the three light companies of Sieur de Trépézec, captain in the Béarn Regiment. From this elevated perspective, they would look down on the French fleet.

At four o'clock on the morning of July 6, 1758, the first English barges approached the shore. Montcalm increased his personnel at the abatis. Why had Brigadier de Lévis not yet arrived with his regular troops? The English began their landing. The French snipers opened fire. That had no effect, as the French were too far away. And so they demolished the bridge over the river. Without being much troubled, the English completed their landing at ten o'clock.

A detachment of scouts commanded by Brigadier Howe made its way toward the Bernetz River (Trout Brook) to be certain that the way was clear, or if not, to free it up. The English army set off at two o'clock with its Royal regiments, its Highlanders, and troops from Massachusetts, Connecticut, New York, and New Jersey. The men entered the forest. The hilly terrain, strewn with stones and covered in decomposed leaves, was slippery. Great fallen trees rotted in the shadow of shrubs. The men could only march slowly, carefully, needled and harassed by mosquitoes. They leaped over bushes, crossed through thickets, worked their way through the tangled branches of dense trees. After five hours of struggle, the ranks were broken, the officers were separated from their men, the guides no longer knew where they were.

The 350 men of Langy and Trépézec, on Mount Pélée, looked down on the landing of the English and described it to Montcalm by waving white flags, according to their established code. Once their mission was accomplished, Langy and Trépézec returned to camp. They followed the Bernetz River at the bottom of the slope. Their native guides had vanished in the direction of the English boats, in search of spoils. But where was the river? Suddenly,

Langy and Trépézec realized they were lost. They heard cracking. Branches stirred, even though there was no wind. Langy asked, "Who goes there?" A voice that was not French replied "*Français.*" It was Brigadier-General Howe with his two hundred scouts, in advance of the main column. "Fire!" ordered Langy. Howe fell, shot in the chest. He didn't move, but according to a captain, one of his hands was trembling. The English battalions, in a frenzy, took off in pursuit of Langy's and Trépézec's detachments. Langy and fifty of his men escaped by plunging into the river and swimming. Others, hidden in the forest, later made it back to Fort Carillon. Trépézec died of his wounds.

That night, Montcalm wrote to Vaudreuil and to André Doreil, the commissioner who was providing for the war. He had no more than "a week's supplies," and "a fearsome army" was approaching. However, the situation was not desperate. The English army "was feeling its way." A French victory was not out of the question. "If by their slowness" the enemy gave the major-general time to complete the fortifications at Carillon, "I will beat it," he promised. His four thousand men had to defeat sixteen thousand English. Otherwise, the French army would have to retreat to Fort Saint-Frédéric, five leagues north of Carillon. That would mean offering Canada up to the enemy, because downstream, Forts Saint-Frédéric, Saint-Jean, and Chambly "do not even deserve to be called bad forts."

On the heights, 640 metres from Fort Carillon, a palisade two and a half metres high was built of tree trunks driven into the ground, sod, and sacks of earth piled up. The palisade was set up in a line broken by angles that flanked each other. That way, the enemy front would be swept by musket shot. The line followed the ridge of the plateau's incline. Montcalm made another inspection. Not all the battery's cannons had arrived, and the palisade needed to be strengthened in the middle.

Early on the morning of July 7, Major-General Abercromby ordered the march on Carillon. Lieutenant-Colonel John Bradstreet commanded an advance guard of five thousand men. At the beginning of the afternoon, Bradstreet arrived at the site abandoned the day before by Montcalm. His advance had been so easy that he hoped to continue on and to surprise the French. Rangers and Mohicans rebuilt the two bridges on the river that had been destroyed by the French. Abercromby, who did not think it so urgent to meet the enemy, asked Bradstreet to wait. Around six o'clock, the English camped near the ruins of the sawmill the French had burned.

The same evening, at about seven o'clock, a reinforcement of three hundred grenadiers from the regular French forces, along with militiamen, arrived at Carillon after having marched and then rowed day and night. They were received with great joy and eau-de-vie. Later in the night, the Chevalier de Lévis finally turned up with a hundred more grenadiers. Montcalm would have under his command some 3,900 men, primarily regular soldiers from a number of French regiments, reinforced by four hundred *Canadien* militiamen and sixteen natives.

Some young British officers who had gone as scouts to assess the French defences returned triumphant: their fortifications were not complete and would be easy to overwhelm. That night, Abercromby's 16,000 men slept half a league from the nearly 4,500 with Montcalm.

At the break of day, drum rolls in the French camp also woke the English. Montcalm had asked for the call to arms to be sounded. There was work to be finished at the fortifications.

Lieutenant-Colonel Bradstreet and the engineer Charles Rivez, a French Huguenot, went off to examine the French defences. On their return, they confirmed what the young British officers had seen. The French structure was weak.

Accompanied by some rangers, Abercromby crossed the river and clambered up Mount Rattlesnake to judge the enemy's positions for himself. The French were working on the fortifications. Was that not proof enough that they were not finished, and that they were not ready for battle?

On July 8, the French made a stone dike to protect themselves against the English projectiles that could rain down on them from Mount Rattlesnake. Scouts had seen movement in that direction. On the north side, they would have to extend the enclosure as far as Lake Champlain. They also had to point a battery in the direction of the lake, where the boats would appear. Montcalm did not have enough men to engage in combat. And he was still waiting for cannons. The English seemed to be sleeping. Nothing stirred, except for the birds and a few white clouds adrift in the blue sky. Suddenly, war cries on the side of Rattlesnake Mountain! Movement in the trees. Probably Mohawks. The scouts had seen some with the English. Then the mountain went silent. Ominous.

At ten o'clock, the first English boats appeared on the La Chute River. An hour later, the rangers in the vanguard clashed with two hundred *Canadien* militiamen in ambush 275 metres in front of the abatis. At noon, the French heard volleys of musket fire in the forest. The alarm was given. The men dropped their shovels and picks and axes, grabbed their muskets, and went back behind the fortifications. At twelve thirty, the colonial regiment from New York was surprised by the *Canadien* militiamen who had confounded the rangers. The colonials reacted with force, and the militiamen scattered! Did that not portend an English victory in the making?

Abercromby's army finally appeared in open country. In the vanguard, the rangers, followed by light infantry. Then came the colonial troops. They began to shoot at the French, whom they could not yet see. Then, heralded by their bagpipes, came the Scots

Highlanders. Finally, the redcoats advanced in impeccable formation to the sound of fife and drum. They were divided up among the colonial regiments. On the heights, from behind their fortifications, the French looked on. Under a brilliant sun, the number of English was even more troubling than they had imagined. A French officer grumbled, "Vaudreuil has sent the army to be butchered, the enemy is six times our size!"

Seeing this sea, "a large number of *Canadiens* jumped over the palisade and ran toward the boats on the shore," Bougainville later related. Rather than die here, they preferred to return to their farms. An officer ordered that the runaways be gunned down. "Those *Canadiens* were not the right type" was the comment of Montcalm's aide-de-camp.

Without waiting for Abercromby's order and without heeding the battle plan, a brigade of regulars, with bayonets at the ready, charged in two columns. The soldiers couldn't find the French. Word spread: "The French have fled!" The English lifted their bayonets, waved their hats. Victory was theirs! In fact, the British had only reached the abatis built to slow down and break up the enemy formations before they could reach the parapets. Suddenly, from the seemingly deserted fortifications, there erupted a hail of balls. "Mowed down like a field of corn," the attackers retreated, injuring themselves on the pointed branches. From their zigzag palisade, the French were hitting their targets face on and on both flanks. After an hour of blood-soaked fury, the brigade commander ordered a retreat. His own musket had been smashed by a ball.

The enemies were great in number, but Montcalm had observed that they didn't seem to know their targets. Their right column advanced toward Lévis's troops but then turned back in the direction of the centre column, which itself moved toward the left. When the columns reached the fortification defended by the La Sarre and Languedoc regiments, three thousand muskets fired. The British reeled, wavered, fell, retreating but reforming, then, determined, resumed their march. Pointing their bayonets, the rangers, grenadiers, and Highlanders climbed onto the abatis, stepping over tree trunks, tearing their clothes, scratching their legs and arms. A hail of balls pushed them back again. Montcalm, in the centre, received the news: 1,500 English were on the ground, "bellies in the air."

Abercromby ordered his three troops to go back on the offensive. Lévis greeted them with brutal hospitality. Not only did he demand from his troops a vigorous reply—a fusilier could shoot nine balls a minute—but he had them emerge from the fortifications so they could thread their way through the abatis and attack the English from the side.

In the midst of the melee, an English officer spotted a Frenchman at the palisade who was waving a red flag to taunt the English forces. Believing this meant a French surrender, the English started to celebrate, shouting, waving their hats and their muskets. The French, believing the English were surrendering, stopped shooting and climbed onto the parapet. The ensign of the Guyenne Battalion waved his green and red flag: "Long live the king!" A French officer ordered the English: "Throw down your arms!" Another officer, more clear-headed, ordered the French grenadiers to "Shoot! Shoot! Shoot!" A Rhode Island militiaman penetrated the abatis, climbed onto the parapet, made his way behind the fortifications, and killed several of the French. One of their comrades shot him, but William Smith had enough strength left to brandish his tomahawk, kill the Frenchman, and get back to his own side. The troops from New England, Rhode Island, New Jersey, and Massachusetts were urged to renew the attack. In the face of this English army that seemed just to keep on growing, a French officer proclaimed: "Monsieur de

Vaudreuil has sacrificed us to have our ears cut off! Let us defend them! Long live the king! Long live our general!" At the centre of it all, beneath a blazing sun, Montcalm took off his hat and his tunic. Braving the gunfire, he moved from one side to the other, encouraging his men, assuring them that the back-up troops were ready to support any battalions in difficulty.

After four hours of combat, the English army had not succeeded in making its numbers felt. The French put their hats on branches and shook them to make it seem as if there were more French soldiers and especially to attract balls that would be wasted. The English launched balls they'd heated red hot in the fire. In many places, the fortifications were burning. Reinforcements brought barrels of water to put out the fires.

At five o'clock, the Highlanders launched an attack on the hill defended by the regiments of La Reine, Béarn, and la Guyenne. Their soles slipped on the piled-up tree trunks, and they injured themselves on the sharpened branches. Several fell under the gunfire, but with tenacity and temerity the others made it to the trenches. Montcalm rushed up with the grenadiers. It was impossible to stop the Highlanders, who got through the abatis, reached the trenches, crossed the parapet, climbed the rampart, and jumped into the midst of the French, brandishing their claymores.

Forward, *Canadiens*! On the right, Lévis came out with his troops from the marine. A bullet tore his hat off. Assailed from the front and both sides, the Highlanders pulled back past the bodies of their companions who had been killed or who were wounded and moaning on the ground. They re-formed, then threw themselves against the Royal-Roussillon, in the centre. The French again forced them to retreat, disheartened and confused. Thinking they were returning enemy fire, the Highlanders were shooting at each other.

From one o'clock to five o'clock, Abercromby's troops attempted at least six assaults. Two thousand of their soldiers and officers had fallen. The battle went on until seven thirty. Before dark, the rangers and colonial troops, behind bushes and mounds, tried to provide cover for their comrades who went to help the wounded. The French had lost 377 men.

Would Montcalm pursue the English army as it withdrew? His forces were far inferior to those of the vanquished army. His soldiers were exhausted, and it was too easy, after nightfall, to lose oneself in the forest. Montcalm was victorious. Why risk transforming victory into defeat in a hazardous pursuit? In the camp, fires were lit. Montcalm and Lévis visited the troops, who greeted them with an ovation that echoed over the lakes and forest. Barrels of beer and wine were handed round.

Montcalm wrote to Doreil, the commissioner of war: "The army, too small, of the king, has beaten the enemy. What a day for France!" The English march on Canada had been halted: "Ah! What troops are ours, my dear Doreil! I've never seen the like." He told his wife about his extraordinary day: "I've beaten an army of twenty-five thousand." There are moments in life when a man cannot be modest.

Montcalm feared, however, that the day was not over. The English knew they were more numerous and would come back, perhaps with reinforcements. During the night, the damaged fortifications were repaired, the unfinished ramparts were completed, the abatis were lengthened, the branches were sharpened, new batteries were set up. Those who had permission to go and sleep woke those who had rested for a few hours, so that they might be replaced.

The next day, July 9, the French buried their dead and those the English had left behind. Montcalm still thought the enemy might return. Work on the defences resumed. Lévis went, along with some grenadiers and fifty or so *Canadiens*, to keep an eye on the movements of the English. On the way to the site of the sawmill, he came across several wounded English soldiers lying on the property. Those who could still move tried to flee. The others, immobilized, wailed in fear of being killed. The French took as many as they could as hostages. How to feed them? All along the portage were the abandoned wounded, wagons, supplies, munitions, sacks, tools, arms, shoes . . .

English deserters insisted that Abercromby and his army had returned to Fort George. A picket went to Lake Saint-Sacrament to make sure. Yes, they had fled, throwing into the lake a hundred and fifty tonnes of flour they didn't want to leave to the French. Some were still afloat; others has washed up on shore. As they had fewer men to transport than when they arrived, the English had sunk several barges and boats.

On his return, Lévis confirmed to Montcalm that the enemy had gone back to Fort George. And so the major-general assembled his victorious army. A missionary sang a *Te Deum*. Then Montcalm had a cross raised made of tree trunks, with an escutcheon on which were transcribed verses he himself had composed, proclaiming that

> *It is the arm of your God . . .*
> *That broke the spirit of the mystified English.*

The English officers did not have a high opinion of their colonial troops. Many would have agreed with Captain Hugh Arnot, who wrote to Loudoun: "For any sett of people in the Universe, they are the worst cut out for war." He added: "The most stupid and most chicken-hearted sett of Mankind."

The officers of the colonial troops were disgusted by the arrogance of the officers from England. Most of the English officers were from families where one was born endowed, through inheritance, with an indisputable superiority, and they could not believe that a farmer from the colonies could leave his fields, pick up a musket, and lead men into combat. After the defeat at Fort Carillon, the colonial officers were not fond of General Abercromby, whom they called "Mrs. Nabbycromby" ("Nabby" being short for Abigail). The chaplains at Fort George, for their part, claimed that the true causes of the army's defeat were the sins of the soldiers, who swore, drank rum, fornicated, and did not respect the Sabbath.

Many wagons with food supplies were left behind during the retreat. Others were seized by the Indians. Abercromby had to ration food. To counter a possible pursuit by the French, he undertook the construction of a palisade. In addition to being wounded at Carillon, many soldiers and officers were sick. Many had trouble leaving their beds, despite treatment with ipecacuanha for nausea. The lash, however, gave energy to those who lacked it. The treatment was administered on a wooden horse, in sight of all. Thanks to this discipline, "Mrs. Nabbycromby's" army, in a few days, raised up a tree-trunk palisade and a parapet.

Three days after Montcalm's victory, Vaudreuil was quick to deplore, in a letter to the minister of the colonies, that once more the major-general had not followed orders. Despite what he had been told, Montcalm refused to pursue the English after their defeat at Carillon.

For his part, Montcalm felt that he did not have enough troops to go after the English army. He did, however, launch a few raids against it. Natives and militiamen pillaged the supply convoys and wagons between Forts Lydius and George. During these brief but effective skirmishes, they surprised the rangers, then vanished into the woods. He told the minister of war how much he admired the French troops: "What pleases me most in this affair, is that the ground troops were second to none in sharing the glory."

Vaudreuil urged Montcalm "not to lose sight of the great advantage we have gained over our enemies by our victory." He emphasized that the final goal of the mission was "to force" the English "to abandon their position, their boats, artillery, campaign support, supplies, etc., and to oblige them to withdraw and abandon forever all hope of reviving their undertaking."

On July 13, five days after the battle, reinforcements arrived at Carillon: more than two thousand militiamen, soldiers from the marine forces, natives ... Montcalm now had an army of 6,669 men. The battle had been won; why did Vaudreuil now send him "useless and temporary troops"? They would "consume to no purpose a great quantity of food."

In Montreal, in Trois-Rivières, in Quebec, in the villages, masses were celebrated to thank God for the victory Montcalm had accorded the French. Songs were improvised based on popular airs:

> *The good Lord, his mother, all are for us*
> *Sacré! I'm Catholic*
> *The English are heretics.*

In a letter on July 15, Vaudreuil repeated to Montcalm, almost word for word, his earlier instructions. The next day, he retracted "all the recommendations I had [the honour] of making to you in the last letter."

Montcalm replied that he always found it "astonishing that Monsieur le Marquis de Vaudreuil thinks he can make judgments, fifty leagues from the conduct of a war in a territory he has never seen, and where the best generals would be confounded after having seen it." The governor general asked him to "aggressively harass the enemies, cut their communication from the former Fort George, and intercept their convoys." Montcalm was scornful. This sentence "is the work of a thoughtless secretary, not a man of war." If Vaudreuil had seen Carillon, he would give orders "that would be clearer and less embarrassing." Montcalm would not refuse to obey the governor general: "But a clear and precise order on your part would be enough for me." However, he warned Vandreuil that such an operation would be imprudent. To assemble enough men, he would have to leave Carillon "unprotected." Then, because of the rapids on the La Chute River, the portage required "would last three weeks." The army would again be exhausted. At a time when supplies were low, the militia-men would once more be away during the harvest. Montcalm ended his letter by announcing that he had requested a recall to France. He asked for the governor general's support in this matter.

Vaudreuil, obstinate, replied: "You now have a considerable force. . . . Your brilliant accomplishment must not remain incomplete."

25

"A great deal of mischief"

In Louisbourg, the officers, superiors, and subalterns had all taken notice of Brigadier Wolfe. Despite an angry sea, he had successfully led a first landing on a shore difficult to negotiate and defended by the enemy. During the seven weeks the siege lasted, Wolfe had built batteries around the port. Despite the risks, he had dug trenches, sometimes 180 metres from the walls. As the youngest officer of his rank, Wolfe had become a familiar figure to the troops.

Early in the crossing to Louisbourg, he had criticized the soldiers for their lack of discipline, their laziness, their drunkenness. But since then, he had seen those men exhausting themselves carrying loads and digging trenches, and he had seen them risking their lives. Brigadier Wolfe now called his men his "soldier brothers."

The news of the fall of Louisbourg, which took place on July 27, 1758, spread through Nova Scotia from one post to the other, then to Boston, to New York, and to all the American colonies. The church bells rang out in joy. Beer and gin were consumed. Songs were sung. Poems were written. Speeches were made. Preachers, with their resonant rhetoric, thanked heaven for this "favour from Divine Providence." Fireworks bloomed over Philadelphia. In Boston, the people gathered around a giant pyramidal fire on Fort

Hill. In New York, there was a great official dinner, punctuated by toasts in honour of the victory. On the shore of Lake Saint-Sacrament, where his army, defeated at Carillon, was camped, Major-General Abercromby had three cannon rounds shot off in homage to the victors at Louisbourg.

Elsewhere, voices were raised in protest. Colonial patriots regretted that so little credit was given to the fighters from the colonies . . . Credit to the colonies? Dr. John Campbell, a writer and friend of Samuel Johnson, had this to say about the American colonists: "Sir, they are a race of convicts, and ought to be thankful for anything we allow them short of hanging."

On August 18, Major-General Amherst's aide-de-camp, his younger brother, arrived in London with a dispatch proclaiming the victory over the French at Louisbourg. William Pitt, Secretary of State for War, embracing him, assured him that he was "the most welcome messenger to arrive in this country for years." After this declaration, Pitt invited the heroes of the Royal Navy, and the infantry as well, to get drunk and celebrate the great victory of both Vice-Admiral Boscawen and Major-General Amherst!

Pitt had published, in the *London Gazette*, Amherst's dispatch, which was picked up by other papers. The French flags taken at Louisbourg were put on view at St. Paul's Cathedral in London. Artillerymen shot off cannons in the parks. From all regions, letters were showered on Parliament, expressing proud admiration for the exploit of the troops.

The officers and soldiers wrote letters to their families. Several mentioned Wolfe's name, talking about this brigadier with red hair who had guided them through danger. Lieutenant Thomas Bell, Wolfe's aide-de-camp, expressed his appreciation: "He commanded, fought and built batteries and I need not add has acquir'd all the glory of our expedition." The papers reprinted these letters in

England and the colonies. One of them affirmed that "Brigadier General Wolfe has acquired no small reputation by his conduct and bravery on this expedition and merits no small share in the reduction of Louisbourg." James Wolfe's reputation was enhanced as well among the army's superior officers and in the offices of the minister of war.

During this time, Amherst imposed English power on Cape Breton Island. He sent Major John Dalling, with a detachment, to occupy Port-Espagnol (Sidney). Commanded by Lord Andrew Rolloe, the 35th Regiment and two battalions of the 60th Regiment went to Île Saint-Jean to suppress the four thousand Acadians there, but most were able to escape. The English captured only seven hundred. They burned down houses, barns, cabins, boats. Elsewhere, in the Baie Française (the Bay of Fundy) and on the Rivière Saint-Jean (Saint John River), Colonel Robert Monckton hunted down Acadians who had taken refuge there when he and Charles Lawrence had put into effect their relocation policy in 1755. These Acadians were receiving help from the governor of Canada (New France). Vaudreuil had even supplied a privateer to a family of pilots so they might harass the English ships. The Acadians monitored the movements of the English fleets and detachments, and then informed the French.

Acadians also withdrew to Saint-Anne (Fredericton), along the Rivière Saint-Jean. Amherst gave Colonel Monckton the order "to destroy the vermin who are settled there." On August 15, 1758, with the exception of the sick and wounded who would not survive the crossing, the prisoners in the port of Louisbourg boarded ships leaving for England.

James Wolfe was bored. He had nothing to do but to gather wild berries. After Louisbourg, why not move on to take Quebec? He was restless and impatient. He couldn't stand inactivity. During the Louisbourg siege, he and Amherst had become close. He didn't hide what he thought: they were wasting too much time at Louisbourg. Amherst explained to his restive officer that organizing the transport of thousands of prisoners to Europe was not an easy task. It was necessary to make sure they didn't escape, to maintain discipline, to arrange for ships, crews, and provisions, to deal with quarrels . . . For example, curious to find out what was under a Highlander's kilt, a French officer had dared to reach up where he shouldn't have. The Scot drew his broadsword and cut off the groping hand. The Frenchman put his other hand on his own sword, but the Scotsman blocked his movement and slit his throat.

Wolfe wanted to know what the major-general intended to do. Amherst assured him that his greatest wish was to take Quebec. He had proposed such a move to Vice-Admiral Boscawen, who had judged it for the moment impossible. Since Vice-Admiral Boscawen didn't want to send troops to Quebec, James Wolfe suggested that Amherst send a brigade to Abercromby for his march on Canada. Wolfe offered to participate. The rest of the troops could launch an "offensive and destructive" war in the Bay of Fundy and in the Gulf of St. Lawrence to avenge "the bloody inroads of those hell-hounds, the *Canadiens*."

In a letter to his mother on August 11, 1758, Wolfe predicted that the French would be driven from this continent, which would then belong to the British and the Spanish. Despite the fact that the English colonies were afflicted with "the vices and bad qualities of the mother country," because that was where Great Britain unloaded its prisoners, it would form "a vast empire, the seat of power and learning." Wolfe was impatient to conquer the territory, but he was kept idle. He considered leaving the army.

While encouraging Wolfe to continue expressing his views, Amherst told him that he wanted to hear no more about his leaving the service of the king. He assigned Wolfe a task: to raze the French settlements along the Gulf of St. Lawrence, the Baie des Chaleurs, and the Baie de Miramichi. When the Acadians were displaced, at least a thousand of them had found refuge at the Baie des Chaleurs. Wolfe was to drive them out.

Wolfe confessed to his father that after the conquest of Louisbourg, he had hoped for a more glorious mission than that of divesting poor fishermen of their nets. "When the great exploit is at an end," he said ironically, he would return to England.

In Amherst's opinion, the mission he was entrusting to Wolfe would achieve two goals. First, it would divert the attention of the French to the St. Lawrence River at a time when Abercromby's army was making its way toward Canada through Lake Champlain and the Richelieu River. Then, since it was known that Quebec was short of foodstuffs, Wolfe would destroy, on the shores of the gulf and the bays, all the provisions that could be sent that way.

His fleet of seven ships and three frigates left Louisbourg on August 28. Off the Îles de la Madeleine (Magdalen Islands), he harassed the fishermen who were hunting sea cows. On September 5, Wolfe's troops landed at Gaspé, a fishing centre where at least three hundred people were active every day. They fled into the forest, with the exception of a few who offered no resistance. Some were taken on as pilots and guides. Wolfe's detachment emptied the storehouse of all its goods, set it on fire along with the fishermen's cabins, then destroyed two thousand hundredweight of dried cod. At Pointe de Penouille, his men slaughtered the livestock, destroyed the cod set out to dry, burned the cabins, staved in the rowboats, set the boats on fire, ruined the nets. At Miramichi, they burned down sixty or so houses, and set fire to eighty rowboats and schooners. The tackle was demolished. The sawmills, houses, and stables were turned into ashes. Men, women, and children were made prisoner.

At Grande Rivière, as elsewhere, the population went to hide in the woods. Wolfe sent a messenger to inform them that, given that winter's cold was on its way, he feared for their survival. If they wanted to return to the village, he would send them boats. On this occasion, Wolfe showed himself to be less aggressive, but his heart had not softened. At Pabos, his men burned twenty houses, a schooner full of cod, forty rowboats, a storehouse containing clothes, eau-de-vie, food for winter, firewood, and lumber. They captured three Frenchmen who were laying out cod to dry. At Mont-Louis, they seized the seigneur's schooner. It would be used to transport prisoners. In several places, the fishermen told Wolfe's officers about the suffering that lack of food was causing to Quebec. That was the reason there were so many fishing boats in the Gulf.

This was the time of year when the French ships that had come to Quebec returned to France. According to the fishermen, the ships bound for Brest were loaded with furs. Wolfe saw there the opportunity to add lustre to his campaign. Studying the map, he saw, on the south side of the St. Lawrence, facing Bic, islands that narrowed the river. His squadron could go to intercept the ships. If he took their furs, what a return that would make to Louisbourg!

However, given the season's stormy winds and tides, it would be a risky move to go up the river that far. Rear-Admiral Charles Hardy refused. Another example of the navy's scandalous fearfulness, thought Wolfe, who, back in Louisbourg on September 29, reported to Major-General Amherst that he had committed "a great deal of mischief." He had spread the "terror of His Majesty's arms through the whole gulf." Still, he had added "nothing to the reputation" of the English troops.

After what he had seen at Gaspé, the impatient Wolfe assured the major-general: "An offensive, daring kind of war, will awe the Indians and ruin the French." And he promised: "If you will attempt to cut up New France by the roots, I will come with pleasure to assist."

James Wolfe boarded the *Namur*, Boscawen's flagship, leaving Louisbourg. He would sail toward England.

26

"Why do we need French troops?"

In Montreal, Governor General Vaudreuil felt he was the victim of underhanded attacks. He had the unshakable conviction that "all those infamies and indecent remarks" concerning his person that were turning up in Versailles were "authored or authorized" by the commander-in-chief of the French troops in North America. In a letter to the minister of the colonies on August 4, 1758, Vaudreuil asked for Montcalm to be recalled to France: "He could serve very usefully in Europe." He even had the delicacy to recommend Montcalm for a promotion.

Montcalm gathered together his officers on August 14. Above all, he forbade them, and asked them to forbid their troops, to hum a "particularly scathing song" about Vaudreuil and the *Canadiens*. French officers and soldiers also had to abstain from saying anything "indecent" about Vaudreuil, the colonial troops, and the militia.

During this time, in Montreal, in Trois-Rivières, in Quebec, and in the villages, colonial officers were asking themselves, "Why do we need French troops? . . . The French troops were hidden behind their fortifications, at Carillon." Many *Canadiens* had no faith in an army that waged war in formation, to the sound of music.

News of "dissension" between Vaudreuil and Montcalm had spread as far as New York, where a newspaper had talked about it. In a letter to Vaudreuil accompanied by a copy of the paper, Montcalm, in an attempt at reconciliation, proposed to the governor general that they seek a new basis for dialogue: "We each thought not to be wrong; and so it must be that we both are." But after this conciliatory paragraph, Montcalm got carried away: "Must you, Monsieur, after three years that I am under your command, force on me pointless or trivial details that I would blush to impose on my lowest captain?" Then, if he did not dare accuse Vaudreuil of corruption, he insinuated that the governor general tolerated it. If he, Montcalm, enjoyed the same privileges as André Grasset de Saint-Sauveur, Vaudreuil's secretary, he would "not require the pecuniary favours of the king."

In the second week of August, at Carillon, Iroquois, Abenakis, Mi'kmaqs, Nipissings, and Mississaugas prepared to return to their villages. Vaudreuil accused Montcalm of treating them badly. Montcalm replied. Yes, he had reprimanded the natives because they had killed animals in the camp, had made off with supplies for the hospital, and had just recently stolen from the tents. Then he shot back at Vaudreuil: "The natives complained in public that you had held them back when they wanted to come to my aid" for the Carillon campaign.

With his allies returning to their villages, Montcalm gave them the go-ahead to seek additional plunder and more scalps. On August 19, thirty Abenakis left to sow terror in Orange and "Sarestoga" (Saratoga), while twenty-three Iroquois went to attack farms on the border with Connecticut.

At Fort Carillon, it was learned from a prisoner that the English were engaged in clearing the Mohawk River of tree trunks, stones, and other obstacles that would impede the passage of barges. The English were preparing to attack a fort "that could only be Frontenac," Montcalm deduced. This fort was guarded by just forty men. The boats barring the way were no longer armed. Montcalm had learned that "their tackle was being used on Monsieur Péan's schooners" to transport goods. If the enemy took Fort Frontenac, they would also take Fort Niagara, whose garrison was also weak.

Despite the French victory at Carillon, which he considered purely accidental, Lieutenant-Colonel John Bradstreet believed that it would be easy to take over Fort Frontenac and to then rebuild the Oswego post the French had destroyed. Fort Frontenac was a link in the chain of French settlements that connected the St. Lawrence River with French posts in the Ohio Valley. It was weakly defended because most of its forces had gone to protect Carillon. Bradstreet's scouts also observed that small armed craft were no longer patrolling Lake Ontario. Persuaded by Bradstreet, Abercromby gave him 3,600 regular and colonial troops from New York, Rhode Island, Massachusetts, and New Jersey.

To get to Fort Frontenac, Bradstreet's army sailed up the Mohawk River and down the Oswego. When the water was not deep enough for the heavily loaded boats to pass, which happened frequently, the men unloaded *matériel* to lighten the boats, or they improvised locks with tree trunks, branches, and sod. On August 21, Bradstreet's troops entered Lake Ontario. During the exhausting journey, six hundred men had deserted. Four days later, after dark, without having been observed, the troops arrived in the vicinity of Fort Frontenac. Nine small boats armed with cannons made fast there. The English set up camp. During the quiet night, the artillerymen aimed their batteries at the fort. In the morning, their balls pounded the limestone walls. The garrison defended itself a little, but to what end? The French knew they were already defeated. The next day, the elderly commander, Pierre-Jacques Payen de Noyan et de Chavoy, surrendered.

Taking possession of Fort Frontenac, Bradstreet's men discovered in the storerooms a surprising abundance of goods: clothes, shoes, tools, muskets, powder, bundles of furs. Bradstreet was also surprised by the generous reserves of food. His men piled up in the enclosure all they could bring back to Oswego. They rolled out hundreds of barrels of victuals. Why so much for such a small garrison? he asked himself. He couldn't know that a French supplier earned fourteen sous more per ration for merchandise that was delivered to posts and forts. But Bradstreet did know that there was a lack of food in Canada, and burning all these edibles when they were so hard to come by was another blow he was happy to deliver to the enemy.

Content, Bradstreet's men lit the fire before getting back on their boats. As they moved off, Fort Frontenac erupted in a triumphant explosion.

On July 26, the fortress of Louisbourg fell into the hands of the English. A month later, Fort Frontenac was razed. And yet Vaudreuil had assured Claude-Louis d'Espinchal, Marquis de Massiac, the new minister of the marine, that Louisbourg was invulnerable and that the British wouldn't dare advance on Lake Ontario.

27

"A distant and disagreeable service"

S tretched out on his bunk on board the *Namur*, James Wolfe was once again brought low by seasickness. His return to England caused some irritation in the War Office. The officer ought to have waited for the authorization of his superiors before leaving his post at Louisbourg. Lord Barrington, secretary of state for war, had signed a rather gruff letter intended for the brigadier, which the War Office had sent to Louisbourg on October 2, 1758. But Wolfe was already at sea a day earlier, certain that he had accomplished his mission.

When the *Namur* anchored at Spithead on November 1, Wolfe still didn't know that his return had exasperated his superiors. As soon as he was on dry land, he completed a report on the Bay of Gaspé campaign, to be submitted to William Pitt. On November 4, he solicited the generous intervention of Lord Barrington in favour of seventy-two soldiers returning disabled to their country after having been wounded at Louisbourg. Then, having been informed of the uneasiness his return had caused, Wolfe made it known to Marshal John Ligonier, commander-in-chief, that he wished to join the British contingent which, with the Hanoverians, the Brunswickers, and the Hessians, was waging war on the French on the Rhine frontier. Wolfe dreamed of grand military manoeuvres.

He had never concealed his admiration for Frederick of Prussia. What is more, Lord Sackville, his protector, was the second in command of the British contingent of which the 20th Regiment, Wolfe's former regiment, was a part.

On his return to London on November 22, Wolfe informed William Pitt that he was not averse to returning and fighting the French in America, "and particularly in the river St-Lawrence, if any operations are to be executed there." Before going back to America, he asked only for the time to regain his health. He wanted "to be better to go through the business of the next summer."

Although Marshal Ligonier had no mission to offer him, he invited Brigadier Wolfe to pay him a visit. After assuring the commander-in-chief that he would return to America as soon as he received the order, Wolfe described to him the siege of Louisbourg and his expedition in the Gulf of St. Lawrence. He reported what he had learned about the "little war" that was waged in Canada, and about navigation on the St. Lawrence River. Ligonier gave Wolfe to understand that the commander-in-chief's staff was studying a plan for laying siege to Quebec. Wolfe didn't hide his interest in a mission that would go up the St. Lawrence River to Quebec and, as at Louisbourg, attack the ramparts and take the city.

On December 7, Wolfe returned to Bath. This man with the long bony body and the pale complexion was one of the heroes who had taken from the French their most forbidding fortress in America. In November and December, the *London Magazine* had published an account of the siege of Louisbourg, written by a naval officer. Wolfe's action was portrayed very favourably. He was shown great respect. His portrait was painted, with a map of Louisbourg in his hands. For a week, Wolfe enjoyed the rest and the admiration that was bestowed on him. Then he was recalled to London.

He had been named commander for "a distant and disagreeable service," James Wolfe announced, but without divulging the secret. In a departure from military practice, the young brigadier asked Sir John Ligonier if he might be granted the privilege of selecting his own officers.

28

"Think now only of making peace"

On September 2, 1758, Bougainville announced to Montcalm, at Fort Carillon, that Louisbourg had been taken by the English on July 26. It was Major-General Abercromby who had given him the news. Bougainville had gone to Fort George to bring Abercromby a letter from Montcalm concerning a prisoner exchange. Bougainville did not believe in the fall of the impregnable fortress. He wagered a basket of champagne "against two beers from London." Bougainville lost the bet. He showed Montcalm a newspaper announcing the taking of Louisbourg. "The New York paper is wrong and fantastical," cried Montcalm. "No one can take Louisbourg. This news was only published to encourage the soldiers and English colonists to fight against the French."

The next day, the last natives prepared to leave Carillon. "These gentlemen don't like bad news," said Montcalm, who sang a war hymn and gave them eau-de-vie and a pig. They decided to stay another week.

The taking of Louisbourg was confirmed officially on September 6. Learning that six or seven warships had been burned in the port, Montcalm judged Governor de Drucour harshly: "With these ships kept in the port, unable to save the stronghold, the trivial honour of a somewhat more drawn out defence was not worth their sacrifice. . . . If Monsieur Drucour had been more of a citizen and less preoccupied with his own interests, he would have spared [France] this loss."

Vaudreuil immediately summoned Montcalm to Montreal. Now that they had become masters of Louisbourg, the English controlled access to Quebec. Their army could descend on the city. What was more, Fort Frontenac had been destroyed. The English were also masters of Lake Ontario. The French could no longer supply Fort Niagara, nor the western posts nor the Upper Country.

Montcalm affirmed that the French had these options: "The utter and imminent loss of the colony, or saving it—that is to delay its taking." But in the current situation, how to "delay the taking" of Canada?

First, all individual or commercial interests had to go by the way-side. Given the large and solid enemy army, a war of ambushes and skirmishes could no longer be waged. This war was up to the regular troops. However, the *Canadiens* and natives had to be part of it. The best marksmen would be incorporated in the ground forces and the marine. In that way, each company would acquire fifteen of them, as well as canoeists and workers. The soldiers and the militiaman "will teach the things they know." Battle-ready men would no longer be excused from military service to work on their farms. Women would take over those tasks. All the militiamen would be paid: those who went into combat, and those who were assigned, with the munitions supplier, to the transport of goods. When Governor General Vaudreuil presented Montcalm's assessment of the situation to the minister of the colonies, he appended this warning: "You will appreciate, Monsieur, . . . the desire to make a mockery of the government, the desire for innovation, and in particular the desire to dominate the colonials."

In the course of conversations that were not very comradely, three decisions were made: the French would go immediately to retake the site of Fort Frontenac, where they would set up a fortified post and build a ship with twenty cannons. A detachment, followed by a supply convoy, would go to reinforce the post of Niagara. Finally, Vaudreuil would send to France an officer who would alert the court to the critical situation in Canada; that would be Bougainville, Montcalm's aide-de-camp, accompanied by André Doreil, the commissioner responsible for managing the wars in New France.

Vaudreuil was quick to explain to the Marquis de Massiac, minister of the marine and the colonies, that he had chosen those two men, who represented Montcalm more than the governor general, to "preserve the union" between them. However, he was duty-bound to warn the minister that "these gentlemen do not know the colony and its true interests well enough to have the honour of talking to you about it with any authority."

Had not Bougainville participated in three campaigns with Montcalm? Had not Doreil been charged, since 1756, with the lodging, the equipment, the clothing, the nourishment, and the hospital care of the regular troops? Did he not deal regularly with Bigot and his high-society associates?

Vaudreuil's true ambassador to Versailles left on August 13, with reports and requests from the governor general. Michel-Jean-Hugues Péan, adjutant-major of the city and government of Quebec, member of high society and associate of Intendant Bigot, left Canada on the pretext that he was going to receive treatment in France for a pain in his arms. The waters at Barèges, it was said, worked miracles. On August 6, 1758, Vaudreuil wrote, in Péan's favour, a letter of introduction to the minister of the colonies: "You may believe everything he says." Suspecting the real reason for Péan's voyage, Doreil, on August 12, warned the minister: "See in him one of the primary causes of the poor administration of this unfortunate country."

In Quebec, people were not blind. Péan, it was said, had fled Canada after having pillaged it. Had he not accumulated a fortune of eight million *livres* in eight years? Like Jacques-Michel Bréard, he would buy a château and land, have influential friends, and evade justice.

After his brief stay in Montreal, Montcalm returned to Carillon on September 13. In his absence, English pickets had been seen marching in the direction of the fort. Montcalm was persuaded that they would come back. That was why he continued to shore up the fortifications.

The French officers complained of having lost their cost-of-living bonus, while the price of merchandise had skyrocketed. A pound of butter, in 1755, cost twelve sous; in 1758, forty sous. A pound of lard, in 1755, cost ten sous; in 1758, it cost twenty sous. The officers criticized Montcalm for not defending their interests.

Fearing that this dissatisfaction would turn into a mutiny, Montcalm brought together the commander, two captains, and two lieutenants from each battalion of the ground troops to go over with them the steps he had taken in their interest with the ministry of war. He read them excerpts from the memos he had sent: "Our officers are at the end of their tether and do not know how to live here. Their situation grows worse every day, and [the price of] food increases every day." He also protested that his troops were no longer being paid "in money." In fact, they were being paid in playing card money, which was proving more and more difficult to exchange for cash.

To forestall a return of the English army, he multiplied his raids. A detachment descended toward the south of Lake Champlain, where the remnants of Abercromby's army, the wounded, the stragglers, and the wagon drivers, were slowly, painfully returning to Fort George. They were easy prey. On the Mohawk River, resident

Iroquois waited for Bradstreet's troops, who, after having left Fort Frontenac, took that way back. A band of Nipissings went to sow terror in the populace of Orange. *Canadien* militia were deployed in Massachusetts. In the course of another incursion along the Belle-Rivière, a detachment of French soldiers killed fifty English.

The season being autumn, the wild geese began to return to lands where the ponds would not ice over. Their triangular flocks glided through the Carillon sky and often set down on the swamps. Thanks to hunting these birds, the soldiers were better fed. On October 4, the first snow whitened the fortifications. Suddenly, everything seemed calm. Too calm.

According to Montcalm's scouts, the English had left Fort George for their winter quarters. He sent a detachment in search of boats, cannons, and munitions that had certainly been hidden away. Perhaps they had sunk the boats, which they would pull out of the water in spring. At the end of October, Montcalm assigned three hundred ground troops to Fort Carillon, along with a hundred troops of the marine. He placed eighty men at Fort Saint-Frédéric. During the winter, the two forts would guard the frontier of Lake Champlain.

And Montcalm left Carillon. A strong wind blew over Lake Champlain, the waves were high, the water was freezing. If the boat capsized . . . Montcalm thought of his son, a *mestre de camp* who, in Austria, "was leading a life of ease" among "a few too many princes and counts from the Empire." He dreamed, "When will I ride in a carriage, rather than a boat and sleigh?"

29

"Canada like a sick man..."

Montcalm returned to Montreal on November 9. En route, he noted: "Agriculture is in decline, the population is shrinking." His first task, once more, was to send the troops out to their winter quarters. He assigned them to villages along the St. Lawrence, at the mouth of the Richelieu, on Île d'Orléans across from Quebec, and to La Prairie on the south shore of the St. Lawrence. From there, they could react quickly to any approach by the English. He was able to give his officers some good news. On his recommendation, the governor general and the intendant were upping their pay.

Over the summer, France had lost Louisbourg and Fort Frontenac. Surprisingly, even though he was tired, and even though he missed his family and his native land, Montcalm asked the minister of war, Charles Louis Auguste Fouquet de Belle-Isle, to ignore his request to be returned to France. "Since affairs in the colony are going badly, it is for me to try to repair them or to delay its loss for as long as it will be possible," he wrote. But he had little hope: "The Court must today treat Canada like a sick man one fortifies with tonic." He was persuaded that "peace is necessary or Canada is lost." Let no one read "discouragement" into his words; he and his troops, he insisted, were "resolved to bury ourselves beneath the ruins of the colony." Hoping for a peace that seemed impossible, Montcalm was determined, all the same, to continue the fight.

It was not without anxiety that Doreil and Bougainville boarded their ship on November 12, 1758, in a season when rough weather was to be expected. "You can be a hero and still be afraid to drown," said Bougainville. On December 1, a storm battered the vessel so powerfully that the sailors, who were not ordinarily a brotherhood of churchgoers, each made a contribution for a mass to be said. Safe on the other side of the Atlantic, Doreil and Bougainville landed at Île d'Ouessant in Brittany. On December 20, their coach entered Paris. At the Ministry of the Marine and Colonies in Versailles, with the arrival of a new minister, there reigned an atmosphere of uncertainty, indecision, and caution that paralyzed the office. Moras, who had left his ministry after sixteen months of service, had been replaced by Monsieur de Massiac, who, after five months, had in turn been replaced by Nicolas-René Berryer, Comte de La Ferrière. In Canada, Bigot lamented this ministerial instability: "We're changing them like shirts; and so our affairs are going badly on the ground and at sea." Montcalm confessed to Colonel Bourlamaque: "Our ministers are changing so often that for the next campaign I would rather have the protection of a Cadet to provide wine at a hundred écus, than that of any of these gentlemen." The protection of a swindler like Cadet, who had accumulated, through his abuse of power, an immense fortune, was more reassuring in the eyes of the commander of the French troops than the policies of a minister. But whatever the circumstances, Montcalm would wage war against the English! And if they took Quebec, he would order a retreat to Louisiana for his eight battalions, his engineering detachments, and the elite of his marine troops. This withdrawal to Louisiana, he promised, "would do honour to the French nation."

On November 29, the last ship sailed out of Montreal for France, leaving Montcalm behind in this snow-covered colony, which would perhaps also be besieged. In a letter on December 9 to Colonel Bourlamaque, he dreamed: "Ah! When will we leave this land? . . . I would give, I believe, half my fortune to be away in my native land enjoying the work I have to do, and aspiring to what Canada can never afford me." The great man was not proud of his thoughts, because he asked Bourlamaque: "Burn my letter."

To busy himself over the winter, Montcalm concentrated on reading Diderot's *Encyclopédie*, an overview of all human endeavour to acquire knowledge, but his mind was uneasy. Informed of another misappropriation linked to "this handling of provisions," he poured out his heart to Bourlamaque. "You must excuse the disorder in my thoughts . . . because I have not slept all this night, what with the thievery at Belle-Rivière, and the incompetence. Poor king! Poor France! *Cara Patria*." He committed to his diary his dark thoughts: "Dear country weighed down with taxes to enrich knaves and the greedy! . . . Will I preserve my innocence as I have done so far in the midst of corruption? . . . Will France never produce at the head of the marine a minister who is enlightened, and an enemy of injustice?"

Montcalm found more and more reasons to be irritated. At one of the dinners he dutifully attended, the governor general again brought the subject back to Carillon. Why had Montcalm not gone after the English? Once more, Montcalm gave his reasons. Madame de Vaudreuil offered her own opinion. Montcalm responded that Madame de Montcalm would not intervene in a discussion between officers. He was telling her to be silent. Then he advised Vaudreuil: "If one is not happy with his second in command, one must wage war on one's own to put into practice one's own ideas." Vaudreuil lashed out through clenched teeth: "That could be done."

Despite a storm that blinded coachmen and horses, Montcalm left Montreal on December 29, 1758. Would he be happier in Quebec, with the charming ladies of the rue du Parloir?

30

"You don't try to save the stables"

The news reached Quebec that Constant Le Marchand de Lignery, the commander of Fort Duquesne, had burned down his post. The French had built this fort four years earlier, at Fourches (Pittsburgh), where the Monongahela River and the Allegheny River came together to form the Belle-Rivière. From there, they had expanded their military and commercial activities into the fertile valley. Then they had developed, cultivated, and strengthened their ties with the natives of those lands.

The Scottish general John Forbes, sent by William Pitt to conquer Fort Duquesne, headed an army of seven thousand men. Lignery, isolated, had received no reinforcements, no supplies, no munitions that spring. Knowing that the enemy was so numerous, the natives deserted. The wretched garrison refused to go down to certain defeat. Lignery felt that he didn't have the right to sacrifice to no purpose fighters that New France needed so badly.

When General John Forbes arrived at Fort Duquesne on the cold morning of November 26, 1758, suffering from "cholick" and pulled on a litter by two horses, all that was left was smoking ruins. A few days earlier, Montcalm had written to the minister of war concerning the Belle-Rivière valley: "I think it's saved for this year."

At the beginning of this new year, Montcalm again had bleak

thoughts: "1759 will be worse than 1758. I don't know how we will manage. Ah! I see all in black." Such was the state of mind of the commander of the French Army in North America, he whom the New England newspapers called "the invincible Montcalm."

On January 2, 1759, Intendant Bigot reduced the bread ration to a quarter of a pound per person. Four hundred women gathered in front of his château to protest the measure. Bigot reversed his decision and authorized a ration of half a pound.

Two days later, Montcalm wrote to Lévis: "The poverty here is extreme." It did not, however, affect the salons of Madame de La Naudière, Madame Marin, Madame Péan, or Madame de Beaubassin. If he disapproved of the prevarication that had enriched their husbands, Montcalm appreciated the conversation of these ladies, and above all that of Madame de Beaubassin. However, he admitted to Lévis, "I am not deriving as much pleasure from it as last winter." The gallant Boishébert, captain of the marine troops, valiant defender of the Acadians, flitted around Madame de Beaubassin a bit too much. Montcalm would have liked to be rid of him: "Send him for me to his Acadians, in Miramichi, on the ice!" If the ladies amused him less, he wrote Lévis on January 12: "Yesterday a delightful party. . . . I was there with the prettiest officer from the Sarre that you might imagine. I assure you that you would have preferred him to [Madame de] La Naudière. But mum's the word; burn my letter." And the party went on! On Thursday, the intendant's ball . . .

At Versailles, Bougainville and Doreil were dealing with the public and private business for which they were responsible. Doreil presented a memoir to the Marshal of Belle-Isle, minister of war. The victory at Carillon against an army three times more powerful was a miracle, he said. But they could not always count on a miracle. The English could bring together 200,000 men in America.

Canada could recruit at the most fifteen thousand men, and that only at the cost of halting land clearing, seeding, harvesting, construction. Doreil advised the minister: "Think only of making peace." Then, through skilful negotiation, it would be possible to save part of New France.

Bougainville described to Berryer, minister of the marine and the colonies, the feeling "of the peoples of Canada." They were "very tired." Many *Canadiens* had lost their lives in the war. Many others had come back maimed and disabled. Their families were deeply affected. Because of compulsory service in the militia, the *Canadiens* did not have time to cultivate their fields. And the intendant had to requisition part of their provisions for the garrisons. Many had not eaten bread in three months. The animals were not well fed. What is more, the populace was obliged to lodge and feed the soldiers in their little houses during the winter. As a consequence of so many constraints, the *Canadiens* were, even after so many years in the colony, in the same state of poverty as when they arrived. In the English colonies, the people lived more prosperously. Merchandise from England cost less than that from France. The English paid their men more generously for their work. If the English were to take Canada, they would leave the *Canadiens* free to practise the Catholic religion. These ideas, warned Bougainville, were common currency in the population. Even some individuals "of higher standing are not reluctant to talk in the same vein."

Bougainville passed on to the minister Montcalm's request for 1,500 soldiers and 500,000 pounds of powder. Montcalm also asked for a large quantity of *poudre des Invalides*, a comestible powder made from roasted corn mixed with other flours, then seasoned with butter, salt, and if possible an egg. For troops destined for long marches in the forest, this powder was easier to carry than sections of pork, beef, or horse.

Canadian officers estimated that the budget allotted for their colony was smaller than the allowance at the disposal of Madame de Pompadour, the king's mistress. Without voicing this opinion, Bougainville did make the point that England invested much more in its American colonies than France did. By the following spring, the English would have from sixty to eighty thousand men under arms in America. Among them, from twenty to thirty thousand came from England. France countered with only 3,400 regular soldiers, 1,200 in the marine, and five to six thousand militiamen, soldiers who lacked for everything. "If the English come to Quebec, our cannon fire will last us for six days," warned Bougainville. Minister Berryer, who had many concerns in Europe, replied, "You don't try to save the stables when the house is on fire."

Montcalm's aide-de-camp had to agree that the eminent gentleman's reply was not far off the mark. France really was in danger. That year, the English had landed at Cancale. They had entered the port of Saint-Malo, where they burned its ships. William Pitt had immediately launched another expedition against Cherbourg, which he bombarded. The city was saved only by bad weather.

Bougainville spoke of the role of "high society, more powerful than the governor general." He compared Intendant Bigot with Verres, the Roman statesman who, to increase his personal fortune, overwhelmed the Sicilians with punishing taxes. Bigot, he said, "is depleting the finances of France, abusing our penury and the danger we are in, and compromising the glory of the nation." Bougainville did not mention that he was courting the same Bigot to obtain an advancement for his cousin. Bougainville and Bigot even lived, according to the intendant, "under the same roof."

The court accorded Bougainville a certain number of "favours." Montcalm was promoted to the rank of lieutenant-general, Vaudreuil received the Cross of Saint-Louis, and Bourlamaque became a brigadier. Twenty-five barrels of flour and as much pork were to be shipped to the colony. The minister endorsed Montcalm's proposition to incorporate the *Canadien* militia into the regular forces. As for his plan to retreat to Louisiana, it was "admired" but rejected. A *Te Deum* was sung at Versailles to thank God for Montcalm's victory at Carillon. The king even mentioned it in one of his letters: "My brave soldiers in Canada". . . Finally, Berryer sent to Canada an administrator who would be "of useful assistance to Monsieur Bigot in his functions." In other words, he would be checking up on the intendant's conduct.

In Quebec, a large country outing took place on January 18, 1759, with fifty-two guests. "I provided," said Montcalm, "the lighting, violins, barley water, beer, wine, and what was needed for twenty-six dishes out of the seventy at the two tables." The following Thursday, he attended a ball organized by the friends of Madame Péan, with whom, he confessed, "I am intimate." He was, however, appalled by the "terrible impecuniousness of the Government of Quebec." Bigot had ordered a levy of grain from the farmers. Montcalm foresaw that this grain would not go where it was supposed to. Life went on: "Balls, entertainments, garden parties, extravagant games of chance at the present time." He confessed: "I am much more often this year in the company of Madame Péan . . . that is proof of idleness." Madame Pennisseault, wife of the munitions supplier Cadet's steward, set a generous table. A number of those who were jealous remarked that the Chevalier de Lévis ate there every day . . . Coming home from an evening at Madame de Beaubassin's, Montcalm felt sad in the freezing air the wind blew off the river: "We amuse ourselves, we think of nothing, everything is going and will go to the devil."

On January 19, Minister Berryer signed a letter in which he repri-manded Bigot in no uncertain terms: "You sold the cargo for 800,000 francs. . . . You repurchased a part for the king at the cost of one million (or 200,000 more than the price at which you had sold all). With such behaviour, it is not surprising that the colony's expenses have become unsustainable. . . . The fortunes of your subordinates cast suspicion on your administration." The minister asked Bigot: "How does it happen that smallpox among the Indians cost the king a million francs? . . . Who is responsible for that? . . . Merchandise is classified as consumed as soon as it arrives and is then resold to the king at an exorbitant price. And so the king buys goods in France and buys them again in Canada."

Bougainville felt that he had succeeded in his mission. He had rehabilitated Montcalm's reputation, which had been compromised by Vaudreuil's correspondence. He would swear to the new lieutenant-general: "You have no enemy, and no one who resents you. I could name all of France if I wanted to name everyone who loves you and wants you to be Marshal of France. Little children know your name."

31

"The business of next summer"

Major-General James Wolfe, on vacation in Bath, was thinking about his mission to "Quebeck." He was studying maps of the St. Lawrence River. It was "a very hazardous enterprise." To succeed, the Royal Navy had to make its presence felt on the St. Lawrence as early as possible, to block any French reinforcements. The night before Christmas, 1758, in a letter to William Pitt, the new commander insisted on that essential condition. To support his view, he included with his letter those of two Louisbourg officers who knew the river.

On the last days of December 1758, William Pitt outlined to Major-General Amherst what his mission would be for the New Year: "By the most vigorous and decisive efforts to establish, by the blessing of God on his arms, His Majesty's just and indubitable rights, and to avert all future dangers to His Majesty's subjects in North America."

Amherst would organize his own "irruption in Canada," either through Crown Point (Pointe à la Chevelure), at the foot of Lake Champlain, or by Fort La Présentation, also called La Galette, on the south shore of the St. Lawrence. The invasion could also be made by both routes at once. After having rebuilt Fort Oswego (Chouaguen), destroyed by Montcalm in 1756, Amherst would continue his progress as far as Fort Niagara, to ensure his mastery of Lake Ontario, and cut all communication between Canada and Louisiana. To attain these goals, Amherst would have under his command fourteen thousand men. Every colony had to provide its share in good time.

To take Quebec, James Wolfe would have in his charge twelve thousand men—ten battalions of redcoats and an impressive array of field artillery operated by three hundred bluecoats from the Royal Navy. Those officers and regular soldiers already serving in America would be backed up by six hundred rangers from Nova Scotia and New England. The ground forces would be transported, escorted, and supported by the Royal Navy's fleet. Pitt asked Wolfe and Vice-Admiral Charles Saunders to co-operate just as Amherst and Boscawen had worked together to take Louisbourg.

Setting their troops in motion toward different frontiers, Amherst and Wolfe would force the French to split up their army. Pitt said to Amherst and Wolfe: "Unite for their destruction."

Still, Wolfe was not thinking only about his enemies. During his stay in Bath, he had courted a "pretty neighbour," Katherine Lowther, who was twenty-five years old. He had met his "little love" during the winter of 1757. In December 1758, he asked for her hand in marriage. The ceremony would take place in autumn 1759, when James was back from Quebec. "First, we must beat the enemy."

Young Major-General Wolfe had had the temerity, contrary to common practice, to insist on making his own choice of officers who would assist him. Colonel Robert Monckton would be his second in command. A few months older than Wolfe, Monckton had fought in Flanders and had been in Nova Scotia for seven years. In 1755, after having orchestrated the taking of Fort Beauséjour, Monckton had overseen the deportation of the Acadians from the region of Les Mines. Just recently, in the autumn of 1758, he had led an expedition that destroyed French settlements along the Rivière Saint-Jean.

Wolfe did not, however, choose his second brigadier. Commander-in-Chief Sir John Ligonier assigned him Colonel George Townshend, who had seen Dettingen, Fontenoy, Culloden, and Lauffeldt when he was aide-de-camp to the Duke of Cumberland. Gifted with astute political savvy, Townshend had hitched himself in 1755 to the rising star of William Pitt. Wolfe had no alternative but to accept the choice made for him by Ligonier.

For his third brigadier, Wolfe chose Colonel James Murray, who had fought the French at Ostend and elsewhere in Flanders, in Brittany, and in India. He had taken part in the expedition against Rochefort, and he had served under Wolfe at Louisbourg. Despite his brilliant service record, he had been stalled at the rank of lieutenant-colonel since 1751 because his elder brother was an active supporter of the Young Pretender to the throne of England.

The French commander, Montcalm, had led his troops to three consecutive victories, but James Wolfe had no great respect for his adversary. On January 29, 1759, he wrote to his uncle Walter Wolfe: "If the Marquis de Montcalm finds means to baffle our efforts another summer, he may be deemed an able officer."

The fleet bearing Wolfe's army to Quebec would be commanded by Vice-Admiral Charles Saunders, one of the 188 men out of two thousand who had survived Commodore George Anson's circumnavigation and returned in 1744 on board the *Centurion* with a treasure of 400,000 pounds taken from the Spaniards. Vice-Admiral Saunders would be assisted by two rear-admirals: Philip Durell and Charles Holmes. Durell, in Halifax, was responsible for the British squadron in North America. He had vast experience in American waters and had contributed to two victories against the fortress of Louisbourg, in 1745 and 1758.

In the summer of 1758, at the end of the expedition around the coast of Gaspé, Wolfe had wanted to go farther up the St. Lawrence to seize the cargos of French ships. Rear-Admiral Hardy had refused to allow the fleet to take that risk. This spring, Wolfe wanted, early on, as soon as the ice had melted, to have a squadron waiting to intercept the French ships at Bic Island. Would Durell agree to undertake that venture? Having experienced the lack of daring on the part of Rear-Admiral Hardy, Wolfe, on December 24, 1758, shared with William Pitt his fear that Rear-Admiral Durell might be "vastly unequal to the weight of the business." Pitt gave Durell a clear order to proceed to Bic Island as soon as the ice had freed up the river. And he asked Saunders to repeat this order to Durell in the most emphatic way possible.

At the end of January 1759, Saunders's fleet was ready to set sail for America. The evening before his departure for Spithead, James Wolfe was invited to a dinner hosted by William Pitt, in London. At the end of the meal, the statesman, who thought he had seen all possible political and diplomatic posturings, could not help being intrigued by Major-General Wolfe, who brandished his sword, whirled it over his head, brought the hilt down on the table, and promised his host that he would perform brilliant exploits on the other side of the Atlantic.

Before leaving London, James Wolfe did not make the short trip to Blackheath to say goodbye to his mother and his father, who was ill. Ten years earlier, his parents had opposed his relationship with Elizabeth Lawson. Were they now less than enthusiastic about his proposed marriage to Katherine Lowther? Celebrated in the papers, on intimate terms with politicians, listened to by his superior officers, Major-General Wolfe limited himself this time to writing a brief note to express his "best wishes" to his mother and to the "General," his father . . .

On February 14, the fleet of Rear-Admiral Holmes left Spithead. Three days later, the rest of the fleet cast off. Vice-Admiral Saunders would join Holmes in the port of New York, where Amherst had begun to assemble the troops and supplies. James Wolfe travelled with Saunders on board the *Neptune*.

With every roll of the *Neptune* on an angry sea, Wolfe felt his stomach doing somersaults, but still he composed an eight-page letter to Major-General Amherst, in very small writing, concerning different aspects of the campaign. When Sir John Ligonier had promised him twelve thousand men, Ligonier was counting on an influx of three thousand recruits from units deployed in the West Indies. The Indies, explained Wolfe, was infested with deadly illnesses and was a cemetery for Europeans. They could not therefore expect the reinforcements they had counted on. Did they not have thirteen thousand men the year before to take Louisbourg? Sickness aboard ships, an epidemic, the loss of men during a potential attack by the French going up the river, would reduce their capacity for taking Quebec. What is more, Wolfe did not have financial support: "There is a great siege to be undertaken and not a farthing to pay the workmen. I am not possessed of a single dollar of publick money." Despite all these obstacles, Wolfe promised to create such a diversion in Quebec that he would make it easy for Amherst to take the forts of Carillon and Saint-Frédéric. That was Wolfe's clever way of lobbying for an increase in his resources. The stronger the army in Quebec, the more men the French would need to counter it. As a result, Amherst would be faced with a weakened defence on Lake Champlain.

James Wolfe opened a book that Katherine Lowther had given him on his departure: *Elegy Written in a Country Churchyard* by Thomas Gray. As was his custom, he scrawled notes in the margin. He underscored the line: "The paths of glory lead but to the grave."

32

"One cannot love you any more tenderly, my heart"

On February 24, 1759, Montcalm no longer had any hope. "The Upper Country is lost; millions spent there, at Detroit, or in Acadia [Louisbourg], for no good reason." The natives had already "adjusted" to the new strength of the English. The previous year, a third of the farmland had not been seeded. This year, only half of it could be sown because there were not enough cattle to pull the ploughs; five hundred barrels full of beef had had to be salted while the people waited for pork to arrive from France. "The colony is lost and there is no peace in sight; I see nothing that can save us." The lieutenant-general was back in Montreal on March 7, 1759. The "invincible Montcalm" was tired. "When will the play we are performing in Canada come to an end?" he asked himself.

Vaudreuil had made a list of all the able-bodied men in the colony, from sixteen to sixty years old, who could bear arms. He could call up fifteen thousand men: 7,511 at Quebec, 1,313 at Trois-Rivières, and 6,405 in Montreal. He had also made an inventory of weapons, munitions, and supplies that were available, but he did not deem it useful to pass on the information to the commander-in-chief of the French forces. "What need does the general of the ground forces have for this knowledge?" said Vaudreuil. "He might plan a campaign proportional to our means and our forces that we would not want to pursue."

Montcalm tried to space out his visits to the governor general. Besides their disagreements, he found it hard to tolerate, in Vaudreuil's entourage, the presence of certain guests such as Le Mercier, whom he saw as "a weak and ignorant man." Montcalm was wary of those officers who had amassed a fortune in Canada, who were gaming friends of Bigot, and who had too much influence on Vaudreuil . . .

As for the coming campaign, Vaudreuil wanted the army to make a number of forays, rather than to shut itself off behind the fortifications. Montcalm saw that his brigadier, the Chevalier de Lévis, also seemed to favour this strategy, which with "a small number of individuals . . . would keep many enemies occupied." Montcalm thought he knew why Vaudreuil preferred a strategy of deployment: "He has to send people to Belle-Rivière, because Saint-Sauveur, Vaudreuil's secretary, and the Chevalier de Repentigny, have each bought half of fifty thousand pounds of merchandise, which, sold on site, and charged to the king, will bring a return of a million. However, it was confirmed, this winter, that given the destruction of Fort Duquesne, Belle-Rivière needs nothing. And it's the same for Acadia. There is no point in sending in supplies just to enrich . . . a bunch of knaves."

Despite their irreconcilable differences, Vaudreuil and Montcalm seemed to agree on one point. The city of Quebec was not in danger. The governor general said: "I would not expect that the English are planning to come to Quebec." The lieutenant general thought that "the only place which we may hope they will not take by force . . . is Quebec."

To forget his cares, Montcalm threw himself into reading the third volume of the *Encyclopédie*, despite an eye infection. His visits to Madame de Lavaltrie and to Madame de Barante did not lift his spirits: "With all that, I am bored to tears." During the winter, Montcalm had noted: "Despite the penury and the impending loss of the colony, the entertainments have never been livelier in Quebec. Never so many balls and games of chance." In a pastoral letter of April 1, 1759, Bishop Pontbriand denounced those "profane entertainments to which the population is abandoning itself more feverishly than ever," and "the intolerable excesses in games of chance." Because of the "crimes that have proliferated over this winter," he admonished, "God is angry. . . . He is lifting his hand to strike us, and . . . we deserve it." This punishment, the faithful understood, could only be the English and Protestant invasion. During the eighteen years that he had been "guiding this vast diocese," the bishop had "with sorrow witnessed its frequent suffering from famine and illness" in this land "almost perpetually at war." He added, however: "This year seems to us in every way the saddest and the most deplorable, because, in fact, you are more criminal. Has such shameful despoilment ever been seen?"

More calmly, the governor general reassured his minister at Versailles: "Whatever the English do . . . the value of our troops, the personal interests of the colonists, their attachment to the king, the number of natives that are ours, all these forces united and infused with the same desire will make the conquest of this colony extremely difficult, if not impossible."

Among the letters and reports leaving for Versailles as navigation resumed, Montcalm had one translated into code. It was addressed to the Marshal of Belle-Isle, minister of war, and was dated April 12: "Barring some unexpected good fortune, such as a great diversion inflicted on the colonies by sea, or some great errors on the part of the enemy," he declared, "Canada will be taken during this campaign, and surely during the next." This catastrophe had been precipitated, according to Montcalm, by the corruption in the country's administration, the most pernicious of epidemics: "The *Canadiens* are disheartened." Making war, they do not cultivate their fields, and the intendant seizes their grain, even their animals. Those responsible for collecting the grain resell it at their own profit. The people fear a devaluation of the playing card money. The colony's government "is worthless." Intendant Bigot "is only concerned with making his own fortune, and those of his circle and his flatterers." Bigot's associates control all the businesses, even that of medicines for the sick and wounded. Those people are anxious to inflate their fortunes before the colony is lost. Many of them even welcome it as "an impenetrable veil over their conduct." Everywhere on the road to war there reigns that ruinous corruption: "Must one put the artillery in working order, make gun carriages, wagons, tools? Monsieur Mercier [Lemercier], who commands the artillery, is an entrepreneur under other names: everything is poorly made and expensive." In the distant posts, "there are only false invoices." Thus, the supplies destined for the Upper Country were resold to the king three or four times: "If the natives" had received "the quarter of what one was supposed to have spent for them, the king would have all of them in America on his side, and the English none." Even the chimney sweep demands the right to cheat. When Montcalm refused to sign "like the others" a receipt attesting to the cleaning of twenty-four chimneys when his residence had only twelve, the sweep could not comprehend the lieutenant-general's miserliness. Such abuses were known to everyone. "I have often spoken of that to Monsieur de Vaudreuil and Monsieur Bigot," wrote Montcalm, "and each blamed the other." What did the people say? "The *Canadiens* who have no part in the illicit profits hate the government; they have confidence in the French general," he flattered himself. He concluded: "Devoted to the service of Your

Majesty, I have expressed my opinion for the best and we will act with courage and zeal, Monsieur le Chevalier de Lévis, Monsieur de Bourlamaque, and myself, to delay the imminent loss of Canada."

As soon as the ice had freed up the rivers and lakes, four thousand men, under Vaudreuil's orders, went to reinforce the garrison at Carillon. It was easier to reach than Quebec. For that seemingly obvious reason, Vaudreuil was persuaded that the English would launch a second offensive against Fort Carillon. As for their coming up the St. Lawrence toward Quebec, that route was littered with obstacles. In 1711, Admiral Hovenden Walker had suffered a disastrous shipwreck there and had lost nine hundred men. The English would not have forgotten . . . Other detachments were sent to Fort La Présentation. Departing on the mission, the commander of the fort, Pierre Pouchot de Maupas of the regular forces, left Montcalm with these words: "My General, it seems that we will see each other again only in England."

At the beginning of May, the birds were singing, flowerets sparkled in the fields, but Montcalm was not joyful: "Ennui is not mortal, that is clear," he wrote to his wife. He was tormented by the battles to come. "My hope is in God; he fought for me on July 8 [at Carillon] . . ." Fortunately, his wife was waiting for him in his Languedoc: "One cannot love you any more tenderly, my heart, and when will I return? The moment I see you again will be the most beautiful of my life."

The fleet returning Bougainville from France, under an uncertain sun, amid blocks of floating ice, entered into a St. Lawrence swollen by melting snow. On May 10, the sailors of the *Chézine* dropped anchor in the harbour of Quebec. Bougainville had to give Montcalm terrible news: as he was boarding the ship, he was informed of the death of one of the lieutenant-general's daughters, but he could not say which one.

In the correspondence that came with the ships, instructions from Marshal de Belle-Isle, minister of war, set out Montcalm's responsibilities. Up to then, despite a military rank higher than that of the governor general, the commander-in-chief of the French troops still had to share his authority with Vaudreuil. This dualism resulted in bitter rivalry. Given the urgent situation, with Canada threatened by an invasion, the king had imposed a compromise: Montcalm would be responsible for military operations, but he had to consult the governor general.

In addition, Berryer, minister of the colonies, had delegated Charles-François Pichot de Querdisien Trémais to uncover "all the abuses that have crept into the different areas of the colony's functioning." Learning of the commissioner's arrival, Bigot demanded from Cadet the reimbursement of a sum of two million, which he accused him of stealing. Cadet also saw the danger. He proposed to Bigot that he return, with the consent of his associates, nine million . . . Bigot forced other associates to give back some of their profits, to show their good faith.

In another letter to Montcalm, the minister of war justified the meagre reinforcements he was sending to Canada. A greater number of troops, he reasoned, "would exacerbate the shortage of food." The minister also feared "that they might be intercepted by the English." This very courageous marshal and minister was afraid as well that "the efforts we would make here to provide you with [additional troops] would only have the effect of provoking the minister of London [William Pitt] into making even greater ones, to maintain the superiority he has achieved on that continent." The marshal reminded the lieutenant-general: "The king counts on your zeal, your courage and your persistence. . . . I vouched for you to the king, and I am certain that you will not prove me wrong," he purred. After having refused Montcalm soldiers, arms, munitions, and supplies, Marshal de Belle-Isle still expected of him that he would avoid "ever submitting to the shameful conditions that were imposed on Louisbourg."

33

"The worst soldiers in the universe"

After five weeks on the Atlantic, James Wolfe's ordeal was about to come to an end. Vice-Admiral Saunders's fleet arrived before Louisbourg on April 21, 1759. The Bay of Gabarus was still blocked by ice. Saunders tried to make his way through, but nothing worked. And so he headed for Halifax. When the fleet entered that port on April 30, Wolfe saw the fourteen ships of Rear-Admiral Durell anchored there, when they ought to have been at the island of Bic, according to his explicit instructions. Durell was not at a loss for excuses. If Louisbourg was paralyzed by ice, you could be sure that, farther north, the entire river was obstructed. Consistent with the navy's tried and true tradition that had so exasperated Wolfe at Rochefort, Durell had not dared face up to the difficult conditions involved in sailing up the St. Lawrence. While Durell dithered, Wolfe presumed, French frigates and merchant vessels had doubtless threaded their way through the ice floes coming down the river.

He'd expected scurvy to have ravaged the Halifax garrison. But over the winter, the men had dined on beef washed down with spruce beer. That had saved them. The four battalions of redcoats were eager to be back in action. Representing a variety of backgrounds, these men were from all the British isles, where they had been farmers, miners, clavichord makers, blacksmiths, weavers, writing masters . . . They had enlisted to escape poverty or an oppressive family, or because they had been conscripted under the War Emergency Law. They were heartened by the arrival of Major-General Wolfe: "Now we begin to live again. . . . I hope to have the pleasure of attending a conquering army," wrote Lieutenant Henry Brown.

While Saunders's ships were being caulked and refitted, Durell's fleet finally moved out of the port of Halifax on May 5, transporting, under the orders of Colonel Guy Carleton, 650 men—in other words, the vanguard of Wolfe's army. James Wolfe still feared an epidemic that might reduce his forces. He demanded cleanliness in the bunks and the bedding, and exercises on the bridge, in the open air when weather permitted. On each ship, guards would make sure everything was clean and in good order, to avoid fires.

The order calling for regiments from the West Indies had been rescinded. The battalions arriving from New York were fewer in number than had been hoped for. And the French, by now, had to have been receiving reinforcements and supplies. It was not before May 13 that Wolfe, along with Vice-Admiral Saunders, boarded the *Neptune*, which dropped anchor in front of the fortress of Louisbourg on May 15. While Saunders's fleet had been in Halifax, ships transporting nine thousand soldiers had gradually arrived in Louisbourg, followed by twenty-two frigates with artillery and munitions, then ships loaded with provisions, and finally straggler ships that had lost their way. Saunders's entire fleet and Wolfe's entire army were now together, ready to attack Quebec.

Winter had been cruel in Louisbourg. After the siege of summer 1758, the cannonballs and the bombs, the garrison's most urgent task had been to build the winter quarters. In October, a hurricane had damaged the ships anchored in the port. Dead bodies, which had lain at the bottom of the water since the siege, rose to the surface.

A dispatch awaited Wolfe. His father had died at the age of seventy-four. Wolfe knotted a black scarf around his left arm and wrote to his uncle Walter: "I am exceedingly sorry it so fell out that I had not in my power to assist him in his illness, and to relieve my mother in her distress."

Was his army up to its mission of taking Quebec? Almost all the battalions had participated in the victorious siege at Louisbourg. He sensed a solid esprit de corps in this "American army." It had acquired skills during its Indian-like skirmishes on rough terrain and in the forest. What is more, this ground army had learned, in 1758, to collaborate with the navy . . . Wolfe was also allotted six companies of rangers newly recruited in the English provinces, "the worst soldiers in the universe," he judged. He imposed strict discipline on them, but when an officer became apologetic that his men could not master a certain exercise, Wolfe replied that if they were "otherwise well disciplined and will fight, that's all I shall require of them."

34

"Against the balls, a relic"

"Nothing is in a condition to meet the English," Montcalm concluded. The sorry state of Quebec's fortifications worried him. In 1757, Vaudreuil had charged Gaspard-Joseph Chaussegros de Léry with improving them. According to Montcalm, the engineer had not known how to take advantage of what "nature had lavished" on the city. What is more, the fortifications were not protected by works that would shield them from a bombardment. The rampart facing the countryside was "a very weak wall." Engineer Nicolas Sarrebource de Pontleroy, who succeeded Léry, was waiting for orders from the minister. But the minister had been replaced. Montcalm had many times tried to alert Vaudreuil.

On May 23, 1759, he brought together at the intendant's residence all the captains of frigates and ships, as well as the port officers. *Carcassières*, rowboats armed with cannons, would be built to fend off the enemy if they tried to land. One thousand four hundred sailors were assigned to this floating battery. Some proposed blocking the St. Lawrence channel between Île d'Orléans and Île Madame by sinking ten large ships. Some wanted to see a battery set up on Cap Tourmente and another farther to the east at Cap Brûlé, to watch for English ships.

Vaudreuil came in turn to Quebec. Montcalm was irritated by his presence: "I have to let him play the role of general. I serve him as secretary and major." Among the officers, it was believed that navigating the St. Lawrence was impossible for a pilot who didn't know its reefs, its diagonal currents, its shallow channels, its shoals, its sudden fogs ... For Bougainville, those obstacles were "Quebec's best rampart."

In anticipation of the Quebec expedition, however, the English had undertaken, in the late autumn of 1758, to recruit pilots who did know the St. Lawrence. They had sought them out among the French prisoners in England. In Canada, Durell had recruited some at Louisbourg, on Cape Breton Island, and in Gaspé. In the spring, Saunders had asked the governors of New York and Massachusetts to assign him two pilots who had already sailed on the St. Lawrence. And so the English had brought together some twenty pilots with experience of the river. Durell was guided by two French pilots who had arrived on board the *Neptune* with Saunders and Wolfe. Captured in Canada, Théodose-Matthieu Denys de Vitré and Augustin Raby had been prisoners in England.

After Louisbourg had been taken, James Cook explored the coast of Cape Breton Island on board the *Pembroke*. He'd been intrigued to see Samuel Johannes Holland, engineer and military surveyor, trace out a map with the help of an instrument he didn't know, a folding wooden frame on which the degrees were indicated: a plane table. Cook asked Holland to give him a demonstration. They became friends, and together, over the winter, they drew a number of maps of the Gulf of St. Lawrence and the river. They also redrew the maps of the Baie des Chaleurs as well as the bays of Gaspé, and of the river, based on maps in Durell's possession. A captain went to the site to verify their exactness. Finally, in the spring, Durell asked James Cook to accompany his fleet on board the *Pembroke*.

On May 11, French fishermen saw Rear-Admiral Durell's fleet proceeding past Gaspé. Seven days later, Durell arrived at Bic Island, five and a half leagues west of Rimouski. With its natural harbour, it served as a base for ships circulating between Gaspé, Tadoussac, and Quebec. Before arriving at the island, Durell raised the French flag on the masts of his ships. According to custom, pilots on the coast came to offer their services to captains who did not know the St. Lawrence. Durell took them prisoner. Questioning them, he learned that French ships had stopped at that island on May 9. As he could still win the race, Durell sped his fleet toward Isle-aux-Coudres.

On May 23, a little before midnight, light signals were transmitted from point to point along the north shore of the St. Lawrence, as far as Quebec. The English were between Les Éboulements and Isle-aux-Coudres! The English had arrived! In the coastal villages, the people ran to the church. In a sleeping Quebec, the news was shouted out from street to street. Young men, fathers of families, old men, children aged twelve and over—all wanted to take up arms. The Sulpicians, who knew of Montcalm's great devotion to the Virgin Mary, had no doubt that he would win another victory over the Protestants. Some nuns gave him a relic that would shield him from the enemy's cannons. They even gave him the first wreath woven from new spring flowers. Montcalm could not suppress a certain sense of satisfaction; it was usually Madame de Vaudreuil who was accorded that honour . . .

Montcalm made the tally of his forces. They included 1,600 well-disciplined regular soldiers who had served at Chouaguen, Fort George, Carillon; six hundred *Canadiens* from the marine troops who had their own ways but feared nothing; nine hundred Odawas, Algonquins, Abenakis, Hurons, and Nipissings, and even Iroquois. There would also be ten thousand militiamen, undisciplined but useful. They were accustomed to the climate and waged war like the natives. In total: 13,718 men. Plus a garrison of two thousand men assigned to guard the city of Quebec.

A few weeks earlier, the Chevalier de La Naudière had proposed to Montcalm that he construct cannon-carrying rafts to block the English fleet around Isle-aux-Coudres. The project had at first appeared cunning, but Montcalm was later irritated to learn that the rafts would be built under false names by Le Mercier and Péan, friends of Bigot, at a profit of at least a hundred *livres*.

Nevertheless, La Naudière left with his artillery on May 22 at the head of a detachment of 150 militiamen and a hundred Abenakis to set up a base on Isle-aux-Coudres. When he arrived, he found the farms deserted. The populace had already fled. La Naudière and his men had barely had time to camouflage their canoes and cut down a few trees to build their *cajeux*, or rafts, when they saw the English fleet coming their way. In their turn, they disappeared into the woods.

Finding the island deserted, Durell set up his camp there. At night, everything was calm. Thinking this was a haven of peace, the English lay down under the stars. Others wandered from their tents, going on foot, by canoe, or on horseback for a moonlit excursion. La Naudière's men, in hiding, made some prisoners. One of them was Durell's grandson. Another was an officer who was on horseback with a young soldier behind him.

In Quebec, preparations were being made to counter the English invasion. Vaudreuil set up a camp near the General Hospital for militiamen who made their way there, as well as for the troops recalled from their winter quarters and distant posts. Montcalm, Lévis, the engineer Pontleroy, and some other officers travelled east on horseback along the north shore of the river. Beginning at the St. Charles River and as far as Montmorency Falls, they constructed a fortified camp. They chose the positions for batteries and redoubts, and decided where the trenches would be dug. At the mouth of the St. Charles, a barrier of posts, of rafts chained together, would block the passage. Farther on, they sank two ships to support a platform bearing twenty cannons. Two bridges were thrown across the river, in addition to the one that already existed. They would be protected by redoubts.

In the city, the people took to their action stations. At the foot of Cap Diamant, upon which Quebec stood, cannons were set up to watch over the harbour and the river. On a hexagonal raft, a twelve-piece battery was installed. Eight fire ships were readied, and 120 rafts were built, to be loaded with explosive materials. These war machines would be loosed on the enemy as soon as they appeared in the harbour. Openings in the houses built onto the cliff were closed up. Obstacles were laid down in the rue du Palais. And the road leading to the upper town would be guarded by two batteries on earthen platforms. At the top of the promontory, the fortifications, unfinished, would have double palisades built onto them. The bishop's palace was transformed into a small fort. So that the provisions might not fall into the hands of the enemy, they were transferred to Trois-Rivières. In anticipation of a landing on Île d'Orléans, the villages were evacuated. A detachment of five hundred *Canadien* militiamen and a party of natives, under the orders of Augustin Le Gardeur de Courtemanche, left to prepare ambushes that would hold up the enemy.

Montcalm was frustrated by the slowness with which the work was proceeding: "Carts are lacking for the fortifications, but not to transport the material needed to make a blockhouse at Madame Péan's." Neither was Intendant Bigot neglecting his own security. He had his château surrounded by a solid palisade armed with several field guns. He also thought it necessary to have the documents from his "financial office" transferred to Trois-Rivières.

Since the arrival in Quebec of Commissioner Pichot de Querdisien Trémais, who had come, at the request of the minister of the colonies, to investigate the abuses in the colony's management, Bigot was persuaded that Bougainville had presented at Versailles a devastating report concerning his administration. And Bougainville was Montcalm's spokesman . . . The meetings of the colony's superior officers had become arenas for altercation.

Finally, the populace was allotted a daily ration of only two ounces of bread, and on the farms, the breeding cattle and the milk cows were requisitioned by the intendant.

35

"Such a tremendous fire, that no human head can venture to peep up under"

As Durell's vanguard neared Quebec, Saunders's fleet was still trapped at Louisbourg by dense fog and thick ice. Major-General Wolfe was extremely anxious. Every day's delay made victory less likely. On May 27, 1759, he was still seeing hardy soldiers making their way from shore to ship, leaping from one block of ice to another. Not until June 6 could Saunders's fleet set sail for Quebec: twenty-two warships, plus 119 for cargo. Raising glasses of port, the men toasted a day to come when the British flag would fly over every fort, over every French post!

The wind was good, the weather was fine, the sea was behaving itself. On board the *Neptune*, the fusiliers of Lieutenant-Colonel Hector Boisrond, a Huguenot who had moved to Ireland, amused themselves by shooting at "sea cows" that came to loiter near the ships. The bullets bounced off their skin as if it were rock. James Wolfe made his will. His first thought was for Katherine Lowther, whom he would wed on his return, but if he were killed in the course of the expedition, the miniature portrait of herself that she had given him before his departure would be returned to her after having been set in jewels with a value of five guineas. Vice-Admiral Saunders and Wolfe had forged a bond of collaboration and friendship. And so

Wolfe left him his dinner service. To the officer who would replace him after his death, he left his camping equipment, his kitchen furniture, his tablecloths, his provisions, and his wine. To every officer on his staff, he left a hundred guineas. To his servant, François, he gave half of his clothing and underclothing, as well as fifty guineas. The rest would be divided among his three valets. His servants would receive wages and a pension until they found a new master or entered another profession. Finally, everything else he owned would go to his "good mother."

Wolfe had studied a report by the engineer Patrick Mackellar. Taken prisoner by Montcalm's army at Oswego (Chouaguen) in 1756, Major Mackellar had been brought to Montreal and Quebec before being exchanged. Mackellar advised against a landing near Quebec, on the river's north shore. The shallow water would be perilous for the ships. He proposed, rather, to land on Île d'Orléans, a little below Quebec, and there to set up a base. James Wolfe adopted that recommendation.

On June 23, a good northeast wind filled the sails. The channel between the cliffs of Baie-Saint-Paul and Isle-aux-Coudres, some fourteen and a half leagues from Quebec, was reputed to be impassable for large warships. What is more, the French had overturned the seamarks on shore and had pulled out the buoys. Saunders had the passage sounded. Two days later, he ordered the pilots to proceed upriver. One of the French pilots, on board the *Goodwill*, refused to co-operate. He predicted that the walls of Quebec would soon be adorned with English scalps. The crew wanted to throw him overboard. Saunders intervened: to conquer Quebec, the English needed every pilot who knew the St. Lawrence.

Another dangerous passage awaited the fleet. The ships had to enter the channel between Île d'Orléans and Île Madame, to tack within the narrow and uneven channel and then in the turbulent shallows of the unforgiving Traverse. Three weeks earlier, on board the *Pembroke*, James Cook had spent two days sounding it. An advance party had placed rowboats at dangerous spots to replace the buoys the French had spirited away. Saunders's fleet slowly passed through the Traverse without incident.

Île d'Orléans was green and peaceful. A few church spires, small whitewashed houses, windmills, stone dwellings, roofs of tile or thatch. Fields separated by picket fences, with wheat, hemp, barley, and peas. On June 26, the *Goodwill*, guided by the reluctant French pilot, dropped anchor in front of the parish of Saint-Laurent on the island's south shore.

Hidden in the foliage, Courtemanche's militiamen and natives watched the manoeuvres. The English put barges into the water. Loaded with soldiers, they approached the shore. The natives could no longer restrain themselves. Faced with this band of yelping Indians, the rowers turned back. But they were determined to return. One English barge was captured.

Finally, with no other opposition, Wolfe's army soon marched into the village and set up camp not far from the church, which became his headquarters. The priest, before fleeing with the elements for the Eucharist and the sacred objects, had left a note for "the worthy officers of the English army," begging them not to damage his church. He added, with sly naïveté, "I would have preferred that you arrive earlier, so as to sample our vegetables, such as our asparagus and turnips . . . which have now all gone to seed." At sunset, a lieutenant and forty colonial rangers went on reconnaissance. Suddenly, in the forest, they found themselves face to face with a group of *Canadiens*. The lieutenant thought they were villagers who had fled. It was in fact the rear guard of Courtemanche's detachment, which killed some of the rangers and then disappeared.

Wolfe was eager to see with his own eyes, in the light of day, this city he had come to conquer. On June 27, accompanied by the engineer Mackellar and escorted by rangers, he walked to the eastern tip of Île d'Orléans. On the north shore of the river, about a league away, Quebec stood out above Cap Diamant. Wolfe peered at it through his telescope. Buildings were silhouetted against the sky. Mackellar pointed them out: the Château Saint-Louis, the cathedral, the seminary, Hôtel-Dieu, the Ursuline convent. Wolfe saw the fortifications, the palisades, the cannons on the ramparts, others at the bottom of the cliff. He had the positions of the buildings, the defences, and the weaponry all noted on a map. To the east, he made out scattered houses and the Montmorency Falls, at least eighty-seven metres high, sparkling in the sun.

Where to attack Quebec? The city was out of range of his cannons. To sail his ships into the basin in front of the city would be suicidal as long as the French had munitions for their own cannons. His map indicated a narrowing of the river near Pointe Lévy (Lauzon) on the south shore of the St. Lawrence. Wolfe's gaze turned toward its steep cliffs. He would position his army both on Île d'Orléans and on the heights of Pointe Lévy. In that way, he would control access to the basin.

The sky darkened. Wolfe returned to his camp. In the afternoon, a heavy rain poured down. Lightning lashed the countryside. In the shelter of the church, the Major-General watched as gusts of wind threw the ships one against the other. Seven transport ships dragged their anchors and ran aground.

Montcalm didn't want to engage in any hazardous attack against the English, but Vaudreuil insisted "that we get rid of them." During the night of June 28, in front of Beauport Church, he oversaw the operation that was underway. Loaded with tar, bombs, grenades, cannons stuffed with grapeshot, and muskets loaded to the hilt, five fire ships and two rafts were set afloat on the receding tide.

The moon gave off enough light that observers could follow their progress. Vaudreuil was delighted—the English would be done for!

Two English soldiers captured by the French at Chouaguen in 1756 had escaped and come to Île d'Orléans with the information that fire ships would try to set the English fleet ablaze during the night. The sentinels had no trouble identifying the black shapes of the ships in the darkness. Suddenly, the cannons of an English frigate began to roar. Under a rain of balls, the fire ships, now floating eruptions, drifted away from their target in a violent, but harmless, spectacle.

The next day, June 29, under the command of Brigadier-General Monckton, regular soldiers, rangers, and Highlanders waited to be transported, at the end of the afternoon, over to the river's south shore. Because of the low tide, some of the troops had to stay on Île d'Orléans. Those who were able to cross took control of the village of Beaumont without meeting any resistance.

It was June, but the cold covered the fields with frost. After shivering all night, those held back by the tide hastened, at dawn, to climb into the boats. When they set foot on land at seven in the morning, a detachment of *Canadiens* and natives fell upon them. The natives took a good twenty scalps. Their women and children mistreated a prisoner who was "of Irish origin and Catholic." Rangers ran up. To take revenge, they scalped nine of their victims and set fire to a house where women had taken shelter with their children.

Monckton had a proclamation from Major-General Wolfe affixed to the church door. It warned the people that they would not be able to resist the English army. It would become stronger still, as more brigades were en route. England and France were at war, but he assured them that England was not hostile to the people of Canada or their religion. Wolfe promised that after Quebec was taken, the people would be able to remain on their land and in their houses. He asked them not to get involved in a conflict between the French Crown and the English. If they took up arms against the soldiers, their homes and their harvests would be set afire, their churches burned. The powerful English fleet would block the arrival of provisions, and during the winter the people would suffer from starvation. They should not count on France; it could not help Canada. It was barely able to defend its own borders. The troops it had sent to Canada consumed the people's food and burdened the populace with all the weight of their oppression.

Few people knew how to read. Those who enjoyed that privilege came to explain the proclamation to the villagers hiding in the forest. They decided that the document should be torn off the church door and delivered to Monsieur de Vaudreuil.

On Sunday, July 1, the Quebec population was attending mass. Suddenly, cannon shot made the windows of the cathedral shake. The least pious rushed outside. In the middle of the basin, in front of Quebec, five French *carcassières* and a battery floating on a raft were pursuing two English frigates. On that day, four French *carcassières* bombarded Monckton's camp at Beaumont. Having suffered losses, Monckton marched his brigade toward Pointe Lévy. But Vaudreuil, who had anticipated the move, blocked their way with three hundred *Canadiens* and four hundred Abenakis and Odawas. Here and there, shots from among the branches reduced the number of English, who arrived in front of the church around three o'clock. It was occupied by *Canadiens* and natives. The battle raged for three hours. Finally, Monckton's men prevailed. During the night, Wolfe suffered an attack of his urinary ailment. He peed "bloody water." The next morning, Monckton's grenadiers found around their camp the bodies of several comrades, scalped and mutilated.

Major-General Wolfe and Vice-Admiral Saunders agreed that they would try to land on the north shore of the St. Lawrence, west of Quebec. The city's sentinels would be keeping their eyes on the English frigates at the western end of Île d'Orléans.

Early in the afternoon on July 4, a small boat approached Quebec, flying its flag for truce talks. Was the enemy coming to demand that the governor surrender the city? Three *carcassières* intervened. A truce for negotiation. A messenger had come with a letter from Major-General Wolfe to Monsieur de Vaudreuil. While he was on his way to Quebec, Wolfe had captured twenty-two Acadian women who were on a French ship. He asked permission to deliver those prisoners to Quebec. Some sailors on the boat had hands that were much too delicate; they were probably officers in disguise who had come to spy. Not fearing the cannons during the truce, an English frigate moved in, and its sailors sounded the depth of the waters in front of Quebec. The next day, the Acadian women were transferred from English to French rowboats between Pointe Lévy and Quebec. Despite the fact that he was suffering that day from "a sad attack of dysentery," Wolfe reminded his officers of the reason for their presence in Quebec: "The object of the campaign is to complete the conquest of Canada and to finish the war in America."

Colonel Murray's detachment, two hundred men in their boats, braved the cannons of Quebec, seeking a suitable site for landing the army on the north shore of the river, west of the city. Some stopped at Anse-des-Mères, between Cap Diamant and Anse-au-Foulon. Others went farther. On his return, the colonel proposed the hamlet of Saint-Michel as the landing site, at least a league west of Quebec, between Anse-au-Foulon and Sillery. Wolfe went to check the site. At the back of a cove, an incline made the terrain higher up accessible. There was no sign that the French were guarding that spot. On his return, he ordered the troops to prepare to make a landing and to attack. But Wolfe and his escort had been observed. Vaudreuil sent five hundred *Canadiens* and natives to monitor the north shore.

At Pointe-aux-Pères, on the south shore of the St. Lawrence, the river narrowed. Quebec was only half a league away. Thirty or so men began building levees. Fire from Quebec's lower town, and a rain of cannonballs, were launched to disrupt the work. But the English persevered, and oxen arrived with cannons and mortars. The engineers, with their lines, set the trajectories for the battery's cannons. Quebec is "a very fair object for our artillery, particularly the lower town," enthused one of Wolfe's young lieutenants, who was looking down on the city from above.

In the east, an English party was spied sounding the Montmorency River. Four canoes filled with natives were sent after them and tracked them as far as Île d'Orléans. Between five thirty and six thirty in the early evening, a floating battery and six French *carcassières* came to bombard the ships anchored at Pointe Lévy. The English, scattered here and there in front of Quebec, seemed not to know what had hit them. Montcalm found that reassuring. The sentinels in the lower town saw a man swimming in the St. Lawrence. Once brought on shore, he explained that he was from Paris, that he had been captured by the English at Louisbourg, and that he had been forced to join the British army . . .

Go all the way up to the village of Saint-Michel and then turn around and come all the way back down to take Quebec? Brigadier-General George Townshend threatened Wolfe with a parliamentary inquiry because he had not consulted his officers before making such a crucial decision. Townshend was very popular with Wolfe's officers. Despite his aristocratic attitude, said one of Wolfe's aides-de-camp, he "may be esteemed an excellent tavern acquaintance." Like all officers who wanted to sketch out their battle plans, Townshend had taken drawing courses at the military academy, but he also had a gift for picking out what was outlandish in someone and translating it into caricature. His drawings had already homed in on the bulbous corpulence of Cumberland. He had dared to render George II's nose in all its majesty. He had made comic portraits of his superiors, who had not always forgiven him for it. At the camp on Île d'Orléans, Townshend enjoyed drawing Wolfe's profile, narrow, with a long nose, projecting chin and brow, red hair braided into a mouse tail. Townshend displayed his drawing in the officers' mess. Wolfe had a different view of his office than that of being the inspiration for caricatures. Glaring at Townshend, he tore one of the drawings off the wall, crumpled it up, and went to consult Vice-Admiral Saunders about the landing at Saint-Michel.

Wolfe was aware that he did not know enough about the positioning of the enemy. And the flat-bottomed boats for transporting his army were still below Quebec. In this instance, Saunders hesitated to use rafts. Targeted by the city's batteries, they would not be very manoeuvrable. An alternative would be to anchor the ships in front of Beauport, east of Quebec, and to attack Montcalm's army camped there. The operation would be risky because, if exposed to the enemy, the English troops would be at a disadvantage. What is more, Mackellar the engineer had warned Wolfe that the long tongues of muddy earth that stretched out along the shore would prevent the boats from drawing alongside. The fusiliers would be too distant to fire salvos, and on landing, they would not be covered. But the impatient Wolfe didn't like shying away from an operation just because it was daring.

In the afternoon of July 8, Quebec's artillerymen tried again to interfere with the English activities at Pointe Lévy, while frigates and cutters took up positions opposite the camp of the marine troops and the *Canadien* militia on the heights above the Montmorency Falls. The cannons and mortars did not fall silent until the end of the day. If they were bothered by this attack, the Chevalier de Lévis's men suffered no damage from it, protected as they were by their elevation and their distance from the attackers.

Before dawn the next day, Wolfe landed three thousand men—grenadiers, soldiers, and rangers—on the shores of the hamlet Ange-Gardien, east of the Montmorency River. After ridding themselves of a band of *Canadiens* and natives that caused them some losses, they began to climb the rocky escarpment, which was wet and slippery due to the mist from the falls. The men grabbed onto bushes and tree branches, and clambered up until they reached the plateau at the top. Suspecting that natives would be lurking in the greenery, they quickly dug trenches, and put up a wall and earthworks. French prisoners had told them of the existence of three fords in winter and two in summer. Scouts went to find them.

The Chevalier de Lévis had watched the army as it approached. He'd been told about the fords higher up on the river. He'd gone himself to look at the sites and had returned persuaded that they were utterly impassable. James Johnstone, his aide-de-camp, a Jacobite Scotsman who had taken refuge in France and become a lieutenant and an interpreter for the marine troops of Île Royale, brought him a *Canadien* who had crossed the river the day before, carrying a sack of grain on his back. Immediately, Lévis sent a thousand men to stand guard at that spot. Barely had they arrived when four hundred natives appeared who for generations had been using the crossing, a league above the falls. On this day, the English were offering themselves up to them like mouth-watering game. The chief proposed to one of Lévis's lieutenants that his warriors and the French join forces to deal a blow to the invaders. The lieutenant sent a message to Lévis with the information and asked him for orders. Lévis sent a messenger to Vaudreuil, at least a league away, to give him the information and ask for orders. Vaudreuil replied by messenger that he would come himself to assess the situation. Two hours later, Vaudreuil arrived and talked to Lévis, who finally went to find the natives along with a strong detachment, while Montcalm rushed to the same place with grenadiers. The natives, so near the English and with such a long time to wait, were unable to suppress their warrior instincts and had come out of hiding. The rangers repelled them. When Montcalm and Lévis arrived, the natives had recrossed the ford.

The English were now dug in across from the French, on the east bank of the Montmorency River, where a ford was practicable. The governor general held a council of war. The forces of the English army were divided: they had men at the Montmorency River, at Pointe Lévy (a league and a half from Montmorency Falls), and at the east end of Île d'Orléans. These units were separated by the river. Each could be attacked without the others being able to come rapidly to its aid. Vaudreuil made his decision. The French had to take advantage of the situation. Intendant Bigot was also in favour of an immediate, forceful, decisive attack. The officers were more cautious. As for Montcalm, he opposed an initiative that might lose him many men.

There was very bad blood between Wolfe and Colonel Townshend, who by virtue of being well born had the support of powerful friends. Although of lower birth, Wolfe was his superior officer. Three years older, Townshend had contempt for Wolfe, this "fiery-headed fellow fit only for fighting." For Wolfe, Townshend was not a soldier. The major-general kept him on a short leash, all the more so because he was outraged that Townshend had threatened him with a parliamentary inquiry. Wolfe reproached Townshend for his slowness in relocating his brigade during a recent operation. On inspecting the parapet that Townshend's men had built at Montmorency Falls, Wolfe gave the colonel a lecture.

Why had he not built smaller redoubts that would require fewer men? When he left the camp for Pointe Lévy, Wolfe did not take the trouble to inform Townshend, even though the colonel was his second in command.

On July 10, the French battery "fired well" on the battery at Pointe-aux-Pères. Montcalm noted: "We have a great number of cannons, enough mortars, four thousand bombs, much ammunition, but we lack powder: and a lot could be said about that," he added, mysteriously. Arriving from the west, a flotilla of canoes came down the river toward Quebec. In the Upper Country, it had been learned that there was war in Quebec. For the Menominee, the Fox, the Saki, and the Cree, a good season of pillage seemed to be in the offing.

Prominent citizens of Quebec offered to form a detachment of volunteers to fight the English. How could Vaudreuil and Montcalm not applaud such patriotism? In the end, guided by Captain Jean-Daniel Dumas and armed with hunting rifles or staffs, two thousand brave bourgeois, workers, farmers, and seminarians, as well as a hundred or so volunteers from the regular army and two hundred Abenakis, marched to Sillery where they got into canoes, crossed the St. Lawrence, and scaled the cliff on the south shore. Once on the plateau, the warriors became very nervous.

Look! The enemy's moving, there, behind the trees! Shoot before they do! Seminarians found that they had shot their comrades. The group was terror-stricken. Captain Dumas was unable to impose order. Each person saw enemies everywhere. Each one fired before the English could attack. Each fled to escape the musketballs. These defenders of Quebec wounded each other, killed each other, mad with fear. Many deserted, sliding down the cliff face. Dumas soon had only 350 men left. They couldn't start a battle against seven hundred Englishmen. Confused and shamefaced, the survivors left for Quebec the next day at six in the morning.

The night before, lost, terrified, they had heard thundering and seen flashes of light. It was the English battery at Pointe-aux-Pères, raining its first projectiles down on Quebec, on July 12 at nine o'clock; "such a tremendous fire, that no human head can venture to peep up under it," in Wolfe's words.

There was dread in the city. The people, on the streets, tried to take shelter between burning houses. Mortars shot *pots-au-feu* charged with incendiary materials. The cathedral was hit, then the chapel and the Jesuit residence. Torn open by a thirty-two-pound cannonball, the presbytery collapsed. With the city in disarray, two English bomb vessels tried to get close to Quebec via the basin. The French battery stopped them. The bombardment calmed on July 13 at noon and then started up again. A ball crushed a woman who, fortunately, said the priest, "had confessed the day before."

And so the English were able to damage the city and terrorize the population. On the Quebec ramparts and in the lower town, the artillerymen asked themselves why Montcalm had expressly forbidden them to respond to the enemy fire in force. It was because the lieutenant-general was afraid of running out of powder. Between nine o'clock at night on July 13 and noon on the fourteenth, the English had unloaded three hundred bombs onto Quebec. On the night of July 15, the seminary was in flames. On the sixteenth, a bomb lit a fire that consumed a widow's residence as well as four neighbouring houses. Despite Montcalm's instructions to hold back, the French artillerymen let loose a "fire from hell" on the battery at Pointe-aux-Pères. In the city, there were wounded and dead. Infirmaries were improvised beneath the storm of iron and fire. Families fled to the neighbouring countryside. Others refused to leave. Some had nowhere to go.

36

"Let him amuse himself where he is"

At Sault Montmorency, on July 17, English grenadiers were busy cutting wood they needed to make oars. Suddenly, a band of natives pounced on them, killed five men, took their scalps, made three prisoners, seized muskets, and disappeared into the forest. The French, thought Wolfe, encouraged this barbarity because they were too cowardly to attack his troops themselves. They would pay the price.

The French received news from Lake Ontario. It was not good. Fifteen or so *Canadiens* who were to "harass" the English at Chouaguen had been killed, and Fort Niagara was being besieged by an impressive number of English troops.

At Quebec, during the night, aided by the rising tide and a favourable wind, the *Sutherland*, the *Squirrel*, two armed sloops, and two supply vessels succeeded in passing in front of the French battery which, at the foot of the cliff, guarded the basin. The flotilla had already passed Cap Diamant when a sentinel on the ramparts, with his megaphone, alerted the artillerymen positioned below. In the darkness, they couldn't see their targets. Drums and bugles called out the troops: the English were preparing to land! At dawn on July 19, Captain Dumas arrived at Sillery, west of Anse-au-Foulon, with six hundred men. He set up a battery there that would go by the name of Samos. Natives came to offer him their services. In the hours that followed, three hundred men and a cavalry unit came to add to the detachment.

Because the sentinels were dozing rather than keeping watch, six English ships had slipped by the French battery, and the English had thereby succeeded in making an audacious breakthrough west of Quebec. Montcalm now feared that the enemy would "intercept all our shipments of supplies and munitions." Vaudreuil and Montcalm had a gallows erected. Two sentinels were hanged for not having sounded the alarm.

Wolfe had made other reconnaissance forays in the area west of Quebec. Anse-au-Foulon, half a league away, seemed a possible site for a landing at Quebec . . .

During this time, on the other side of the city in the east, the French and English were camped on opposite sides of the Montmorency River above the falls, within hearing of each other, within mutual musket range, behind the breastworks their detachments had thrown up. Snipers traded shots from one shore to the other. On any pretext, the battery fired. Montcalm called for more restraint: "We must ask our natives, our soldiers, and our *Canadiens* to contain themselves somewhat when it comes to firing, because even though we may kill some of their people, I would deplore that our own may die."

It even happened that Lévis and Monckton, each on his own side, reviewed their troops at the same time. Separated by the river, they could size each other up. From time to time, one of the armies would wave a flag of truce. They lowered their arms. They accused each other of unwarranted aggression. They negotiated the freeing of prisoners. They threatened each other with destruction. Sometimes there was even a civilized conversation between officers. A meal was shared, with rum, with wine. On one of those occasions, an emissary from Montcalm said to Wolfe: "We have no doubt that you will destroy the city, but we've resolved that your army will never set foot inside its walls." Wolfe replied: "I will be master of Quebec if I have to stay here until the end of November."

Why was the French army, so near to its enemies, being kept waiting? wondered some of the soldiers busying themselves with work that would be unnecessary if they moved immediately to crush the adversary on the other side of the river. Montcalm struggled to keep his officers from being dragged into a confrontation. When the Chevalier de Lévis urged him to move quickly against the enemy, the lieutenant-general replied: "Let them amuse themselves where they are. If we drive them from there, they could go somewhere where they would do us harm." The *Canadien* militiamen were concerned. Food for their families and for their animals would be even scarcer if they did not return for the harvest . . . Despite the threat of harsh punishment, many deserted. What is more, the officers couldn't prevent famished settlers from coming out of the woods and going to Pointe Lévy to beg food from the English. On the ramparts of the upper town, an artilleryman saw a swimmer in the river, coming toward Quebec. He was English. He was interrogated. Montcalm couldn't ascertain whether he was a deserter or a spy.

One of Wolfe's officers congratulated himself on the work his artillerymen were doing, bombarding Quebec: "We have been so successful as scarce to leave a house in the place that is not battered down by our guns or burnt to ashes by our mortars." An English prisoner claimed that General Wolfe had had to reduce his troop's rations. That was good news for the French: the enemy was going to die of hunger! The prisoner also revealed that Wolfe encouraged his troops to go to farms and kill pigs and sheep to serve their own needs. The militiamen and the troops of the marine became worried. How would their aged parents, and their wives, be able to defend their animals? Under Carleton's orders, a reconnaissance picket approached shore between Sillery and Cap Rouge. A French sentinel, instead of sounding the alert, jumped into the river, swam through the strong current, and approached one of the English boats. He was helped aboard. It was well known that red English tunics had also deserted to the French.

As for Wolfe, on board a barge, he once again surveyed the river's north shore. From Cap Diamant to Cap Rouge, three leagues to the west, there was a steep cliff. Above, the land covered with spruce and beech was easy to defend. However, farther on, five and a half leagues from Quebec, the shore was more welcoming. On July 21, six hundred English soldiers landed at Pointe-aux-Trembles (Neuville). Houses they didn't burn, they pillaged. They killed cattle and sheep. They forced two hundred women, their children, and a missionary, Father Jean-Baptiste Labrosse, to get into the boats. Several women had come to the village to escape danger in Quebec. One of the officers leading the operation tried to reassure them. He spoke French, he knew Quebec, and he knew the members of its high society. This was Robert Stobo, who in 1745 had been a hostage in Quebec. Wolfe had promised that the English would let the French practise their Catholic religion. Father Labrosse was given permission to confess the women and to celebrate mass on board ship.

The next day, one of Wolfe's aides-de-camp asked to negotiate with Vaudreuil. He went to offer him the women, children, and Father Labrosse in exchange for permission to allow a barge loaded with wounded soldiers to pass in front of the Quebec batteries. Vaudreuil gave his consent. Landing at Anse-des-Mères around five o'clock in the evening, the women said they had been "treated with all possible consideration." Wolfe demanded that the sailors and soldiers give back everything they had taken from the French. They had to return to Father Labrosse the sacred vessels they had seized at the church. Some ladies had been invited to General Wolfe's table, where he had joked about the French generals who didn't want to fight. One of them found the English general "tall, extremely thin . . . and very ugly."

During the night of July 22, a dozen houses in Quebec were aflame on the rue de la Fabrique. A spark flew to a flag that was used to send messages to Montcalm's officers from the top of the cathedral steeple. The fabric caught fire, shreds of it fell onto the steeple's cedar shingles, the steeple burned and collapsed, and its three bells hurtled to the ground. By dawn, eighteen houses had been reduced to ashes.

Wagering that the French sentinels were dozing, Saunders tried to slip past the artillerymen. But they were not asleep. Nor were their cannons. Wolfe's aide-de-camp then accused the French of being "dirty fellows."

On July 24, Wolfe asked for another "lowering of arms." Many of his soldiers were ill at the camp on the Montmorency River. He needed permission for his boats carrying the sick to Île d'Orléans for treatment to pass in front of the French trenches at Beauport. The French hesitated. Isaac Barré, the son of a French Huguenot who had fled to Dublin, was Wolfe's adjutant-general. He made reference to the natives' massacre of English troops after Montcalm's taking of Fort George in 1757 and threatened that the French, *Canadiens*, and Indians would be "treated like a cruel and barbarous horde thirsting for blood." Montcalm penned Vaudreuil's response: "Nothing in all that will render us fearful nor barbarous." During the night, the English went for supplies to the stables of Ange-Gardien. The priest accused them of stealing twenty bulls and cows. In Quebec, the rumour circulated that they had taken a hundred and fifty.

Wolfe tried on many occasions to provoke a clash. For three weeks, the French held back. The parties exchanged balls and shot, but there was no battle. The French troops were like wet wood that would not catch fire. But when a flock of passenger pigeons appeared over the Montmorency River, in no time six hundred militiamen were after them! Wolfe was furious at Montcalm's elusive, persistent, exasperating defensiveness. Weeks had passed, and nothing had been accomplished. On July 25, he ordered his troops to "from now on burn and destroy everything, not sparing churches or buildings serving different purposes. Women and children, as I have already ordered, are not to be molested under any circumstances." That day, Major John Dalling's rangers plundered the humble dwellings in the village of Saint-Henri, about three leagues south of Pointe Lévy, and took 250 prisoners, men, women, and children. They also made off with livestock and horses. Major Dalling left a notice on the church door: "His Excellency, offended by the lack of regard on the part of the residents of Canada concerning his notice of June 29 last, is resolved no longer to heed those human feelings that would incline him to bring comfort to people blind to their own interests." Montcalm judged that now the English "would attack nowhere, but would seek to cut off our supplies and to render the land desolate."

Since Wolfe's proclamation, the *Canadiens* had been profoundly uneasy. If they defended their country, whatever they owned would be destroyed by the English. And Montcalm would not tolerate that the populace make "its separate peace." On July 25, he wrote in a letter to the Chevalier de Lévis: "We would need a large detachment of natives and *Canadiens* to bring them to heel."

The movements of the English west of Quebec seemed to indicate that they were preparing an incursion from that direction. Montcalm posted eight hundred men between Anse-des-Mères and the mouth of the Jacques-Cartier River. At Sault Montmorency, the days were punctuated by reciprocal gunfire over the river. Then everything would go quiet . . . and begin again. In Quebec, every night, cannonballs fell.

The ruined dwellings, the abandoned storehouses, shops, and workshops were tempting to thieves. Anyone found in possession of objects not belonging to him was condemned to death and executed the same day.

One night, two young French soldiers—sixteen and twenty years old—stole a barrel of eau-de-vie from the basement of a gutted building. Thinking that the noise from the bombardment would hide what they were doing, they rolled the barrel along the rue Saint-Roch, but they were caught. Their trial took place at ten in the morning, and by the afternoon their two bodies were hanging from ropes.

In the dead of night on July 28, seventy rafts loaded with incendiary material and explosive projectiles drifted toward the English ships moored at the west end of Île d'Orléans. The explosions were at first modest; then the percussive fire increased in intensity, and they became volcanic. But no English ship was damaged. A priest interpreted the misadventure: "It seems that God does not want us to burn our enemies."

37

"That man must end with a great effort, a thunderbolt"

Wolfe had a new plan. He would take possession of the two French redoubts located on the Beauport coast, west of the Montmorency River rapids. Feeling that he would die during the battle, he added codicils to his will.

At eight in the morning on July 31, at Pointe Lévy, the grenadiers from the 60th Royal American Regiment of Foot who had served under Wolfe's command at Louisbourg, and two regiments of soldiers, boarded their boats. The fleet moved into the channel north of Île d'Orléans. From the Quebec ramparts, the French watched the manoeuvre. Montcalm had warned the officers of the tricks the English would play to dupe them. "They will make a false attack, they'll try to make it seem serious by covering the water with boats and barges holding only three or four men in each one." But the officers could see through their telescopes that the boats were full. At ten o'clock, the *Centurion*, an English frigate with fifty-four cannons, came to moor in the channel between Île d'Orléans and the Beauport coast. The tide was high, but the water was shallow. At eleven thirty, two transport ships, each armed with twenty cannons, approached the shore. They ran aground in front of the redoubts. Therefore the *Centurion* advanced cautiously. Still far from shore, it ran aground as well, but nothing stopped its cannons, which began firing fiercely. At almost five hundred yards from the redoubts, the balls caused only minor damage. At the same time, from the cliff-top at Montmorency Falls, the English battery fired its six mortars and thirty cannons. The French defended themselves. Wolfe, on the bridge of the *Centurion*, took in the situation. A ball wrenched away the stick he held in his hand.

At one thirty, two thousand Englishmen from the Montmorency camp headed toward the height of the river, in the direction of the ford. Montcalm put out the call to arms and rushed to Lévis's camp. "We agreed that we would fight as seemed best at the time," said Lévis. Five hundred militiamen, regulars, and natives sealed off the ford from the colonial enemy.

Despite the setback he'd encountered at the two redoubts, Wolfe took the measure of the French defences: "Their confusion and disorder incline me to attack them," he said to one of his officers. And so 350 boats moved out from Pointe Lévy and entered the channel north of Île d'Orléans. From their fortifications on the north shore, the French watched this army forming before their eyes. At four in the afternoon, the tide dropped. The strips of sand forced the ships to stay far from shore. The English battery on the Montmorency River, the cannons and mortars of the *Centurion*, the muskets and guns of the two stranded transport ships, as well as the boats that had just arrived, let loose on the French fortifications. At five o'clock, when Wolfe judged that their adversaries had been weakened by the bombardment, he gave the signal to attack. The row-boats made a dash for shore, but strong currents carried them off course. Some brave fighters jumped into the water to walk to land, not thinking that their munitions would be soaked. Wolfe's soldiers were exposed to French fire. Monckton, the soldiers of the 60th Royal American Regiment of Foot, and the Louisbourg grenadiers managed to land not far from the redoubts, while Townshend's and

Murray's brigades, which had landed below Montmorency Falls, prepared to cross the river to join up with Monckton's army. Instead of waiting for them, Monckton's men fixed their bayonets to their muskets and advanced with their drums beating out the *March of the Grenadiers.*

Wolfe found this behaviour "strange." Apparently, the night before, a Scottish officer and a "German comrade" had clashed in a sword fight. One had been seriously injured, but he'd insisted on coming to fight against the French, despite his "scratch." When the troops set foot on land, the two officers found themselves by coincidence side by side. One challenged the other. Without waiting for orders, the officers spurred their grenadiers into a race toward the enemy.

At the top of the slope, behind their embankments, the *Canadien* militiamen watched the grenadiers, out of breath, struggling up the spongy terrain. They were being cut down both by the projectiles from the fortifications and by those from the eastern redoubt.

Above the falls, the English column that was going to try to cross the ford turned about when it saw the French. Lévis directed the fire of his militia and grenadiers down onto the assailants. Under the onslaught, bodies tumbled into the legs of those scaling the steep incline. The sky was heavy with black clouds. Rain began to fall, whipped by the wind. The thunder of the storm joined with that of the cannons. The English withdrew.

Townshend's and Murray's troops crossed the river at the foot of the falls. They attacked the second redoubt, on the west side. It was seven o'clock. The rising tide would soon cover the ford. The boats would be farther off from shore. Wolfe's brigades would be prisoner to the French. Half his army would risk death from fire or water. Wolfe ordered a retreat.

The wounded were loaded into the boats. The soldiers, wet

through, smeared with mud and blood, didn't want to stop fighting. Soldiers and officers defied the French to come out of their fortifications, to come down the slope, to confront them face to face. "The *poltrons*, who were twice our numbers, dared not come down to us," said one officer. Their bravado didn't last. Natives came running. The soldiers threw themselves into the river and headed for the boats. In the rising tide, the boats were far from shore. Several men drowned.

Montcalm rushed up and congratulated Lévis. What a glorious day for France! The Quebec garrison celebrated the victory. Montcalm judged that "the *Canadiens* have done very well."

Vice-Admiral Saunders had his two transport ships that were stranded in front of the redoubts set afire to keep them from falling into French hands. In the smoking ruins, the French found twelve cannons, munitions that hadn't exploded, provisions, ploughshares, and thirty-four picks.

It was a bitter defeat for Wolfe. Forty-seven of his men had been killed and four hundred wounded. The attack was a "foolish business." The next morning, in the orders of the day, he severely criticized the grenadiers for their "impetuous, irregular and unsoldierlike" conduct. Wolfe blamed Vice-Admiral Saunders for having landed his men in front of the French redoubts, rather than east of the Montmorency River, where they could have landed safely. From there, they could have crossed at the ford to then march on the French.

To make up for this defeat, Wolfe had to make clear to the enemy his determination to take Canada. The battery at Pointe-aux-Pères rained incendiaries and balls on Quebec. Wolfe ordered the destruction of the Baie-Saint-Paul settlements, and the burning of the buildings running from the village of Saint-Joachim to the Montmorency River. He ordered the settlements razed between the Chaudière and Etchemin rivers. He sent Monckton to destroy the arms and munitions depot the French had moved to Trois-Rivières.

In a letter to Wolfe, a wounded English captain whom a French soldier had transported to the General Hospital described the fine care he had received from the nuns. Wolfe expressed his gratitude and promised them protection when the army took control of their convent. He enclosed in his letter a sum of twenty pounds for the soldier who had saved the captain. Vaudreuil returned the money to Wolfe—the soldier, he explained, was only doing his duty.

Since his arrival, Wolfe had made several plans for taking Quebec. One of Vice-Admiral Saunders's officers complained of Wolfe's indecision to Governor Lawrence in Halifax: "Within the space of five hours, we rec'd at the general's request, three different orders of consequence, which were contradicted immediately of their reception; which indeed has been the constant practice of the gen[eral] ever since we have been here; . . . I'm told he asks no one's opinion and wants no advice."

The bombardment of Quebec continued "as usual," but some English soldiers no longer seemed to want to fight. On August 4, five deserters gave themselves up to the militia, near the Chaudière River. Three other English deserters took refuge in the forest with the inhabitants of Pointe Lévy.

Montcalm learned, on August 5, that Fort Carillon had been destroyed during the last week of July. Its garrison had blown it up so that the English could not take it. The French flag had flown there since Samuel de Champlain had raised it in 1608. After holding on for four days against the English army, the unfortunate garrison had put its cannons out of commission and withdrawn on the night of July 26, blowing up the fort. The explosion woke the enemy.

South of Lake Champlain, all that was left to the French was Fort Saint-Frédéric. So that the English wouldn't take it, supplies and munitions were loaded into boats. Then women, children, workers, farmers, the sick, the wounded, soldiers, volunteers, and sailors got on board. On July 31, the engineer stuffed the furnaces with explosives. The blast was heard far off, from the boats.

At two o'clock on the night of August 6, English boats slipped past the Quebec batteries and joined up with thirty other allied boats gathered around four ships in front of Pointe-aux-Trembles. Three English regiments were posted across the way, on the south shore of the river. In the face of this new threat, Montcalm immediately reinforced Bougainville's detachments, which were inadequate and, what was more, scattered on the north shore above Quebec. An English deserter claimed that French warships had been spotted to the east, lower down on the river. Montcalm didn't dare believe it, but he hoped it was true.

On August 8, boats bearing a few hundred men under Murray's orders tried with difficulty to land at Pointe-aux-Trembles, seven leagues from Quebec. Rocks were poking through the water. Two hundred men commanded by Bougainville were waiting for them in ambush. Bougainville did not let the enemy step on land. Under fire, the English turned on their heels and scrambled toward their boats. Several didn't make it. Other boats arrived. And still others, more than a thousand men. In the end, the English lost four hundred men, according to the French. The English reported a loss of a hundred and forty.

At night, the mortars rained incendiaries on Quebec, and fire consumed several buildings, including the church of Notre-Dame-des-Victoires in the lower town. To the east, the hundred and fifty rangers of Captain John Gorham, having arrived at Saint-Paul, executed Wolfe's orders and set fire to everything the populace had built and grown, as well as all they possessed.

Governor General Vaudreuil convened a council of war. Two armies were marching on Canada: one toward Fort Île aux Noix, and the other toward Fort La Présentation. Should they relax Quebec's defence to go and contain the advance of those armies?

Chevalier de Lévis was to leave to study the situation on those two frontiers. He would take command of the one he judged was most threatened. Montcalm thought of Bourlamaque, who was at Lake Champlain, then of Lévis, who would be at the frontier of his choice, then of himself, at Quebec. His thoughts were darker than the night sky: "I don't know which of us will be defeated first."

During the "standard cannonade" of the city, the enemy boats coming up the river at night to defy the batteries were more and more numerous. The English seemed to want to retreat from the Montmorency River. Boats brought no fewer than twenty-five cannons to face Pointe-aux-Trembles and Saint-Antoine-de-Tilly on the south shore, where the English burned down houses and barns. The church, which they spared, served as their hospital.

According to three deserters, German Catholics, Wolfe would lift the siege on September 1 if Amherst's army didn't come to join his own. According to what the deserters said, the Battle of Montmorency had cost the English dearly. Wolfe had no more than five thousand men in combat condition, and sickness was ravaging his troops. What is more, the deserters insisted that they had sighted twenty-six large French ships and several frigates. Could Montcalm still believe this good news? Other deserters, an Englishman and two Germans, had also talked about an imminent departure of the English army.

In the villages and the hamlets, the people feared more than the English. Natives stormed into houses, helped themselves from the cooking pots, grabbed objects that tempted them, went to the stable, took a bull, a cow, a horse, fowl . . . In one instance, under the very eyes of the horrified owner, they killed thirteen sheep.

On August 18, a thousand Englishmen landed at Deschambault, on the north shore, nine leagues west of Quebec. In their search for an arms and munitions depot, Brigadier Murray's men burned three houses. The French had stored the officers' silverware in one of them. They had also hidden there 1,800 *livres* in cash. After emptying out the arms depot, the English led a hundred horned animals to the church, which they turned into an abattoir. When Bougainville's cavalry came up, they re-embarked. The villagers had taken two prisoners. One of them swore that Vice-Admiral Saunders had been ordered to return with his fleet as fast as he could, to defend Ireland, which had been invaded by the French.

Every day, Captain Gorham and six hundred rangers laid waste to houses, stables, mills, and grain harvests on the south shore. They burned down the village of Saint-Nicolas. They destroyed the village of Saint-François on Île d'Orléans. On August 22, the rangers set up their field cannons at Saint-Anne-de-Beaupré. Thirty or so parishioners, alerted by the priest, barricaded themselves in a stone house and fired from the windows. On August 24, the houses of Ange-Gardien and Château-Richer were in flames. At Saint-Joachim, the rangers came upon a dozen old men and invalids who, gathered around the priest, threw themselves on their knees and begged for mercy. It was said in the streets of Quebec that they were killed with sabre blows. The rangers set the church on fire, even took some scalps, despite Wolfe's warning not to emulate "the inhumane practice of scalping except when enemies are Indians, or *Canadiens* dressed like Indians."

The English had scalped the populace! Montcalm was furious: "The English, faithfully imitating the ferocity of our savages, have taken the scalps of some of our people on the south shore. Can one believe that a civilized nation would set itself in cold blood to mutilating the dead?"

Other English deserters claimed that Boston was being besieged by a Spanish fleet. Louisbourg and Chibouctou (Halifax) were threatened by a French fleet . . . This information, impossible to verify, brought a little hope to a besieged Quebec, whose defenders were more and more despairing. Two French soldiers at the Montmorency River ran toward the woods to desert. One was brought down by musket fire. The other, who was captured, had his head "broken" in front of the governor general's residence.

Despite rumours to the contrary, the English remained well dug in at the Montmorency River. As the soldiers slept in their tents at night, the natives riddled them with balls. Montcalm noted in his diary: "If we could have the natives with us and make them act with caution, we'd destroy the English army."

During the night of August 27, the frigate *Lowestoft* and three smaller vessels passed in front of the Quebec batteries, but French *carcassières* forced them to turn back. In the morning, an English sergeant from the Montmorency River camp presented himself, with his hands up, to the French. He said he had fled after having killed an officer in a quarrel. The enemy troops, he revealed, were much affected by fever and diarrhea. General Wolfe himself was very sick. It was said that he might not survive . . . And England was calling on help from all its armies to counter a French invasion in Ireland. The sergeant also knew that before heading back to Great Britain, Vice-Admiral Saunders would attempt a landing in the Quebec harbour.

At about nine o'clock at night, five English ships were before Quebec. In his haste, a cannoneer set fire to a powder charge which, on exploding, killed two French artillerymen and wounded thirteen others. The ships went through, and the next day, in front of Saint-Augustin (about three leagues west of Quebec), the two largest ships in the fleet, with twenty-four and fourteen cannons respectively, were blocking any convoy from carrying supplies and ammunition to Quebec.

Wolfe was feeling better, to the "inconceivable joy of the whole army," exclaimed the young lieutenant John Knox. On August 29, he felt strong enough to dictate a letter to his brigadiers Townshend, Monckton, and Murray, asking them to consider the best way to attack the enemy, and to examine the three alternative plans he'd devised for the final assault on Quebec. First, a general attack with all the ships of the fleet, which would moor in front of Beauport. Or a part of the army might cross the ford above Montmorency Falls and march through the woods to come out behind the French at Beauport, while the rest attacked face on. Or, finally, the entire army might cross the ford at the mouth of the Montmorency River, march west along the shore, and make a frontal attack on the French fortifications.

France had not forgotten Canada. On August 29, Berryer, minister of colonies, signed a devastating letter to Intendant Bigot: "You tell me that instead of sixteen million, your drain on the treasury for 1758 will come to twenty-four million, and this year will rise to thirty-one to thirty-three million. It seems that there are no limits to the expenses in Canada." These expenses "have made the fortunes of all those who had a hand in them . . ."

Wolfe's brigadiers, after consulting Vice-Admiral Saunders, informed him that they rejected all three plans.

38

A "wary old fellow"

Despite his poor health, Wolfe was determined not to return to England defeated, "to be exposed to censure and reproach of an ignorant populace." He would not come before Miss Katherine Lowther as a vanquished man. His brigadiers advised him to land on the north shore, upstream from Quebec. Wolfe saw many difficulties in that proposal. Had they not already lost enough men? He would not sacrifice the rest of his army in an action that was too risky. But if it succeeded . . . what a victory it would be!

On August 31, he wrote to his mother: "The Marquis de Montcalm is at the head of a great number of bad soldiers, & I am at the head of a small number of good ones . . . but the wary old fellow avoids an action, doubtfull of the behaviour of the army."

At eleven o'clock at night, five English ships, including the frigate *Sea Horse*, manoeuvred in front of the Quebec battery, while other ships from the English fleet, in the west, bombarded the church of Saint-Augustin, where the parishioners were holed up, armed with their hunting rifles. After 150 cannon shots from their ships, the English soldiers landed. It was reported in Quebec that twenty villagers had forced the English army and navy to retreat. Those *Canadiens* were said to have had more courage than the soldier from the Royal-Roussillon who went that day to offer his services to the English.

On September 1, the English struck their tents at the Montmorency River camp. No fewer than seventeen English ships sailed up the river to Sillery during the night. Admiral Charles Holmes's squadron, above Quebec, now numbered twenty-two ships. One of the last to arrive, the *Terror of France*, a schooner, had passed in broad daylight in front of the Quebec artillerymen. Furious at such insolence, they had let loose with their cannon fire. The schooner had continued on its way as if everything were normal. During the night, two frigates even came to moor alongside Vaudreuil's headquarters at La Canardière. They were driven off by the battery before they dropped anchor.

On the north shore, to the east, from the Montmorency River to Cap Tourmente, five and a half leagues from Quebec, houses, stables, barns, and storehouses had been razed. The English had also destroyed the preserved fish and the boats. Fortunately, the grain was sometimes too green to catch fire.

The officers and the population feared a new English attack. Others thought the English were preparing to leave Canada, because at the Montmorency River the troops had brought their cannons, belongings, and provisions down to the boats. On September 3, the last of the English left the camp, setting fire to the fortifications. Montcalm congratulated himself on having resisted those who had urged him to attack the English as they left. He wrote: "Monsieur Wolfe was waiting in ambush with two thousand five hundred men."

Below Quebec, the English had abandoned Montmorency Falls. Above, nineteen French ships were on guard, and Bougainville's troops patrolled the north shore. Montcalm breathed more easily: "I am doing my best, and I have not removed my clothes since June 23."

On the night of September 4, no fewer than forty English boats passed safely in front of the cannons at Quebec. A deserter claimed that the English were going to feint an attack on Cap Rouge but that the real landing would take place at Quebec. If the English failed, they would leave Canada. While sceptical, Montcalm asked the Guyenne Regiment to take up position on the Plains of Abraham. This was how people referred to a field, not far from the ramparts, belonging to the farmer Abraham Martin.

The next day, September 5, Murray's five battalions marched toward the Etchemin River on the south shore of the St. Lawrence, followed by the three battalions of Townshend and Monckton. The battery at Samos (Sillery), on the opposite shore, erupted to no effect. Those 3,600 men boarded Rear-Admiral Holmes's ships, which were waiting for them. Laid low by a recurrence of his illness, Wolfe was carried on by soldiers.

Vice-Admiral Saunders was anxious to head home before the autumn, with its stormy seas. The Montmorency River camp had been abandoned, the batteries at Pointe Lévy had been dismantled, and several ships were sailing east toward Kamouraska. Meanwhile, troops were boarding ships above Quebec. All these movements seemed to confirm the reports of prisoners and deserters: The English were leaving! Vaudreuil asserted: "Everything indicates that the English grand design has failed." But he did not let down his guard. He reminded Bougainville and his men, who were with the natives at Anse-au-Foulon, Sillery, and Cap Rouge, that "the salvation of the colony is in your hands."

Wolfe often said: "A good spirit will carry a man through everything." On September 6, he was back on his feet. Townshend rejoiced in his fashion in a letter to his wife: "General Wolfe's health has been very bad and in my opinion his generalship is not a bit better." Once more, despite his weakness, Wolfe scanned the north shore of the

St. Lawrence through his telescope. He observed, at the top of the cliff at Anse-au-Foulon, the presence of a few tents. He noticed on the escarpment, among bushes and scrub, a steep path that seemed to lead upward. So it was possible to scale that cliff...

That night, in the cabin of the *Sutherland*'s captain, he met with Rear-Admiral Holmes and Captain James Chads. Then he went to bed, more than ever determined to apply in Quebec the lessons he had learned during the failed operation at Rochefort in 1757. Time must not be frittered away in futile debate when the moment had come to draw your sword. No obstacle should be considered insurmountable before you had tried to overturn or overcome it. He wrote: "In war, something must be allowed to chance or fortune, seeing it is in its nature hazardous and an option of difficulties." Being a major-general, Wolfe had the lives of his men in his hands, but "in particular circumstances and times, the loss of 1,000 men is rather an advantage to a nation than otherwise, seeing that gallant attempts raise its reputation and make it respectable." Wolfe wrote out his instructions to his officers.

On September 7, a clear day, Rear-Admiral Holmes's ships sailed up the St. Lawrence. At the Quebec batteries, the French artillerymen saw the bridges crowded with men in red uniforms. On the south shore of the St. Lawrence, four thousand English soldiers were marching to the west in the direction of Saint-Antoine-de-Tilly. Two thousand French soldiers and militia rushed to Pointe-aux-Trembles on the other side of the river to prevent a landing on the north shore. Holmes's ships dropped anchor in front of Cap Rouge. The gorge into which the river flowed was defended by a floating battery, and the shore by a long parapet of earth and tree trunks. Bougainville and his soldiers from the regular army, troops from the marine, plus his militiamen and his cavalry watched the enemy approach.

At the sight of Holmes's ships, the cavalry dismounted from their horses and, with the infantry, formed a line that, on command, ran shouting to take up position behind the parapet. On one of the ships, a captain mocked the noise made by the French: "How nobly awful and expressive of true valour is the customary silence of British troops."

In the afternoon, the English artillery bombarded Bougainville's fortifications with cannon fire, while the English troops left their ships to board boats that went up or down the river. It seemed obvious that the English were looking for a place to land. Because of the heavy rain that began to fall, Wolfe was forced to cancel the landing. The boats returned one by one in the direction of the ships. The rain didn't stop. The soldiers were soaked. The officers were concerned, because even more men would be sick. Half the force was brought back on land. The soldiers set up their quarters in the village of Saint-Nicolas. Had they not burned down the houses a few days earlier, they would have had roofs over their heads and stoves where they could dry their clothes.

On September 9, the natives from the Upper Country left for their villages, disappointed that the war had not taken place. Some, it was said, had to travel seven hundred leagues to get home. That day, in the city of Quebec, where the population was subject to the constant, crippling fear of being invaded by a heartless enemy, a master cannoneer and a young seventeen-year-old sailor, both part of the battery on the ramparts, were hanged for having robbed the residence of Sieur Marin, a member of high society.

In front of Cap Rouge, the boats of Holmes's squadron went upriver with the tide and back down as the tide lowered. Persuaded that the enemy was going to land, Bougainville did not want to be taken unawares. Night and day, his men, exhausted, drowsy, walked along the shore to keep watch.

On September 10, Major George Scott's detachment, fulfilling its mission of ravaging the south shore, arrived in Kamouraska, where it set fire to 165 houses, stables, and other buildings. That day, the commanders of the Royal Navy held a meeting on the flagship. The officers of the ground forces were demoralized by the campaign's lack of success. Their men were sapped by illness. Autumn was coming with its storms and strong currents, both on the river and at sea. Almost unanimously, the officers advocated lifting the siege.

Wolfe pleaded for a bit of patience. Along with Townshend, a few other officers, and the engineer Mackellar, he went back to examine the cliff at Anse-au-Foulon on the north shore of the river, to see whether it would be possible to scale it. If the cliff proved too steep, Wolfe would return to England, saddened by his failure but satisfied that he had done all that was possible. Vice-Admiral Saunders agreed to delay his fleet's departure.

That night, Montcalm predicted to Bougainville that the enemy would stay "another month or perhaps less." He raised the numbers in Bougainville's detachment keeping watch on the coast between Cap Rouge and the Jacques-Cartier River to three thousand. As for the cliff at Anse-au-Foulon, Montcalm thought it impassable. Vaudreuil had never shared that opinion, but Montcalm, on July 29, had mocked the governor general's fears: "We must not think that the enemy has wings, that he might in the same night cross over, land, negotiate broken terrain, and climb." Montcalm then assured him, with conviction: "I swear to you that a hundred men positioned there will stop their army." And if that were not the case? "Captain Vergor . . . in case of an unlikely emergency . . . could ask for help from the Guyenne Battalion, which is camped not far from the Plains of Abraham." Nearby also was the Samos battery, held by seventy men, and a little farther on, the heights of Sillery, guarded by 130 men. If the alarm were sounded, they could rush to Vergor's aid. Bougainville's detachments could also intervene. On September 12, much preoccupied by the enemy's movements, Vaudreuil insisted that Montcalm send a battalion to back up Vergor. "We'll see to it tomorrow," promised the lieutenant-general.

During this time, Major Scott's rangers continued their destructive mission. At Cap-au-Diable, they set fire to fifty-five buildings and stole animals from the farms. At Rivière-Ouelle, they torched 121 buildings, including many houses. A messenger by the name of Danseville, from the fort at Île aux Noix, France's last obstacle to the English progress toward Montreal, reported that the *Canadien* militiamen had deserted and gone back to their fields to take in the harvest. Brigadier Bourlamaque raged against Vaudreuil's spinelessness in not having the traitors shot.

Where and when would the British attack? The French could not say. Perhaps they would leave without attacking . . . Many hoped that would be the English general's decision.

The French army's reserves of ammunition were limited; the food stocks for the army and the people were lower still. The British had the capacity to block any supply convoy. The *Canadiens* were exhausted by these wars. They were tired of their poverty and of paying too much for necessities. They were tired of the privileges of those ladies and gentlemen who lived a life of abundance. There were detachments of the French army, it was said, that were ready to join the British forces.

Major-General James Wolfe finally announced that on that night, September 12, 1759, the King's Army would launch its assault on the city of Quebec. The decision had to be kept absolutely secret. The first detachment to reach shore had to march immediately on the enemy's defences, whatever they were, and crush them. That was the key to victory. The officers were to make sure that the detachments would not fire, whether in error, clumsiness, or neg-lect, into the backs of those preceding them. After scaling the cliff, the battalions would re-form and would hold themselves ready to charge, forcing the French to fight. Officers and men in the ranks had to think of what Great Britain expected of them. They had to keep in mind what determined, experienced, and hardened soldiers were capable of achieving in war.

On the south shore, at Saint-Nicolas, the English troops that had gone down to camp in the village ruins were recalled to their ships.

On board Holmes's ships, 3,600 men and officers were at the ready. Wolfe had asked Colonel Ralph Burton to transfer to him all the men who were not indispensable at Pointe Lévy or Île d'Orléans. That would increase his forces by 1,200 men.

Although he wished he had already left Quebec, Vice-Admiral Saunders supported Wolfe's operation. Despite certain differences of opinion, the two officers had forged a friendship grounded in their commitment to serving the king. While Wolfe would go west to Anse-au-Foulon, Saunders would launch a diversionary man-oeuvre in the east.

The bombardment of Quebec began again, as if the mortars could still set fire to what had already burned. At Île d'Orléans, the English sailing ships moved about, exchanging signals that the French could not interpret. While the day was still bright, Saunders's fleet, perfectly visible, positioned itself in front of Beauport. An officer ran to Montcalm: boats, in great number, filled with the enemy, were approaching shore! A general alarm. The troops had to arm themselves and go to the fortifications! Montcalm was to be kept informed of all the English movements above Quebec. His secretary went to Vaudreuil with the latest information. Saunders's aggressive move on Beauport proved to Montcalm that the English activity west of Quebec was only a diversion. Taking the measure of the enemy fleet in front of his camp, he congratulated himself on having increased the number of cannons, but he feared for the boats that were to bring in supplies this night: "I tremble that they might be taken, and that this loss be our ruin, with no recourse, because we have provisions only for a few days."

In front of Cap Rouge, Holmes's squadron stood fast: thirty-five large ships at anchor, to which empty boats were moored. On board, the men did not yet know that they would be fighting that night. Wolfe had seen to it that no deserter would warn the French. Only a few officers knew where the landing would take place. Colonel William Hall was in charge of the advance party, made up of twenty-four volunteers. During the day, two French deserters from Bougainville's camp had confirmed that the heights at Anse-au-Foulon were weakly protected. They also indicated that, at low tide that night, a supply convoy would be headed to Montcalm's camp at Beauport. Deserters often lied, but Wolfe did not dismiss this information.

He slept a little in the evening. His faithful servant, François, woke him, shaved him, served him some food, helped him put on his linen shirt with the cuffs and jabot for which he had paid "too dearly," his white trousers, his embroidered vest, his leather gaiters, his scarlet tunic with gold buttons, and his sword belt embroidered with gold thread. Dressed in his three-cornered hat, Major-General Wolfe called a school friend, the officer John Jervis, to his cabin. Wolfe told him that he expected to die in this battle. Jervis tried to reassure him: doubtless these dark thoughts were due to fatigue. Wolfe took from his neck a miniature portrait of Katherine Lowther and asked his comrade to return it to his fiancée after his death.

39

"I don't think you'll make it . . ."

During the night of September 13, at one in the morning, two lanterns were hung on the trestle tree of the *Sutherland*'s maintop. They signalled to the troops where they would meet. Wolfe, on the bridge, received the latest reports: Adjutant-General Barré had distributed the troops among the boats, and there remained seven hundred men in reserve on the ships. Colonel Howe had given his advance party the information it needed: Captain Chads would guide the convoy toward the landing spot that he had carefully surveyed with Wolfe. Chads confirmed that the boats loaded with men were gathered together in good order near the *Sutherland*. Rear-Admiral Holmes announced that at three in the morning the ships, one by one, would start down the river toward the landing site.

All the lamps were out. Captain Chads demanded absolute silence from his men. In every boat, there were ten oarsmen. With the ebb tide pressing them on, Chads asked them to avoid the creaking of the oarlocks under pressure from the oars. The men were seated back to back, their muskets upright between their knees. Major-General Wolfe, wearing a frock coat, found himself a place with Captain William DeLaune and his picket of grenadiers, who would be the first to try scaling the cliff.

One after the other, the boats soon formed a four-hundred-metre ribbon between the black water and the dark sky. They could be attacked without warning by French *carcassières*, by Indian canoes . . . Many of the soldiers they carried would be dead before morning. The men were pensive, under the stars. The boats kept their distance from the rocks on the south shore. Nor could they go too near the north shore, where French sentinels were watching. The operation unfolded as planned. The rumbling of cannons echoed far off in the night. The feigned attack on the Beauport fortifications, some three leagues to the east, was in progress. A great reader, Wolfe thought of Alexander the Great before Hydaspes: a larger army was waiting with its elephants on the opposite side of the turbulent river. Thanks to deceptions that forced the enemy to divide its troops, Alexander was able to cross the water when the enemy was not expecting it. Wolfe thought also of the poem *Elegy Written in a Country Churchyard*, which Katherine Lowther had offered him when he was leaving for the campaign in Canada. He repeated a line that haunted him: "The paths of glory lead but to the grave."

Holmes gradually let the cargo ships leave, which would provide support for the soldiers on the boats. Around three thirty in the morning, the rowers began to tire in the strong currents. Following Chads, their guide, the boats turned in the direction of the dark wall that was the cliff on the north shore. The night obscured any possible landmark. The cliff was the same everywhere. Chads didn't know exactly where he was. He could barely make out the signals of light from the *Hunter*, anchored at least a nautical mile from the south shore. In the darkness, the landscape's features blurred together. Suddenly, a French voice called out: "Who goes there?" Having anticipated possible encounters with the sentinels, Wolfe had taken the precaution of including two French-speaking

Highlanders in Chads's boat. One of them replied: "France! Long live the king!" The voice in the darkness asked: "What regiment?" The Highlander replied: "The Queen's." The sentinel said, "Speak louder, we can't hear you." The Highlander shot back: "Be quiet. There are English nearby, they're going to hear us." Another French voice ordered: "Let them pass. They're our people with supplies." Chads was almost certain, then, that he was in front of Sillery, facing the Samos battery.

Anse-au-Foulon was less than half a league away. Chads asked the rowers to go slowly. He didn't want to pass their destination. His eyes scanned the cliff, lost in the darkness. The "naked rock," the opening, the path he'd scrutinized so carefully with Wolfe, seemed to have vanished. Given the time that had passed, Chads estimated that they must have reached the place chosen by Wolfe. He signalled that they should approach the shore. At four o'clock, the first soldiers jumped onto the gravel strand, happy to be able to move their stiff limbs. Wolfe didn't recognize the cliff he'd studied during the day. Chads had gone a hundred yards too far downstream; he'd reached Anse-des-Mères rather than Anse-au-Foulon.

The cliff rose up, forbidding. Could they climb here? Time was of the essence; they had to surprise the French. Wolfe challenged DeLaune and his front-runners. "I don't think you'll make it but you can try." DeLaune immediately grabbed onto the cliff, and his twenty-four grenadiers followed behind. Their hands clutched at branches, bushes, their feet sought support on slippery rocks. Branches cracked, broke under their weight. Their feet slipped on rotten leaves. Stones came loose, rolled down. Their fingers clung to razor-sharp shale. Weighed down by their fourteen-pound muskets and their bags, the grenadiers slowly scaled the rocky wall. The tools hooked to their belts clinked against each other.

The sentinels would surely have heard the grenadiers had the cannons from Pointe-aux-Pères and those farther on from Beauport been silent.

When the first men got to the top, among the spruce, a sentinel from the other side of a stream asked, "Who goes there?" A Highlander captain replied in French: "I've come with a detachment from Quebec to relieve this post." DeLaune and his men had already surrounded the French camp when the sentinel saw through the trick. He gave the alarm. Coming out of their tents, a few militiamen, not really awake, heard him and, grumbling, went for their muskets. The French and English exchanged fire. Vergor, the camp's commander, half dressed, tried to slip away, but he was wounded. DeLaune assigned a few men to guard the prisoners. Vergor had been court-martialled after his surrender, in 1755, at Fort Beauséjour in Acadia. That night too, Vergor and his men had been sleeping deeply.

The Guyenne Regiment on the Plains of Abraham, a short distance from this camp, would have rushed to Vergor's aid had it not been recalled, earlier that night, by Montcalm, who thought it would be of more use facing the English ships and boats at Beauport than on the heights of Anse-des-Mères. Like the engineer Pontleroy, Montcalm thought the cliff was unscalable.

Wolfe, walking on the beach, finally found the path he'd been looking for on the cliffside at Anse-au-Foulon. Signalling, he called Howe and his two hundred soldiers. What was happening up top? They'd heard shots. Then everything had gone silent. Had DeLaune failed? No. A cry summoned the detachment to climb on up. At four forty-five, the soldiers started up the path (today's Gilmour Hill) which led, obliquely toward the northeast, to the clifftop. Other soldiers followed, then the infantry regiment. Alerted, the Samos artillerymen turned their four cannons and their mortar toward Anse-au-Foulon. Howe's men ran behind the battery and captured the artillerymen. At the break of day, the *Lowestoft* and the *Squirrel* were pouring men onto the beach.

Earlier, in the darkness, some boats, including that of Chads, had gone past Anse-au-Foulon. Landing lower down, the soldiers moving up the beach on foot encountered a French patrol, exchanged fire, escaped, and found themselves being shot at a bit farther along by some escapees from Vergor's camp who were at the top of the cliff. On the river, the English boats, more and more visible in the dawning light, awaited their turn to land.

At five thirty, at Beauport, Montcalm could see the English ships and boats, unmoving, their cannons silent in front of the fortifications. The enemy was allowing itself some sleep. Some soldiers on patrol said they'd seen some boats going up toward the city. Montcalm asked some militiamen to follow them along the shore. Seeing no sign of an imminent landing, Montcalm released the troops guarding the fortifications. The soldiers retired to their tents. Montcalm returned to his quarters. He had not slept all night. He drank a cup of tea with his aide-de-camp. With no news from the supply convoy that should have arrived, the lieutenant-general assumed it had been captured by the English.

With his telescope, Wolfe scanned the surroundings: a plain crossed by the Chemin de Sainte-Foy going toward Quebec. On the other side of the road, isolated houses, and farther on, the St. Charles River. On his right, the gently rolling plain ended in a wooded ridge that hid the city from him. Where was the enemy? Where was Montcalm, that "wary old fellow"? His telescope returned to the field the people called the Plains of Abraham. It was large enough for him to deploy there his troops and reserves. On the left, a hill would protect his army's flank, and the army would be facing the ramparts of Quebec, a kilometre away. Wolfe knew, from the descriptions of the English ex-prisoner Stobo, that those walls were neither solidly built nor well defended.

While his men pushed, pulled, and hoisted cannons by main strength toward the cliff's summit, Wolfe, a bit after six o'clock, marched at the head of the grenadiers who had fought with him at Louisbourg. After their sleepless night, his troops were tired, but proud. They had fooled the French watchmen on the river, they had scaled that steep cliff, they had surprised Vergor's camp, and without having lost a single man, they were advancing toward the battlefield. Their flags waved in the wind, drums beat out their every step. The strident sound of the bagpipes was a bit sad perhaps, but resolute. Some Highlanders felt uneasy: were they not going to be fighting enemies who were Catholic, like them? The regiments sang together words written by a sergeant killed during the attack on Montmorency: "Wolfe commands us, my boys, we shall give them hot stuff."

At that moment, a French officer convalescing in the General Hospital opened the shutters to his window, as he did every morning, and saw the English army. He ran into the courtyard, jumped on a horse, and galloped toward the St. Charles River to the redoubt, crying that the English were on the Plains of Abraham!

Montcalm had heard the cannons at Samos firing that night. But he had not been concerned, because at night they often opened fire on English boats trying to infiltrate. At six o'clock, more curious than alarmed, the lieutenant-general started toward Quebec, taking some of his officers with him. On his way, a messenger came to tell him that Vaudreuil wanted to see him.

At six thirty, Montcalm arrived at Vaudreuil's headquarters, where there was great confusion. During the night, at three o'clock, the governor general had been informed that the English were preparing to land in front of his camp, at La Canardière. He had positioned cannons there and had summoned a detachment from the city. At four o'clock, the city's signal lights had warned him that the enemy had been seen at Anse-des-Mères, between Cap Diamant and Anse-au-Foulon. A few moments later, it was announced that the enemy had landed at Anse-des-Mères. That news could have been true because Montcalm had heard the cannons at Samos. A bit later, they had gone silent. Vaudreuil then concluded that the English had been repelled. At four forty-five, one of Vergor's militiamen came to inform him that the English had taken their camp. No one believed him. Marcel, Montcalm's secretary, later said: "We knew so well how hard it was to get through at that point, as long as it was defended, that we didn't believe a word of the man's story, thinking that fear had turned his head." At five forty-five, Chevalier Armand Félicien de Bernetz, commander of the city in the absence of Jean-Baptiste-Nicolas-Roch de Ramezay, came to inform Vaudreuil that according to one of Vergor's orderlies, the English had landed at Anse-au-Foulon. Bernetz had heard gunshots, but then everything had gone silent, and he thought the English had left. None of this muddled information persuaded Vaudreuil that the English really had landed at Anse-au-Foulon. So much activity could have only one purpose: to distract the French from the ongoing attack on the coast at Beauport. However, to be certain, Vaudreuil asked Montcalm to go and assess the situation.

The lieutenant-general took a hundred militiamen with him. They passed in front of the redoubt surrounded by palisades and earthworks. They crossed the boat bridge on the St. Charles River, and on a hill half a league from the redoubt, they made out against the grey sky the red line of English army uniforms.

Montcalm reined in his horse and told his aide-de-camp: "This is serious; go back to Beauport as fast as you can and ask them to send reinforcements at once to the Plains of Abraham." Montcalm went back to Vaudreuil. They had a brief exchange. To the officers nearby, their dialogue did not seem cordial. A few weeks earlier, during an attempted landing by the English at Pointe-aux-Trembles, Montcalm had noted in his diary: "We can be beaten, that is the common fate of the weaker party; but the height of misfortune is to be surprised."

After his interview with Montcalm, Vaudreuil dictated a dispatch to Bougainville: "It seems certain that the enemy has landed at Anse-au-Foulon. . . . We heard some small gunfire. . . . The enemy forces appear substantial." The horseman carrying the message had to travel the four and a half leagues that separated the two men.

At the General Hospital, convalescents, refugees, and the mentally ill jostled each other, hauling themselves to the windows to see the English. "The English are at our doors!" Rumours circulated: the English were digging trenches on the Plains of Abraham! They had invaded the lower town! They "were running down the hill to massacre the people at Saint-Roch"!

At six forty-five, on the coast where Bougainville's troops were stationed, the *Sutherland*, in front of Saint-Nicolas, raised anchor. All were made uneasy by the manoeuvres of the English.

Montcalm arrived at the Buttes-à-Neveu. From this fifteen-metre elevation dominating the Plains of Abraham, he could clearly see the front line of the enemy army, extending more than a kilometre. It was not as numerous as the French had feared: fewer than two thousand men, it seemed to him. Montcalm saw no artillery or trenches. If he could quickly muster his forces, they would push the English to the bottom of the cliff.

An orderly brought him an urgent message from Vaudreuil: it was "in our interest not to be hasty." The governor general advised against Montcalm's attacking the English before being able to face them with both the city's garrison and Bougainville's detachments, "by which means they will find themselves surrounded on all sides." Vaudreuil predicted that, faced with those combined forces, "their retreat would be . . . assured."

For the lieutenant-general, to wait for Bougainville and his men would be to give the English army time for more forces to come and swell its ranks, time to set up its artillery, time to transport munitions and dig trenches. Montcalm gave his orders: all available militiamen were to immediately block paths, roads, and bridges around the Plains of Abraham, making it impossible for the English to set foot on the terrain, and if they did so, to prevent them from escaping. The Guyenne Regiment was to take up position on the Buttes-à-Neveu. He sent Johnstone, his aide-de-camp, to deliver to the other French regiments, at Beauport, his order to present themselves immediately on the Plains of Abraham.

When Johnstone arrived, he found that a messenger had already delivered orders from Vaudreuil. The governor general had directed that no unit was to withdraw from the fortifications on the Beauport coast, which was threatened by the English fleet moored before it. Johnstone then described the English army that Montcalm and he himself had seen from the Buttes-à-Neveu. He insisted: the enemy is at Quebec's doors! He argued that an order from the commander of the French forces should take priority over one from the governor general. He feared that they were losing precious time arguing and had Montcalm informed of this setback.

The lieutenant-general rode flat out to confront Vaudreuil. In a bitter altercation, the two men made mutual accusations. Who had authority over the other? Vaudreuil refused to weaken the Beauport coast, which would be invaded by an English fleet. The English brigades at the Buttes-à-Neveu were only a diversion, he insisted. If they dared to attack, the Guyenne Regiment, the Quebec garrison, and the militia would block their march. Besides, Bougainville's troops were en route. Montcalm repeated that the enemy fleet was continuing to unload men at Anse-au-Foulon, and waiting for Bougainville's troops would only favour the enemy: "If we give them the time to dig in, we'll never be able to attack them with the troops we have." In a European-style formal battle, on exposed terrain, against a disciplined army, Montcalm had little confidence in his own forces. Too many of his men knew only the native strategy of ambushes and skirmishes. He announced to his officers his determination to attack: "I, Marquis de Montcalm, by the will of the king, being the officer responsible for operations on the battlefield, have decided that we must crush the enemy before noon."

Vaudreuil couldn't understand Montcalm's sudden haste. He tried again to persuade him to wait for Bougainville's troops to arrive. In the end, he agreed, reluctantly, that the Beauport troops should be moved to the Buttes-à-Neveu. He would retain 1,500 men.

Soon the Quebec population heard the fifes and drums on the ramparts. They saw advancing, in rows, under flags, the French troops in white uniforms, the troops of the marine in grey uniforms, then the militia in their everyday clothes, and the natives, bare-chested, tattooed, feathers in their hair. The militiamen were armed with guns they had brought from home. For bayonets, they had hunting knives tied to their gun barrels.

For the French officers who had fought on several fronts in Europe and Canada, this was another battle to get through. For the ordinary soldiers, poorly nourished, who had barely slept the night before, farmers with no land, workers with no work, illiterates who had been forcibly recruited in the city slums, in the ports, in the doorways of taverns, who had been pushed onto ships leaving for Canada, and who hoped to acquire some land one day when they were no longer soldiers, this battle was a nightmare in the course of which they hoped not to lose their lives. The *Canadiens* in the militia and the troops of the marine knew that the English would set fire to the houses of those who had left for the war. And the harvests had not been taken in.

At seven thirty, Wolfe positioned the two last regiments to arrive along the Chemin de Sainte-Foy and along the cliff, to protect his flanks. Brigadier Townshend, in charge of the left, called for help, amazed that the red uniforms of his men, on the green field, were drawing fire. His men were being shot by invisible snipers hidden among cornstalks. Grenadiers ran up. The snipers disappeared into the natural world. The grenadiers took refuge in the house of Louis-Borgia Levasseur. Militiamen and natives, reappearing, fired on them. The grenadiers came out. Other Englishmen came to help them. The militiamen fired "from one side and another without forming a body that could stand up to the enemy."

At seven forty-five, all of Wolfe's men were on the plateau facing the Buttes-à-Neveu. The major-general had seen to it that his flanks were well guarded, that his reserves were in the centre, well protected, that his supply line to the river was secure, and that the Chemin de Sainte-Foy was being carefully watched. In front of Anse-au-Foulon, the English fleet had the strength to impose absolute control on the river.

At Île d'Orléans and Pointe Lévy, Wolfe had run his soldiers through detailed exercises: loading the muskets (no more than twelve seconds), priming (taking care with the spring of the safety catch), maintaining the flint, reloading quickly. Unlike other officers, he did not believe in the virtues of the lash for disciplining a soldier. He preferred to parade them, dressed in feminine attire, through the quarters of those women who followed in the wake of regiments.

Wolfe gave his final instructions. He demanded that, on the front line, there be between each of the nine hundred men a gap of forty-five centimetres. In the following line, each man would position himself behind that space. When the order came to shoot, the men in the second line would thus have a clear view, and their balls, synchronized, would cut down the French like a scythe. The order to shoot would be given in different ways, depending on the circumstances. If there was confusion due to the smoke, the drum would give the signal.

At nine o'clock, Wolfe saw the French arrive on the Buttes-à-Neveu. The commander of the Guyenne Regiment positioned the elite marksmen behind mounds where the ground was uneven. Montcalm was "frustrated" that his troops were so slow to arrive. Had Vaudreuil tried to hold them back at the St. Charles River bridge? As soon as they appeared, Montcalm gave them assignments: the militia and the marine troops on the two flanks, the French regiments in the centre. Montcalm had decided to attack the enemy both frontally and on the flanks. The French regiments would deal with its front line, which they would force to retreat as they descended the hill, through their strength in numbers and their cannon fire. The marine troops, aided by militiamen and natives in ambush along the Chemin de Sainte-Foy and in the bushes at the top of the cliff, would push the flanks toward the centre. Thus choked off, the British army would retreat. It would then come up against Bougainville's detachment, which would arrive soon.

The soldiers of both armies were keyed up. There were gunshots here and there . . . Neither *Canadien* militiamen nor the natives wanted to miss out on an easy target just because an officer had not shouted at them to fire. Thinking they spotted Indians in hiding, Wolfe's marksmen shot at stands of corn waving in the breeze.

Wolfe asked the colonels to remind their men, once again, of the disastrous consequences of firing too early. As soon as the French began to advance, the English army would move forward a hundred paces. The sergeants traced lines on the ground where each regiment was to stop. They made another mark, twenty-five yards farther on, where the first firing against the French would take place. Wolfe had placed in the centre of the front line one of the two bronze cannons that had been hauled, at great effort, to the top of the cliff. This cannon would inspire some fear in the French, who at ten o'clock on the Buttes-à-Neveu seemed numberless. On the side of the English army, 1,800 muskets, bayonets fixed, were ready to fire.

40

"Each waiting for the other to fire first"

At the top of the Buttes-à-Neveu, Montcalm's army, which Wolfe estimated at 3,500 men, took a first step forward a little after ten in the morning. The slope was gentle, uneven, strewn with scrub. As they moved forward, the lines became straggly. An English cannon discharged its six-pound balls on the Royal-Roussillon Regiment. The marine troops and the *Canadien* militiamen released a crackling of gunfire, even though the enemy was still out of range of their muskets. Wolfe, on horseback, in his scarlet, gold-embroidered uniform, in the centre, in the rear, then on the flanks, urged on his officers. A ball from an elite marksman hit him in the wrist. Someone helped him wrap a handkerchief around the wound to stop the blood. Wolfe immediately got back in his saddle and was given his stick.

At two hundred paces, the English, immobile, imperturbable, awaited the French army. A few of their soldiers had fallen. Their bodies were pulled out of the line. Other soldiers took their places in the ranks.

Despite his wound, Major-General Wolfe was "radiant and joyful beyond description," one witness said. He had observed that Montcalm's men were great in number on the flanks, so that the centre seemed weak; his regiments were separated by fifty paces and sometimes more. With a certain contempt, Wolfe observed that "disorderly floating of lines." He had no fear of the marine troops, that "disorderly peasantry" camouflaged behind trees. If those soldiers risked coming out of their hiding places, his fusiliers would take their heads off.

The French advanced in their white tunics, under a sun that made their weapons gleam. At a hundred paces, they paused, pointed their muskets at the English, who were waiting with their own musket hammers at rest. "All were observed for two or three minutes, each waiting for the other to fire first," remembered the Highlanders' chaplain.

Those French, those English, would in a moment perhaps not be alive. A light-headedness took possession of their bodies. English, Scottish, French, *Canadiens*, had to think only of killing so as not to be killed.

Finally, the French attacked the English with a confused, disorganized fire. One of their balls hit Wolfe on his left side, a bit above the groin. The thick cloth of his tunic lessened the shock. Wolfe's face tensed. Muskets on their shoulders, his soldiers were waiting for the order to shoot. The French were advancing. The distance between the enemies shortened with agonizing slowness, punctuated by the beating of drums.

At seventy-five paces from the English, the French front line came to a halt. Would Wolfe give the order to fire? His officers had their eyes riveted on him. The major-general waited for the enemy to come closer before striking. Would his officers be able to control the fearful impatience of their men? The French, at seventy paces, were walking more and more slowly . . . They were at sixty paces . . . The drums were beating. Hearts were beating. The seconds passed interminably.

When the French arrived at forty paces, Wolfe, despite a burning pain in his groin, brandished his stick at the end of his arm. It was ten twenty-seven. At the signal, Carleton cried out to the Louisbourg grenadiers: "Present . . . arms! Ready! FIRE!" Their balls tore into the Guyenne Regiment. The English drums rolled. Four hundred muskets of the 28th Regiment, in a single volley, drove into the flank of the Béarn Regiment, whose front line, six seconds later, was cut down by the three hundred muskets of the 43rd Regiment. The Languedoc Regiment was slashed by the oblique fire of the 47th Regiment, while six hundred muskets ripped into its front line. The 58th Regiment directed its fire at the La Sarre Regiment and the troops of the marine.

Despite his two wounds, Wolfe dismounted from his horse. His long body erect in its stiff scarlet tunic, he stood between the Louisbourg grenadiers and the "butchers" of the 28th Infantry Regiment, waiting for the white smoke from the musket fire to dissipate so that he could see what damage they had inflicted. A ball shattered his ribs. He staggered, but did not fall. He sat down. Two lieutenants ran up, another grenadier came to their aid, and they carried their major-general to a depression in the ground.

The smoke had settled. The Louisbourg grenadiers were within fifteen paces of the French. The front line of the Guyenne Regiment was decimated. In the second line, many soldiers were lying on the ground. The third and fourth lines of the regiment were responding with desperate fire. Several grenadiers crumpled to the ground. The survivors of the Guyenne Regiment stood upright among the bodies of their dead comrades or those who were wounded, doubled up in pain, groaning and cursing. At a signal from the drums, the grenadiers fired their weapons at the French who were still on their feet and, pointing their bayonets, threw themselves upon the French. From the other side came a joyous clamour: the Highlanders were whirling their gleaming claymores at arm's length. Exalted by their own cries and the drone of their bagpipes, they charged the Languedoc Regiment, which collapsed, and then that of the La Sarre.

The French officers attempted to re-form their ranks, but panic was stronger than discipline. Pursued by claymores and bayonets, the French soldiers struggled to flee. The marine troops retreated into the woods on the other side of the Chemin Sainte-Foy. Despite the officers' shouted orders, the Royal-Roussillon also turned on its heels. The French army climbed back onto the Buttes-à-Neveu ... On his horse, sword in hand, Montcalm waved his arms, ordered his companies to rally. His arms extended, he tried to intercept the escapees. Two balls hit him, one in the thigh, the other in the groin. He was about to fall from his horse, but two of his men placed him back in the saddle.

Wolfe, after having been wounded, had passed his command to Brigadier Monckton, who, just a few minutes later, received a ball in the chest. Brigadier George Townshend then took over. Major-General Wolfe lay on the grass, his head resting on his folded tunic. The surgeon examined his wounds. Blood flowed freely. Wolfe murmured his own diagnosis: "It's all over with me." He had a perforated lung. One of the men around him cried: "They run, see how they run!" Run. The word revived the dying man. "Who runs?" murmured Wolfe. "The enemy, sir!" said the man. "By God, they give way everywhere." Wolfe, in a barely audible voice, ordered: "Go, one of you, to Colonel Burton: tell him to march his regiment with all speed down to the Charles River—to cut off retreat of the fugitives to the bridge."

Wolfe had already written that victory was "the highest joy to him who commands." Now that it was so near, he lost consciousness. A few moments later, he revived briefly to sigh, "Now I can die content." The last word he pronounced was both English and French.

41

"New France descended into the tomb"

On the Plains of Abraham lay the 150 Frenchmen who had been killed and the hundreds of wounded. The English counted sixty-one dead and 603 wounded. Among the French and *Canadien* escapees fearing the punishment the victors would inflict on them, Montcalm, who had escaped the shame of being taken prisoner, was led mounted on his black horse to Quebec. So that he would not fall, he was supported on each side. He entered by the gate of Saint-Louis. He could hardly breathe. People rushed up to see him. His white uniform was bloodstained. Women lamented: "My God! Oh my God! They've killed Monsieur le Marquis!" Painfully, he turned toward them: "It's nothing, my good friends; don't concern yourselves about me, it's nothing."

Realizing that their army had been routed, the garrison's soldiers and the populace ran with their hunting rifles and their staffs into the thicket not far from the city gates. They waited for the English, who were descending on the city. A number of Highlanders fell under fire from snipers. Some natives, off to the side, were waiting to loot the battlefield.

Several wounded officers, among whom there were French prisoners, were led on board the *Lowestoft*. At eleven o'clock, they carried on "ye corps of General Wolf." Lieutenant Browne remembered: "Even the soldiers dropped tears, who were but the minute before driving their bayonnets through the French."

At that moment, Bougainville and his two thousand men arrived at Sillery. Leaving a hundred soldiers to attack a stone house occupied by an English party, he continued his march toward the battlefield. "When I arrived ready to fight, our army was beaten," he wrote simply.

In his house on the rue Saint-Louis, the surgeon André Arnoux cleaned and dressed Montcalm's wounds. He did not hide from the lieutenant-general that they were serious . . . Montcalm asked: "How many hours do I have to live?" The surgeon replied: "Not much past three in the morning." Montcalm responded, "So much the better, I will not see the English in Quebec."

At the windows of the General Hospital, patients and refugees lamented the "sad spectacle" of the defeat. A nun would report: "We were in the midst of the dead and dying that they brought us hundreds at a time."

Johnstone, Montcalm's aide-de-camp, whose tunic had been torn by four balls, rushed to Vaudreuil's headquarters to inform the governor general of Montcalm's imminent death. Johnstone found Vaudreuil and Bigot, solemn, talking in lowered voices. "You have no business here!" Vaudreuil barked at him.

The officers of François-Gaston de Lévis, who replaced Montcalm, were in discussion. Some said that to prevent the English from crossing the St. Charles River, they had to quickly destroy the boat bridge on the river. But were they going to sacrifice to the English several divisions of the French army that had not yet crossed over? They had to preserve the redoubt. Other officers were resigned: with or without the bridge, the English were going to take the redoubt. "Destroy the bridge!" ordered some officers. Others broke in: "We must surrender."

Canadien militiamen and soldiers from the troops of the marine came together near a flour mill, where they waited for the battalions pursuing the French troops. Almost all the *Canadiens* were killed, but they slowed the progress of the enemy. The French soldiers were able to cross the river.

Brigadier Townshend wanted to rein in the "great disorder" of his army. He ordered all the battalions that had set off in pursuit of the French to present themselves on the Plains of Abraham. Fearing the return of Bougainville's army, which had disappeared without attacking, he re-formed the battle lines. His men cut down bushes, dug trenches, built parapets, replaced artillery. Townshend posted elite marksmen in houses and set up cannons in the flour mill.

At the council of war led by Vaudreuil and Intendant Bigot, several officers were absent: thirteen had been killed, others were still involved in skirmishes, and several had been taken prisoner. Two officers proposed surrendering without suffering any more damage. Johnstone was opposed: to surrender would be shameful. An old officer whose face was marked by scars listened with pity. The enemy was overwhelmingly superior; all that was left for the French was to return to their native land while the sea was not too perilous. The engineer François-Médard de Poulariez swore that he would spill his blood rather than cede the colony to the English.

Even though he knew Montcalm was dying, Vaudreuil sent to ask his opinion. The lieutenant-general replied that the French had three options: to continue fighting, to capitulate, or to retreat to the Jacques-Cartier River. However, perhaps to avoid his advice being rejected one last time by Vaudreuil, he refused to reveal what would be his own decision.

Vaudreuil and Bigot hoped to renew the attack the next day. The French officers had many objections: the superiority of the English army, the weakness and demoralization of the French army, the lack of supplies, the broken lines of communication. They proposed, rather, that the army retreat to the Jacques-Cartier River. At four o'clock, Vaudreuil wrote to the Chevalier de Lévis in Montreal, to inform him of the day's events: "We have just experienced a very unfortunate occurrence." Despite "our tenacity," he announced, "the enemy has forced us to retreat. There are many dead and wounded. Monsieur le Marquis de Montcalm has himself been wounded. We fear for his life." He added, "No one more than myself wishes that it not be so." Vaudreuil told Lévis of the decision he had made: "I am leaving this evening with what is left of the army to take up position at Jacques-Cartier. . . . I will never agree to surrender for the entire colony." In conclusion, he ordered the Chevalier de Lévis to come and take command of the troops at the Jacques-Cartier River "as soon as you receive my letter."

At six o'clock, Vaudreuil wrote to Montcalm: "I cannot tell you enough how grieved I am at your wounds; I would like to think that you will heal in a short time, and that you are mindful that no one is more concerned than myself that that be the case, given my affection for you at all times. . . . I here enclose, Monsieur, the letter I have written in this regard to Monsieur de Ramezay [commander of the Quebec garrison], with the instructions I am giving him, concerning the terms of surrender that he must ask of the enemy. You will see that they are the same that we agreed upon together. Have the goodness to transmit them to him once you have read them; spare yourself, I pray you, think only of your recovery."

The night would be cold. The Pointe Lévy guns still battered the city, where no one slept. The French army left the Beauport camp at nine o'clock. The soldiers took with them some cannons, munitions, and enough supplies for four days. The rest was abandoned. They put out of service the cannons left behind, they blew up the reserves of powder, they destroyed the bridges and set the floating batteries afire.

Marcel, Montcalm's secretary, replied to Vaudreuil's letter: "Monsieur le Marquis de Montcalm, grateful for your attentions, has given me the honour of writing you that he approves all; I read him your letter, and the document for surrender that I submitted to Monsieur de Ramezay as you intended, along with your accompanying letter."

After reading the terms for surrender that Vaudreuil had instructed him to demand of the enemy, Jean-Baptiste de Ramezay asked for more precise instructions. Montcalm replied: "I have no more orders to give; I must concern myself with more important affairs, and the time left to me is short." Montcalm asked his secretary, who watched by his side, to give all his papers to the Chevalier de Lévis: "I leave the affairs of the king my master in good hands; I have always had a high opinion of Monsieur de Lévis." He made his secretary promise to visit his family when he returned to France. Then Bishop Pontbriand heard the lieutenant-general's confession.

The commander-in-chief of the French forces in North America died a little after five o'clock on the morning of September 14, the day after his defeat. Marcel shut his eyes. Montcalm would never again see his mother, nor his wife, nor his sons, nor his daughters, nor his olive trees, nor his mill. Bougainville, on his return from France in the spring, had told him that one of his daughters had died. Montcalm never knew which child he'd had the misfortune of losing.

In the terror-stricken streets of Quebec, there was panic: the French army had abandoned the camp at Beauport! It wasn't true! Look, you can see the tents! The tents are there, but the soldiers have gone! Who will defend the people? Even the city's garrison has lost its nerve. The army has abandoned Quebec... Ramezay would remember: "The disheartenment everywhere was extreme;

the grievances and grumblings against the army that had abandoned us became a public outcry."

In the general disarray, no one could be found to make a coffin worthy of the Marquis de Montcalm. An employee of the Ursulines, "old man Michel," agreed, tears in his eyes, to build a box with his aged, trembling hands, using boards he had scavenged around houses destroyed by bombardments.

Thinking to distribute in the starving city the food left behind by the army, Bigot sent his wagons to Beauport. By the time they arrived, the camp had already been looted. The day after the battle, the bourgeois, the merchants, officers of the militia, and other important citizens met at the home of Monsieur Daine, lieutenant-general, civil and criminal, of the provostship of Quebec. Making the case that the population, famished for several weeks, had food for only a week, the notables and the merchants voted to present to Monsieur de Ramezay a "request for surrender."

At eight o'clock, a horse pulled a wagon that carried the coffin of the Marquis de Montcalm. On every street, on either side, there were collapsed walls and sections of roofs, charred beams and floors. The French had been defeated. The Beauport army had deserted. The English cannons were mute. The horse's hoofs echoed in the silence. Even the sky seemed sad. Holding a few lanterns, men, women, and children, in tears, followed the coffin behind Ramezay, the garrison's commander, and his officers. There was no tolling of the bell, as the steeple of the Ursulines' chapel had been destroyed. The convent had suffered greatly during the siege. "Every day, a great number of bombs and cannonballs struck our house," one sister recounted.

The chapel was filled with the saddened faithful. Montcalm's coffin was placed on trestles between chandeliers that cast weak light. The priest sang the *Libera me*, to which responded the cannon and the choir of eight nuns who, despite the bombardments, had remained at the convent. Near the pulpit, a bomb had shattered the floor and made a hole in the ground. Fearing that the boards of Montcalm's coffin might pull apart, eight men worked together to lower the wooden box into this grave. The lieutenant-general was buried with no bugle, no cannon shots, but with tears and sobs inside the church. The chronicle of the Ursulines affirmed: "It seemed that New France descended into its tomb along with the remains of the general." Just as Quebec was saying farewell to Montcalm, an old nun breathed her last. The Ursulines' annalist, she had faithfully kept a diary of the siege of Quebec, which ended with these words: "The land is laid low."

Some militiamen took advantage of the night to slip away. To take in the harvest was not a betrayal. French or English, a master was a master. Some soldiers in the army crossed over to the stronger side. Others suggested blowing up the city to turn it into a "desert." But still others preferred to be taken by the English rather than see-ing their city destroyed. There were altercations between officers. A major struck two captains with the flat of his sword. Proclaiming his opposition to those who wanted to capitulate, Louis-Thomas Jacau de Fiedmont, commander of the city's artillery, unleashed the fury of his cannons upon the ships at Pointe Lévy and the fortifications Townshend had set up on the Plains of Abraham. Vaudreuil prom-ised to offer the British the resistance that Montcalm had not known how to inspire. He would retake Quebec. If he failed, he would have the city razed, so that the English would not be able to enter it.

On September 17, at the beginning of the afternoon, eight of Admiral Saunders's frigates approached the lower town. Near the Porte Saint-Jean, English soldiers scoured the underbrush where snipers might be hiding, while a convoy of wagons brought cannons and howitzers that the enemy set up in front of the city's ramparts.

Behind the walls, Ramezay wanted to avoid pointless losses. He had white flags hoisted on poles, on the St. Lawrence and on the side of the Plains of Abraham.

That day, returning from Montreal, Lévis and his detachments arrived at the Jacques-Cartier River. The chevalier shared Vaudreuil's conviction: the French army had to return to Quebec to repair "the error that had been made."

A missionary had informed Vaudreuil that Montcalm had entrusted him with letters to be delivered to Madame de Pompadour at Versailles. Vaudreuil also knew that Montcalm had entrusted his papers to the Chevalier de Lévis. Would those letters and those papers contain more insinuations and accusations against Vaudreuil and high society? That worried the governor general, who asked for access to the documents. The chevalier resisted: "I am formally responsible to my minister and to the family of Monsieur de Montcalm for his papers, which ought not to be seen but by me alone."

On the night of September 18, a bit before sunset, Ramezay opened the city gates. Preceded by drums and the British flag, Brigadier George Townshend, three companies of grenadiers, and a detachment of artillery and a field cannon entered the upper city in procession. Ramezay gave the brigadier the keys to the Château Saint-Louis, the governor general's residence. Salvos of cannon shots saluted the British flag as it was hoisted on its mast. At the gates of the city, the sentinels in white uniforms were replaced by sentinels in red uniforms. The sailors, down from their ships, were treated to the less-than-friendly hospitality of the people. A detachment of five hundred men left to dislodge the *Canadien* militia who refused to surrender, from the redoubt on the other side of the St. Charles River. The English troops set up their camp under the ramparts.

On September 21, Brigadier Murray published a proclamation. He gave the people of Quebec and its surroundings permission to peacefully reacquire their belongings. What belongings?
Their houses and their stables had been destroyed, their animals
had been slaughtered. Women came out of the woods with their
children in rags, dirty, sick, starving. They searched for their men,
they searched for food. That autumn, there was no roof over their
heads, no stove for a fire, and in some cases no more husband.

The soldiers repaired the foundations and built up the ramparts.
They cleared the streets of their rubble, rebuilt damaged houses,
cut down trees for floors, beams, firewood. Some were lodged in
the intendant's château, at the Ursuline convent, in other religious
institutions, or with families. The English army saw to it that strict
discipline was maintained in the city and its surroundings. Day and
night, it patrolled.

According to the capitulation agreement, the soldiers, sailors,
and citizens who so desired would be transported to France on
English ships. Before his departure, Montcalm's faithful secretary,
Marcel, made a last visit to his general's tomb.

After Montcalm's death, Vaudreuil wrote to the Marshal de
Belle-Isle, minister of war: "I've missed him greatly." However, his
true feelings were displayed in a diatribe contained in a letter to
Berryer, minister of the marine, on October 30, 1759:

*From the moment Monsieur de Montcalm arrived in this col-
ony until his death, he never ceased to sacrifice everything to his
overweening ambition. He sowed ill-feeling among the troops,
tolerated the most indecent outbursts against the governments,
consorted with the worst individuals, conspired to corrupt the
most virtuous, whose cruel enemy he became when he could not
succeed. He wanted to become governor general. . . . He showered*

with favours those officers, in particular, who embraced his ideas, and promised them protection. He spared no effort in displaying his affection for different peoples in their stations in life, while through him and his troops on the ground he had them bear the weight of a most terrible yoke. He defamed honest people, encouraged subordination, shut his eyes to the soldiers' pillage, which he tolerated to the point of seeing them sell off the food-stuffs for animals that they had stolen from the farmer.

I deeply regret, Monseigneur, having to paint you such a portrait of Monsieur le Marquis de Montcalm. While its truth is indisputable, I would have desisted had it only been a ques-tion of his personal hatred for me; but the loss of Quebec is too sensitive a matter for me to hide the cause, which is widely and publicly known.

42

"America's succeeding flame"

M ajor-General Wolfe's body, transported to Pointe Lévy, was embalmed in the church that had been requisitioned to serve as the military hospital. Then it was taken to Île Madame, where the *Royal William* was moored. The cannons of Quebec saluted his remains with thundering solemnity. The soldiers believed his body had been plunged into a barrel of rum to preserve it; a lot of rum for just one man, one of them joked . . . On September 25, the warship set sail for England.

The news of the conquest of Quebec reached Boston on October 11, 1759. That night, windows in homes and shops were brightened by candles in joyous celebration. Passers by lingered in front of drawings displayed to tell the story of the victory. One of them showed the British flag flying over Quebec, while the French flag was in tatters on the ground, at the foot of its broken mast. The governor of Massachusetts proclaimed a day of thanksgiving. Parades, salvos of cannon fire. Notables were invited to a great banquet. For all there were bonfires, music, and roasted meat.

In the churches, sermons took as their subject Wolfe's victory over the French. Pastor Thomas Foxcroft, in Boston, declaimed: "The Lord hath done great things for us . . ." Pastor John Mellen, at Lancaster, prayed for the vanquished: "May the blessings of

Heaven be ever upon those enemies of our country that have now submitted to the English Crown." He prophesied that one day America would be populated by sixty million people. In the village of Brookfield, Pastor Eli Forbes explained to his faithful: "God had given us to sing this day the downfall of New France, the North American Babylon, New England's rival." In the joy of this victory, his faithful had, however, "to lament the fall of the valiant and good General Wolfe, whose death demands a tear from every British eye, a sigh from every Protestant heart." After Wolfe's victory, the Boston newspapers were able to envision the prospect of an America without the French.

It was a bit later that the news of Wolfe's victory reached England. On September 2, Wolfe had written to the secretary of state, William Pitt, to bring him up to date on the situation in Quebec. Since the end of June, he had lost 850 men, killed or wounded. Almost as many officers and soldiers were ill with a fever caused by food that had spoiled in the extreme heat. Despite those setbacks, he wrote, "be assured that the small part of the campaign which remains shall be employed, as far as able, for the honour of His Majesty and the interest of the nation." Wolfe's letter, which gave no reason to hope for a victory in Quebec, arrived in London on October 14. Having read it, William Pitt regretted his decision to have entrusted this mission to a young officer with little experience. Saddened by the impending defeat, Prime Minister Newcastle was nevertheless not unhappy to see Pitt in an uncomfortable situation.

On October 16, the *London Gazette* published Wolfe's letter, omitting the paragraphs that spoke of the villages and farms put to the flame by Major Scott and Captain Gorham. The British army in Quebec was about to experience "a bloody failure," predicted the writer Horace Walpole.

On the evening of that same day, Pitt received a dispatch from Quebec that he hastened to read. Immediately, he scribbled a note to the prime minister: "Mr. Secretary Pitt has the pleasure to send the Duke of Newcastle the joyful news that Quebec is taken, after a signal and compleat Victory over the French army." Was such a reversal of fortune credible? Dispatches from Vice-Admiral Saunders and Brigadier Townshend confirmed the British victory in Quebec.

The next day, the *London Gazette* trumpeted the news. Victory over the French army! Quebec has been taken! At the market, the butchers celebrated by banging their cleavers on their stalls. People drank beer and gin. Public notices celebrated General Wolfe. House and shop windows were decorated. At night, candles were lit, and there were bonfires in the street. People danced. They had defied the enemies of invincible England!

That same day, October 18, the English fleet left Quebec. Brigadier Townshend, who had not wished to winter in that glacial colony, was returning to London. Brigadier James Murray would be governor of Quebec and commander of His English Majesty's army of 7,300 men.

The news of the "signal victory" spread across the kingdom. In Bath, which preachers denounced as the fortress of Satan, the cannons thundered, and a ball was organized in honour of James Wolfe, who had regularly spent time in that spa centre along with his family during his winter holidays. At the Fakenham Market in Norfolk, the minor nobility of the countryside joined with the shopkeepers and landowners in a banquet of mutton, beef, and pork on a spit. At Bradford on Avon, the populace marked the news with toasts drunk to the "brave country men in America and the immortal memory of their late brave commander General Wolfe." At Salisbury, the bells rang for thirty minutes to honour Wolfe's death. Then, to celebrate his victory, the drums rolled, and the fusiliers let loose with salvos of gunshot. In the evening, beer flowed freely in the city, lit by bonfires "more splendid than ever known before." At Blackheath, where James Wolfe's mother lived, the people refrained from celebrating, out of respect for this woman who had lost her son.

King George II was congratulated on every side for the capture of the Niagara, Duquesne, Carillon, and Saint-Frédéric forts by the Royal Army, as well as the island of Guadeloupe in America. These conquests added to the recent British victories at Cap de Lagos (Portugal), Minden (Germany), the Island of Gorée (Africa), and Pondicherry (India). The lord mayor of London paid him homage for "successes which, under the divine blessing, have attended your Majesty's army by sea and land within the compass of this distinguished and ever memorable year." As one of those victories, the conquest of Quebec had succeeded, said the mayor, "against every advantage of situation and superior numbers." General Wolfe had left "to future times an heroic example of military skill, discipline and fortitude."

For Katherine Lowther, "the intended bride" of James Wolfe, the death of the general was a "dreadful calamity." On October 25, Captain Thomas Bell went to return to her the miniature portrait that Wolfe had sent back, along with one of her letters that the general had not had the opportunity to open. The *London Magazine* of November 1759 published an ode to Mademoiselle L: "You, gentle maid, above the rest, his fate untimely mourn."

Aware of their readers' interest in the Major-General Wolfe who had won an impossible victory in Quebec, the newspapers told the story of his past accomplishments: at Lauffeldt during the Austrian War of Succession, Wolfe's conduct had merited him the Duke of Cumberland's praise; at Rochefort, the English would probably have succeeded in their mission had they put into practice the tactic recommended by Wolfe; at Louisbourg, the year previous, when he was only second in command, Wolfe's actions had led to the taking of that supposedly invincible fortress. The papers published the letters of officers who had served in Quebec. In October 1759, in the *Chronicle Magazine* in London, an officer gave Wolfe full credit for the conquest: "singly and alone in opinion, he formed and executed that great, that dangerous, yet necessary plan, which drew out the French to their defeat, and will for ever denominate him the conqueror of Canada." By the end of October, two volumes relating the Quebec campaign were being printed.

The minister of war had already been informed that this "glorious and successful" campaign was marred by differences between Wolfe and his brigadiers. Those disputes in Wolfe's headquarters were revealed openly when Brigadier George Townshend's letter declaring victory in Quebec was published in London. It barely mentioned Wolfe's name. Did Townshend want to appropriate the honours for the conquest? Several people raised the question in the taverns and the inns. Immediately, a letter arrived from Townshend, expressing his sorrow at having lost his "friend" Wolfe: "If the world were sensible at how dear a price we have purchased Quebec in his death, it would damp the general joy." As Townshend was at sea, returning to England, it seemed that someone was manipulating public opinion in his favour. Behind this rivalry between Brigadier Townshend and Major-General Wolfe, was there a struggle between Newcastle and Pitt? Some thought so.

The *Royal William* dropped anchor at Spithead at seven in the morning, November 17, 1759. Two cannon shots boomed out as Wolfe's body was lowered into a barge that then brought it to Portsmouth Point. In this unsavoury part of the port, the coffin was greeted at nine o'clock by the regiment of Invalides and an artillery company that honoured it with the traditional salvos. All along the route, people applauded this general who had vanquished the French. James Wolfe had come home. On November 20, dressed in an embroidered gown, he was buried beside his father in the family vault at St. Elphege's Church in Greenwich.

The day after the burial, William Pitt proposed to the House of Commons that a monument be raised in Wolfe's memory. The members of Parliament were in agreement. The general deserved, through his victory and his death, a monument in Westminster Abbey, whose cost would be assumed by the public.

Even though the major-general was in his tomb, Townshend's animosity toward Wolfe did not lessen. In January 1760, the editor of *Scots Magazine* wrote that the "brave Wolfe" ought to share his glory with Monckton, but most especially with Townshend. Others reproached "poor Mr. Wolfe" for having lacked resolve during the Quebec campaign. Why had he suddenly abandoned the brigadiers' plan? Why had he not shared with all the officers his own plan for landing at Anse-au-Foulon?

Brigadier George Townshend's brother, Charles, who had become secretary of state for war, affirmed that "some artful insinuations had been industriously though secretly propagated" with the view of depriving the brigadiers of the least credit for the victory at Quebec.

Informed of these quarrels between officers, the elderly George II asked: was Wolfe mad? It's said that he was, a little . . . "Then all the better," said the king. "I hope he bit a few of the brigadiers before he died!"

In his generous will, James Wolfe had given away three times what he possessed. Buoyed by the nation's sympathy, his mother addressed herself to William Pitt. It would give her "the greatest of pleasure" to execute her son's last wishes, but she could not do it, she wrote him, "without distressing myself to the highest degree."

Might she not request a pension from the king that would allow her to carry out the "generous and good intentions" of her son? A deft bureaucrat, Pitt replied that the question should more appropriately be put to Prime Minister Newcastle . . .

In February 1761, vouchers were issued for the payment of the officers on duty in Quebec during the summer of 1759. Henrietta Wolfe saw that her son had a right only to a payment as major-general and not as commander-in-chief. At the War Office, it was explained to the combative mother that her son was under the orders of the commander-in-chief, General Jeffrey Amherst. General Amherst was not at Quebec, protested Henrietta, but at the other end of the colony. A bureaucrat showed her a document signed by her son, in which he declared himself fully satisfied with his treatment.

On October 25, 1761, George II lost his footing in the bathroom, fell, and succumbed, the victim of a heart attack. The tireless and persevering Henrietta Wolfe addressed herself to the new king, George III, who was said to be peace-loving. In conquering Canada, had not James Wolfe brought peace to America? The secretary of state for war informed Henrietta Wolfe of the king's decision: General James Wolfe had no right to payment as commander-in-chief. Henrietta died twelve days later, having honoured James Wolfe's entire legacy. She would never read, in the monument erected in memory of her son, which would not be unveiled until 1773, these words carved in marble: "Major-General and COMMANDER-IN-CHIEF of the British Land Force on an Expedition against Quebec."

43

"If the king does not see fit to send us help"

On October 25, 1759, the Chevalier de Lévis, at his camp on the Jacques-Cartier River, informed the Marshal de Belle-Isle, minister of war: "We'll be lucky if we can keep ourselves going; we're going to end up eating what's left of the cattle and horses." Canada was in dire straits, but Lévis thought it could still be saved "if the king wants to support this colony and if it pleases him in the month of May to send a squadron that arrives here before the English and makes us master of the river, with six thousand men who will land and four thousand recruits for the battalions and the troops of the marine that are here…" But "if the king does not see fit to send us help, I must advise you that you will be able to count on us no more, come the end of the month of May."

Behind Quebec's walls, those with a roof over their heads had to lodge one or two Englishmen, with their muskets. Powerless, some could only insult the intruders in a language they didn't understand. Others tried to engage their sympathy. Resisters unreconciled to surrender criss-crossed the countryside between Sainte-Foy and Beauport, looking for enemies. They stole to acquire food, to have something of their own, to wreak vengeance for having lost everything. Farm families lucky enough to still own a cow feared having it stolen by soldiers. They took the precaution of hiding one or two sheep in their cellar.

Patrols kept an eye on the population. Candles in houses had to be doused at ten at night. After that hour, no one on foot or in a horse-drawn cart could circulate without a lantern. The nuns, overwhelmed, were taking care of the sick, of whom there were too many, plus many of the English, who had no confidence in their "detestable military hospitals."

At the end of November, in the woods of Sillery and Sainte-Foy, English troops were cutting up trees for firewood. Every group of woodcutters was protected by an armed escort, as were the wagons that brought in the wood. One morning, freezing rain spread a coat of ice over the city. The English patrols watched, amused, as the people came down the Côte du Palais or the Côte de la Montagne, sliding on their behinds. As the soldiers didn't have the proper clothes for the winter cold, they improvised bizarre costumes, a "masquerade" mocked by the populace. The Highlanders, less foreign to this cruel climate, swaddled themselves in their kilts. The Ursulines knitted long woollen socks to hide their naked legs. It seemed that some did adapt to winter. In February, English soldiers were skating on the river in front of Pointe-aux-Trembles. Some natives discovered them and delivered the six sportsmen to Captain de Repentigny, still holding out in the church.

In Montreal, the Chevalier de Lévis's soldiers did not receive their pay. The army's coffers were empty. A small privileged community managed, however, to distract itself from the prevailing indigence. French and *Canadien* officers, merchants, and distinguished ladies ate, drank, and gambled, risking large sums of money.

At Versailles, a few people thought of expressing some sort of gratitude to Montcalm, who had lost his life in Canada. At a time when war was draining the country's resources, could the royal treasury afford such an expense? The Comte de Noailles persuaded Louis XV to acknowledge the merit of this lieutenant-general, "whose value and talents were an honour to French arms." His Majesty accorded a pension to Montcalm's widow and to each of his children. In addition, Montcalm's eldest son assumed command of his father's regiment.

On April 24, 1760, the Chevalier de Lévis's army arrived by canoe at Pointe-aux-Trembles. Determined to retake Quebec, the chevalier had ladders made to scale the ramparts. Accomplices in the city stole from the English anything that could be of use to the French army. They hauled to his camp sleds of food that was essential, but far from sufficient. Others became spies. Lévis learned from them that scurvy was ravaging the English troops. While waiting for the earth to thaw before digging graves, the English had buried in the snow no fewer than seven hundred victims.

Governor James Murray had the populations of Quebec, Sainte-Foy, and Lorette evacuated. In that way, the French army would not receive any support from the French people. So that the French could not approach the fortifications by going from house to house, Murray had razed what remained of the neighbourhoods of Saint-Roch and Sainte Famille. To have enough men for this task, he had to release two hundred soldiers from the hospital. Lévis wanted to surprise the English, but it was Murray and his 3,200 men who surprised Lévis on April 28, on the Plains of Abraham. From the Buttes-à-Neveu, the soldiers attacked the French, but the Béarn Regiment below resisted, on a terrain that had become swampy due to the melting snow. Bogged down in the mud, the English artillery was left in the rear. The Béarn Regiment repelled the English soldiers who, as they retreated toward their comrades, prevented them from firing. The Berry Regiment took possession of the English cannons. The La Sarre Regiment then engaged in man-to-man fighting. Murray had to sound the retreat. Among the fallen, 259 of his men were dead and 829 wounded. Lévis had won a victory on the Plains of Abraham. It had cost him 193 officers and soldiers, dead, and 640 wounded. But the English were still masters of the city of Quebec.

Before the enemy could get help, Lévis posted his troops in front of the ramparts to besiege the city. On May 9, a first frigate dropped anchor in the port of Quebec. It was English. Lévis didn't have enough men, or cannons, or munitions, or food, but the next frigate to arrive might be French ... Lévis bombarded the city. The English response was "vigorous." Four days later, three large sailing vessels came up the St. Lawrence: they were English warships. Lévis ordered his army to withdraw to Montreal.

By the end of the summer, three English armies were threatening that city: Brigadier William Havilland's army from Lake Champlain; Major-General Jeffrey Amherst's from Chouaguen, southwest of Lake Ontario; and James Murray's army from Quebec.

On August 16, Havilland arrived at the fort of Île aux Noix on the Richelieu River, which was on the way to Montreal. Bougainville, commander of the fort, knowing that he could not hold out for long against the invaders' intense bombardment, conceded defeat. Leaving to the enemy the wounded, fifty-six cannons, seven mortars, fourteen stone catapults, plus munitions, behind palisades breached everywhere by the bombardment, Bougainville and his men went to the defence of Montreal.

General Amherst's troops, ten thousand soldiers and seven hundred natives, headed for Montreal along the St. Lawrence, navigating its rapids. Almost a hundred men drowned in the turbulent waters. On September 6, 1760, this army landed at Lachine, west of Montreal. Murray's army, having arrived from Quebec, was already camped east of Montreal. That of Havilland was posted on the south shore of the St. Lawrence.

Six metres high, with a perimeter of half a league, Montreal's ramparts couldn't hold back such a host of enemies. They numbered at least eighteen thousand. Governor General Vaudreuil also feared that, if the enemy encountered strong resistance, it would exact fearsome revenge after its victory, which was most probable. Reluctantly, Lévis acknowledged that surrender was inevitable. Hoping that France and England would make peace in Europe, Vaudreuil and Lévis asked Major-General Amherst for a truce that would last until October 1. If, at that date, there was no peace between the two countries, they would capitulate. They also asked that the honours of war be accorded their army. Finally, they asked that the belongings of the population be protected, and that their laws and the right to practise their Catholic religion be respected. Bougainville was delegated to negotiate the terms of surrender. Uncompromising, Amherst rejected the request for a truce. And as the French army offered no resistance, it did not deserve the honours of war.

Refusing these humiliating conditions, Lévis wanted to terminate the talks, leave the confines of Montreal, and fall back on St. Helen's Island, where his army would resist the English. Vaudreuil opposed this option; it would mean consenting to certain massacre of the French troops. He would submit to the English general's intransigence. During the night, Lévis had the regimental flags burned along with the companies' flags, so the French would not have to turn them over to the enemy. The next day, September 8, Vaudreuil affixed his signature to the bottom of the act of surrender for Montreal. The French troops deposited their cannons and muskets at the Place d'Armes, and Amherst's army, to the sound of bagpipe, fife, and drum, came to take possession of Montreal.

To the French soldiers who had married *Canadien* women, Amherst offered the possibility of staying in Canada, as long as they left the army. Many seized the opportunity.

According to the terms of surrender, the defeated French offi-cers, soldiers, and officials had to return to France on board ships provided by the conquerors. But the English didn't have enough ships to "fulfil the stipulations of the surrender." They proposed "to have our battalions pass through New York to be more conven-iently sent off." Lévis rejected this offer, fearing that "on this route" soldiers would desert "of their own free will, or as subordination."

Many of the French preferred not to return. In a letter of November 25, 1760, to Marshal de Belle-Isle, secretary of state for war, Lévis estimated at "more than five hundred" the number of those who "have left since the surrender." Why so many "desert-ers"? "This evil is a result," he explained, "of an abuse from the outset, of their having been allowed to marry, to acquire land, and to be granted their leave once the war in Canada was concluded."

44

Wisps of straw swept away

Canada now belonged to England. Étienne-François de Choiseul, the French secretary of state for foreign affairs, did not seem overly troubled by the defeat of France in Canada. On October 12, 1760, he wrote to his friend Voltaire, living in Switzerland: "I have learned that we have lost Montreal and with it, Canada. If you are counting on us for furs this winter, I advise you that you must address yourself to the English." Were not the statesman's words but a distant echo of Voltaire's thinking when, in 1753, in his *Essay on the Manners of Nations*, he described Canada as a "land covered in snow and ice eight months of the year, inhabited by barbarians, bear and beaver"?

No sooner had Governor Vaudreuil landed at Brest in France on November 28, 1760, than he received a letter expressing the king's astonishment that Canada had succumbed to the enemy without offering a defence. A last attempt at resistance would at least have forced the English general to accord the French army the honours of war. Louis XV was displeased that Vaudreuil had not sacrificed a few hundred men to obtain the privilege of beating the drums . . .

As soon as he arrived in France at the beginning of the winter of 1760, Intendant Bigot, for his part, was imprisoned in the Bastille. The munitions supplier Cadet first went to Bordeaux where, having anticipated Quebec's inevitable fall, he had already installed his family. Going up to Paris on business, he was taken and imprisoned in the Bastille on January 25, 1761. François Morin, the assistant munitions supplier, brought back from Canada, in his trunk, almost two million *livres*. Like Péan, Bréard, Pennisseault, Marin, Corpron, Le Mercier, and other members of high society, he was accused of misappropriation of funds, of embezzlement, and of having, through his fraud, contributed to the fall of Canada.

Back in France as well, Colonel Bougainville tried to persuade his connections, including Madame de Pompadour, that their country should erect, in Quebec, a monument in honour of Lieutenant-General Montcalm. He sought the support of the *Académie royale des inscriptions* (the Royal Academy of Inscriptions), whose secretary was his brother. The academy agreed to his request and proposed the following lines to honour Montcalm's memory:

> *He made up for*
> *Fortune with courage, and for the number of men*
> *With skill and effort.*
> *For four years, he delayed through his measures*
> *And his valour, the imminent loss of the colony.*

Before this inscription could be engraved on the stone that would be placed on Montcalm's tomb, a question was raised: had France the right to honour a general whose body lay in a land that had become English? Bougainville asked his brother to appeal to William Pitt, in London. On April 10, 1761, Pitt replied, in a letter written in French: "It would give me pleasure to facilitate in every way possible such remarkable intentions."

In December 1761, the Châtelet Commission began to sit in judgment of the "Canadian Affair." According to public opinion, which had condemned them in advance, Bigot, Cadet, and Péan deserved to be hanged. The judges had before them masses of incriminating documents. The prosecution demanded that the guilty parties be condemned to torture and death. Vaudreuil and Bigot denounced each other. However, a few weeks earlier on October 15, the former governor general of Canada had defended his friend to the minister of the colonies: "There is no better citizen than him . . . no one takes more to heart the interests of the King." Vaudreuil was condemned to be imprisoned in the Bastille on March 30, 1762, but was granted provisional freedom the following May 18 and was exonerated on December 10, 1763. Not only did he later receive the Cross of Saint-Louis, but to compensate for his humiliation, the government increased his pension.

Bigot was banished from France in perpetuity. His properties were confiscated, and he had to reimburse an enormous sum. He went into exile in Switzerland, where he lived under an assumed name. The other accused defended themselves by incriminating each other, but they all blamed Cadet, who swore he did only what his partners had done. But could Cadet explain why, after the fall of Quebec, he had maintained relations with the enemy? He was simply trying to sell good French products to the English, he said. Cadet was condemned to reimbursing a colossal sum and was banished from Paris for a period of nine years. On March 5, 1764, however, he was freed from prison, the sum he was to reimburse was reduced by half, and his banishment was lifted. At the end of the "Canada Affair," among the other accused, ten were found guilty, six were acquitted, three received a warning, two were dismissed for lack of proof, and seven were condemned *in absentia*.

Quebec and Montreal were not France's only defeats. On July 31, 1760, 35,000 French clashed with the allied troops of Great Britain,

Hesse, and Hanover at Warburg in Germany. The French troops withdrew after a brief altercation. In India, on January 16, 1761, the army of Commander Thomas Arthur de Lally attempted to retake the fort of Vandasivi, near Pondicherry, but it was crushed by Colonel Eyre Coote's Indian and English soldiers. At the beginning of June 1761, the redoubts of Belle-Île-en-Mer, in Brittany, were not strong enough to resist a body of eight thousand Englishmen who landed with their cannons. Their frigates' artillery demolished the palace citadel on the heights of the port, and the garrison surrendered. On July 16, 1761, the Prussian army of Prince Ferdinand easily repelled the French of the Duc de Broglie and Maréchal de Soubise, who had advanced upon Kirch Denken, in Germany.

Since the beginning of this interminable Seven Years' War, France had lost Acadia, the Upper Country, the Ohio Valley, and Canada. Of the former colonies, all that was left to France were the Saint-Jean and Royale islands, depopulated, Louisiana, and the very fragile colonies of Saint-Domingue (Haiti) and French Guiana.

In 1762, the French ambassadors began to talk of peace. From the start of the negotiations, a letter from Choiseul, secretary of state for foreign affairs, to Charles Wyndham, Count of Egremont, let it be understood that the King of France "found it just that England retain Canada" if "Martinique and Guadeloupe" were restored to him. However, the French marine wanted to show the English that France was not yet beaten. In June of 1762, 650 soldiers invaded St. John's in Newfoundland. The British retook the city less than three months later.

That did not silence the rumours in London that the French were preparing to retake possession of Canada. Ambassador Charles Alexandre Léon Durand de Linois told Choiseul about the rumour. Choiseul made France's position clear to his ambassador: "there is no intelligence in Canada, nor any interest in having any." In that context, "intelligence" meant communication between people who were conferring in secret.

French and English emissaries negotiated for months. The bourgeois, the "philosophers," the officials, and the court, in both countries, discussed the value of territories lost or gained. In England, they talked of this British America, augmented by Canada, which would be a counterweight to the Spanish colonies. Some were concerned, however, by the American colonists' spirit of independence. Would they want one day to be free of the Crown? In France, it was known that Canada had proved very costly. The expenses had never stopped growing. Under the administration of Intendant Hocquart, they were two million *livres* per year; under the administration of Bigot, who had replaced him in 1748, the expenses had risen to nine million *livres*. If Canada returned to France, it would cost even more because they would have to rebuild the city of Quebec and provide Canada with a strong army to ensure its protection from the neighbouring English, who were more and more numerous. And what would Canada return to the royal coffers?

Guadeloupe would be much less expensive. And did it not already produce sugar and *guildive*, a fermented sugar cane juice? And the export products would be more and more abundant if they imported from Africa the labour force need for farming. A naval base there would protect France's presence in the region. Choiseul advised Louis XV to give up Canada.

With the Treaty of Paris, signed on February 10, 1763, France ceded Canada, the Royal and Saint-Jean islands, as well as that part of Louisiana east of the Mississippi, to Great Britain. The other part of Louisiana west of the Mississippi, including New Orleans, would go to Spain. France recovered Guadeloupe, Martinique, Marie-Galante, and Sainte Lucie, for the price of a few other islands in the West Indies and its trading posts at Pondicherry. France also lost its trading posts in Senegal, with the exception of the island of Gorée. It obtained from the English that they relinquish Belle-Île-en-Mer in exchange for Minorca. It was happy to acquire, in the dealings, the archipelago of Saint-Pierre and Miquelon. Its fishermen would have access to Newfoundland's Grand Banks. The signing of the treaty was celebrated on the Place de Grève in Paris, in front of the city hall. An elegant crowd danced beneath fireworks that bloomed in the night like the dawning of a new age.

Montcalm, Wolfe, officers, soldiers, militiamen, and indigenous people had been wisps of straw swept away by the raging currents of a war between narcissistic tribal chiefs.

Index